# VOICES OF DIVERSITY

## Twentieth-Century Perspectives on History and Government

### SECOND EDITION

**PAT ANDREWS**
*West Valley College*

***Dushkin/McGraw-Hill***
*A Division of The McGraw-Hill Companies*

**Book Team**

Vice President and Publisher *Jeffrey L. Hahn*
Editors *Theodore Knight, Ava Suntoke*
Production Manager *Brenda S. Filley*
Director of Technology *Jonathan Stowe*
Developmental Editor *Richard Morel*
Designer *Charles Vitelli*
Typesetting Supervisor *Juliana Arbo*
Permissions Editor *Rose Gleich*

**Dushkin/McGraw-Hill**
A Division of The McGraw-Hill Companies

Cover © UPI/Corbis-Bettmann
Cover Research *Pamela Carley*

The credit section for this book begins on page 239 and is considered an extension of the copyright page.

Library of Congress Catalog Card Number 98-74980

ISBN 0-07-366156-2

Printed in the United States of America

1234567890BAHBAH5432109

http://www.mhhe.com

# About the Author

Throughout her teaching career Pat Andrews has specialized in American history and government. She is chair of the Department of History/Political Science at West Valley College in Saratoga, California, coordinator for Women's History Month, and teaches online at http://www. wvmccd.cc.ca.us/wvc/ss/ps/tele.html. She has been a faculty member at Cabrillo College and Presentation High School, both in California, and a guest lecturer at Repton and Greylands Colleges in England. Following completion of her B.A. at San Jose State University and attaining lifetime teaching credentials in history and government from California Community College, Pat Andrews earned M.A. degrees in social science and political science at California State University, San Jose. An active member of the teachers' unions at West Valley and Cabrillo Colleges, she also served as coordinator of West Valley's Cultural Diversity Task Force and has been honored with several outstanding teacher awards. In addition to this book, she has written a number of freelance articles on politics and current issues.

Pat Andrews and her family make their home in San Jose.

*I want to acknowledge my life's real treasures—my family, who is growing every day—*

*Lisa, Jennifer, Danielle, and our newest addition, Faustino, and the great joy they all bring me;*

*my partner in life, Robert Mora, and the love we share;*

*my mother who is my dearest friend;*

*my father whose loss has left a huge hole in my life;*

*my brother, the idea man, who keeps the family together;*

*and, always, Christopher who never leaves my mind or my heart.*

# Preface

Women and minorities have played an essential role in the advancement of American ideals and institutions in the twentieth century. *Voices of Diversity: Twentieth-Century Perspectives on History and Government,* showcases some of the key players and events.

This book brings together two kinds of primary sources: the often eloquent words of American women and minority group members raised in protest at the unfair treatment they confronted in American life; and the responses of government to their grievances.

In chronological order, and beginning with Alice Stone Blackwell on "Why Women Should Vote," essays, speeches, letters, proclamations and other documents provide a snapshot of some essential contributions made by people from underrepresented groups to the expansion of democratic values. Also featured are government documents that benefit those groups and promote the ideals of liberty and equality.

The selections in chapters 1, 3, 5, and 7 represent the voices of many people who were long excluded. One hears from such well-known figures as Martin Luther King Jr., Cesar Chavez, Betty Friedan, Clarence Thomas, and Ronald Takaki, and becomes acquainted with less-known people, such as Bert Corona, Armando Rodriguez, Joaquin Avila, John Mohawk, and James Chin, to name only a few.

Found in chapters 2, 4, 6, and 8, are the federal statutes, executive orders, state laws, judicial decisions, newly created government agencies, that serve as a testament to the effective role that these and other voices have played in forging a more inclusive democracy.

Voices of Diversity demonstrates to students how democracy works and that people do have power. Each chapter begins with a capsule summary of the history at that moment; each reading begins with a summary of the author's background and ends with several study questions. Few collections feature such a sweeping view of democratic values as they evolve through the thoughts and deeds of minority groups and women along with a historical look at the work of government redress.

An excellent supplementary text to American history and government classes, this book can also be utilized as a primary text in sociology, race and relations and multicultural curricula.

I would like to thank the reviewers who provided some excellent recommendations for the second edition. They include:

Maria Brown, *El Camino College*

Norman Love, *El Paso Community College*

Michael Miller Topp, *University of Texas at El Paso*

I would like to give special thanks to Richard and Beth Morel for their wise editing, to Laurie Trulock for her expert marketing advice, to Ava Suntoke for her oversight of the entire project, and to Dushkin for its support of a second edition.

Pat Andrews

# Contents

## Chapter 4: The Blessings of Liberty    74

## Chapter 5: Redefining Democracy    111

## Chapter 6: One Nation, Many People      153

## Chapter 7: The New Politics      187

## Chapter 8: Democracy in the Twenty-First Century    223

# Introduction

**D**iversity has played an essential role in the advancement of American ideals and institutions in the twentieth century. *Voices of Diversity: Twentieth-Century Perspectives on History and Government,* Second Edition, showcases some of the key players and events and pays tribute to the profound impact that women and minorities in the United States have had upon American society and its democratic values.

In chronological order, and beginning with Alice Stone Blackwell on "Why Women Should Vote," essays, speeches, letters, proclamations and other selections provide snapshots of some essential contributions made by people from underrepresented groups to the meaning of democracy. One hears from well-known figures such as Martin Luther King Jr., Cesar Chavez, Betty Friedan, Clarence Thomas, and Ronald Takaki, and becomes acquainted with less-known people, such as Bert Corona, Armando Rodriguez, Joaquin Avila, John Mohawk, and James Chin, to name only a few.

Juxtaposed with the chapters devoted to the underrepresented are those that highlight federal and state statutes, executive orders, judicial decisions, presidential speeches, and newly created government agencies, which serve as a testament to the effective role that all have played in forging a more inclusive democracy.

Each chapter begins with a capsule summary of the history at that moment; each reading begins with a summary of the author's background and ends with several study questions. Few collections feature such a sweeping view of democratic values as they evolve through the thoughts and deeds of minority groups and women and through a working representative government.

In *Voices of Diversity* you will read the actual words that people spoke and wrote, rather than the interpretations historians and political scientists. You will witness government in action at great moments of history. You will judge for yourself the works of these individuals and of government in promoting democratic ideals.

Woefully absent from American government textbooks are real life examples of the workings of government such as executive orders or state laws. Absent from American history survey texts are the portraits and words of individuals from underrepresented groups. This collection of primary source documents enriches history, government, and multicultural curricula. And I hope the book enhances one's appreciation of the vital role that pluralism plays in the United States.

"So two cheers for Democracy: one because it admits variety and two because it permits criticism. Two cheers are quite enough; there is no occasion to give three," wrote E. M. Forster. Perhaps we have found the occasion for the three cheers: that Democracy works.

# We, the People

From the European colonists who first settled in the New World to the men who drafted the Constitution more than 150 years later, the majority of early Americans pledged allegiance to three basic ideals for their new nation: individual liberty, equality, and representative self-government.

The Declaration of Independence, America's founding document, asserted that government derived its power from "the consent of the governed" and was responsible for protecting the "unalienable rights" of men.

The United States Constitution speaks of "We, the People," and, in its Bill of Rights, includes constitutional guarantees for "all persons."

Despite such statements, women could not vote or participate in government. Once married, a woman became a member of a household with a single voice represented by its male head. Women were often denied rights to property, to business ownership, employment and educational opportunities, even jury duty. Marriage and divorce laws, as well as issues of child custody, were decided by men.

When the cotton gin triggered a demand for mass labor, Black servants became slaves owned by their masters. The Constitution, with its three-fifth's compromise, allowed states to count every five slaves as equal to three free persons for purposes of representation in Congress. It legitimized the institution of slavery by allowing such people to be imported until 1808.

Native American tribes were defined as separate nations. Treaties determined their relationship to the federal government and their territorial rights. Nevertheless, expansion soon forced Indians off their land in violation of treaties in order to make room for settlement. The federal government stood by and witnessed the slaughter. The total Native American population, which had been over 8 million in the 17th century, fell to

250,000 between 1880 to 1910. Indians were forced to accept an allotment plan, called the Dawes Act of 1887, for the purpose of promoting property ownership, a farm existence, and more rapid assimilation, that distributed reservation land in 160-acre plots to Indian families.

Latinos had an experience similar to that of Native Americans. Following the Mexican-American War of 1848, the Treaty of Guadalupe Hidalgo promised former Mexicans, now Americans, citizenship and protection of their property. However, a gold rush into the Southwest quickly ended that commitment. Mexican Americans were treated as second-class citizens and it was quite common for land to be "grabbed" from them either through fraud or intimidation.

Chinese immigrants came to California during the Gold Rush of the late 1840s to mine and were also recruited as "coolie" labor for large construction projects. They kept mainly to themselves and organized their own community institutions. Their success caused resentment; their settlements brought about fear of their unfamiliar cultural practices. Eventually, California denied them citizenship, and the United States suspended Chinese immigration. Japanese Americans had a similar experience. These groups sought fulfillment of the democratic ideals outlined in the Declaration of Independence, the Constitution, and the Bill of Rights. Their dissenting voices demanded change.

By the start of the 20th century, they had made little progress. Women still did not have the vote. Alice Stone Blackwell represents only one of many women's suffrage organizations that had been formed to lobby for women's rights. The League of Latin American Citizens was created to combat discrimination and promote equal protection for Latino Americans who were segregated in schools and other facilities, not entitled even to serve on a jury.

Native Americans were living on poverty-stricken reservations. Luther Standing Bear is a lone voice defending Indian culture. Asian Americans faced many discriminatory laws and practices, and were often segregated. Because of the Japanese government's attack on Pearl Harbor, Mike Masaoka went before Congress to defend Japanese American patriotism as the United States entered World War II. Nevertheless, Japanese Americans were interned in prison camps for the duration of the war.

The Civil War had brought an official end to slavery but not a practical end to prejudice and discrimination. In 1896, *Plessy v. Ferguson* legalized segregation and consigned southern Blacks to live under "Jim Crow" laws and northern Blacks under *de facto* discrimination.

From the very beginning of the Republic, many voices had been raised on behalf of liberty and equality for all, but it was not until the 20th century that the country began to experience real change.

In *Lincoln at Gettysburg,* noted scholar Garry Wills wrote, "By accepting the Gettysburg Address, its concept of a single people dedicated to the proposition (of equality), we have been changed. . . . Because of it, we live in a different America." We had changed the definition of "We, the People," and allowed a much broader interpretation of the Constitution without overthrowing it.

---

## Reading 1

Alice Stone Blackwell, 1917

### "Why Should Women Vote?"

From the beginning of the Republic, women had called for their voices to be recognized. They worked in the abolitionist crusade that became the seminal crusade for women's rights.

"It is fair and right that the people who must obey the laws should have a voice in choosing the lawmakers," wrote Alice Stone Blackwell (1857–1950).

Alice Stone Blackwell was a journalist, suffragist, and supporter of Black rights. After graduating from Boston University, she edited a publication of the National American Woman Suffrage Association, called *The Woman's Journal*, that was founded by her parents, Lucy Stone and Henry Blackwell.

Her argument rests in large part on an argument for the American Revolution: that one must have a voice through a vote in the decision to tax. She challenges every commonly held reason for excluding women from having this voice.

The reasons why women should vote are the same as the reasons why men should vote—the same as the reasons for having a republic rather than a monarchy. It is fair and right that the people who must obey the laws should have a voice in choosing the lawmakers, and that those who must pay the taxes should have a voice as to the amount of the tax, and the way in which the money shall be spent.

Roughly stated, the fundamental principle of a republic is this: In deciding what is to be done, where everybody's interests are concerned, we take everybody's opinion, and then go according to the wish of the majority. As we cannot suit everybody, we do what will suit the greatest number. That seems to be, on the whole, the fairest way. A vote is simply a written expression of opinion.

In thus taking a vote to get at the wish of the majority, certain classes of persons are passed over, whose opinions for one reason or another are thought not to be worth counting. In most of our states, these classes are children, aliens, idiots, lunatics, criminals and women. There are good and obvious reasons for making all these exceptions but the last. Of course no account ought to be taken of the opinions of children, insane persons, or criminals. Is there any equally good reason why no account should be taken of the opinions of women? Let us consider the reasons commonly given, and see if they are sound.

## Are Women Represented?

*Women are represented already by their husbands, fathers and brothers.*

This so-called representation bears no proportion to numbers. Here is a man who has a wife, a widowed mother, four or five unmarried sisters, and half a dozen unmarried daughters. His vote represents himself and all these women, and it counts one; while the vote of his bachelor neighbor next door, without a female relative in the world, counts for just as much. Since the object of taking a vote is to get at the wish of the majority, it is clear that the only fair and accurate way is for each grown person to have one vote, and cast it to represent himself or herself.

## Men and Women Different.

American men are the best in the world, and if it were possible for any men to represent women, through kindness and good will to them, American men would do it. But a man is by nature too different from a woman to be able to represent her. The two creatures are unlike. Whatever his good will, he cannot fully put himself in a woman's place, and look at things exactly from her point of view. To say this is no more a reflection upon his mental or moral ability than it would be a reflection upon his musical ability to say that he cannot sing both soprano and bass. Unless men and women should ever become just alike (which would be regrettable and monotonous), women must either go unrepresented or represent themselves.

## Women Not Represented in the Laws.

Another proof that women's opinions are not now fully represented is the lack in many states of humane and protective legislation, and the poor enforcement of such legislation where it exists; the inadequate appropriations for schools; the permission of child labor in factories, and in general the imperfect legal safe-guarding of the moral, educational and humanitarian interests that women have most at heart. In many of our states, the property laws are more or less unequal as between men and women. A hundred years ago, before the equal rights movement began, they were almost incredibly unequal. Yet our grand-fathers loved their wives and daughters as much as men do today. . . .

## Would Unsex Women

*It will turn women into men.*

The differences between men and women are natural; they are not the result of disfranchisement. The fact that all men have equal rights before the law does not wipe out natural differences of character and temperament between man and man. Why should it wipe out the natural differences between men and women? The women of England, Scotland, Canada, Yucatan, Ireland, Australia, New Zealand, the Scandinavian countries and our own equal suffrage States are not perceptibly different in looks or manners from women elsewhere, although they have been voting for years. . . .

## Suffrage and Feminism

*Suffrage is a branch of Feminism and Feminism includes free love.*

Feminism merely means the general movement for woman's rights. The word is used in this sense in England and Europe, and is coming into use in America. There is no more authority for saying that Feminism means free love than that the woman's rights movement means free love—an accusation often made against it without warrant. Mrs. Beatrice Forbes Robertson Hale (a strong opponent of free love) says in her book, "What Women Want":

"Feminism is that part of the progress of democratic freedom which applies to women. It is a century-old struggle conducted by large groups of people in different parts of the world to bring about the removal of all artificial barriers to the physical, mental, moral and economic development of the female half of the race."

In this sense the woman suffrage movement, of course, is a part of it.

## Suffrage and Marriage

*Suffragists and Feminists are the enemies of marriage and the home.*

The National American Woman Suffrage Association at its annual convention in Washington in December, 1915, passed the following resolution by a unanimous vote:

"That we believe the home is the foundation of the State; we believe in the sanctity of the marriage relation; and, furthermore, we believe that woman's ballot will strengthen the power of the home, and sustain the dignity and sacredness of marriage; and we denounce as a gross slander the charges made by opponents of equal suffrage that its advocates as a class entertain opinions to the contrary." . . .

# Questions for Review and Reflection

1. According to Alice Blackwell,

   a. What is the fundamental principle of a republic?
   b. Based upon the principle of a republic, why should women vote?
   c. Based upon the differences between men and women, why should women vote?
   d. Compare feminism today with the feminism described by Blackwell.

# Reading 2

LULAC, 1929

## Aims and Objectives of the League of United Latin-American Citizens (LULAC)

The League of United Latin-American Citizens (LULAC) is an organization created in 1929 that coalesced several groups promoting economic and social opportunities for Latinos. With approximately 10,000 members today, LULAC offers job training programs, scholarships, and classroom instruction in English, working toward "justice and equality of . . . treatment in accordance with the law of the land."

LULAC's work began because of U.S. segregation policies toward Mexican Americans. The Treaty of Guadalupe Hidalgo that incorporated Mexican land into the southwest United States and settled the Mexican-American War of 1848 promised Mexicans residing on the land United States' citizenship. But, in fact, Mexican Americans confronted discriminatory laws from the beginning.

Well into the 20th century, Mexican Americans in the Southwest attended segregated schools, were restricted in some public facilities, and were excluded in some states from serving on juries. LULAC was responsible for court cases that resulted in landmark decisions that broke down barriers and extended the equal protection of laws. Their aims and purposes as expressed in this founding statement in 1929 continue today.

The Aims and Purposes of This Organization Shall Be:

1. To develop within the members of our race the best, purest and most perfect type of a true and loyal citizen of the United States of America.
2. To eradicate from our body politic all intents and tendencies to establish discriminations among our fellow citizens on account of race, religion, or social position as being contrary to the true spirit of Democracy, our Constitution and Laws.
3. To use all the legal means at our command to the end that all citizens in our country may enjoy equal rights, the equal protection of the laws of the land and equal opportunities and privileges.
4. The acquisition of the English language, which is the official language of our country, being necessary for the enjoyment of our rights and privileges, we declare it to be the official language of this organization, and we pledge ourselves to learn and speak and teach same to our children.
5. To define with absolute and unmistakable clearness our unquestionable loyalty to the ideals, principles, and citizenship of the United States of America.
6. To assume complete responsibility for the education of our children as to their rights and duties and the language and customs of this country; the latter, in so far as they may be good customs.
7. We solemnly declare once for all to maintain a sincere and respectful reverence for our racial origin of which we are proud.
8. Secretly and openly, by all lawful means at our command, we shall assist in the education and guidance of Latin-Americans and we shall protect and defend their lives and interest whenever necessary.
9. We shall destroy any attempt to create racial prejudices against our people, and any infamous stigma which may be cast upon them, and we shall demand for them the respect and prerogatives which the Constitution grants to us all.
10. Each of us considers himself with equal responsibilities in our organization, to which we voluntarily swear subordination and obedience.
11. We shall create a fund for our mutual protection, for the defense of those of us who may be unjustly persecuted and for the education and culture of our people.
12. This organization is not a political club, but as citizens we shall participate in all local, state, and national political contests. However, in doing so we shall ever bear in mind the general welfare of our

people, and we disregard and abjure once for all any personal obligation which is not in harmony with these principles.

13. With our vote and influence we shall endeavor to place in public office men who show by their deeds, respect and consideration for our people.

14. We shall select as our leaders those among us who demonstrate, by their integrity and culture, that they are capable of guiding and directing us properly.

15. We shall maintain publicity means for the diffusion of these principles and for the expansion and consolidation of this organization.

16. We shall pay our poll tax as well as that of members of our families in order that we may enjoy our rights fully.

17. We shall diffuse our ideals by means of the press, lectures, and pamphlets.

18. We shall oppose any radical and violent demonstration which may tend to create conflicts and disturb the peace and tranquility of our country.

19. We shall have mutual respect for our religious views and we shall never refer to them in our institutions.

20. We shall encourage the creation of educational institutions for Latin-Americans and we shall lend our support to those already in existence.

21. We shall endeavor to secure equal representation for our people on juries and in the administration of governmental affairs.

22. We shall denounce every act of peonage and mistreatment as well as the employment of our minor children of scholastic age.

23. We shall resist and attack energetically all machinations tending to prevent our social and political unification.

24. We shall oppose any tendency to separate our children in the schools of this country.

25. We shall maintain statistics which will guide our people with respect to working and living conditions and agricultural and commercial activities in the various parts of our country.

 **uestions for Review and Reflection**

1. Does the League support U.S. citizenship?
2. Based on their statement, how do they expect to achieve their goals?
3. Based on their statement, what do you think their position would be regarding bilingual education?

# Reading 3

Luther Standing Bear, 1933

## *Land of the Spotted Eagle*

Luther Standing Bear (1868?–1939) was an Oglala Sioux who grew up on the Pine Ridge Reservation in South Dakota. He was one of the many Indian children sent to an assimilation school (part of the Dawes Act of 1887) that was designed to eradicate Indian culture and educate Native Americans in the white man's way.

As a young adult, Luther Standing Bear left the reservation, became a teacher, and later an actor. When he finally returned to Pine Ridge many years later, he found dismal conditions of physical and psychological deterioration.

He denounced assimilation and urged that his people be allowed to live as Indians, raise cattle, practice their own culture, and be left alone. "Regarding the 'civilization' that has been thrust upon me since the days of reservation, it has not added one whit to my sense of justice; to my reverence for the rights of life; to my love for truth, honesty, and generosity."

His ideas contributed to what Franklin D. Roosevelt hoped would be the "New Deal" for Indians: self-determination, freedom from government control, and self-sufficiency. This reading comes from Luther Standing Bear's 1933 book.

### What the Indian Means to America

The feathered and blanketed figure of the American Indian has come to symbolize the American continent. He is the man who through centuries has been moulded and sculpted by the same hand that shaped its mountains, forests, and plains, and marked the course of its rivers.

The American Indian is of the soil, whether it be the region of forests, plains, pueblos, or mesas. He fits into the landscape, for the hand that fashioned the continent also fashioned the man for his surroundings. He once grew as naturally as the wild sunflowers; he belongs just as the buffalo belonged.

With a physique that fitted, the man developed fitting skills—crafts which today are called American. And the body had a soul, also formed and moulded by the same master hand of harmony. Out of the Indian approach to existence there came a great freedom—an intense and absorbing love for nature; a respect for life; enriching faith in a Supreme Power; and principles of truth, honesty, generosity, equity, and brotherhood as a guide to mundane relations.

Becoming possessed of a fitting philosophy and art, it was by them that native man perpetuated his identity; stamped it into the history and soul of this country—made land and man one.

By living—struggling, losing, meditating, imbibing, aspiring, achieving— he wrote himself into inerasable evidence—an evidence that can be and often has been ignored, but never totally destroyed. Living—and all the intangible forces that constitute that phenomenon—are brought into being by Spirit, that which no man can alter.

The white man does not understand the Indian for the reason that he does not understand America. He is too far removed from its formative processes. The roots of the tree of his life have not yet grasped the rock and soil. The white man is still troubled with primitive fears; he still has in his consciousness the perils of this frontier continent, some of its fastnesses not yet having yielded to his questing footsteps and inquiring eyes. He shudders still with the memory of the loss of his forefathers upon its scorching deserts and forbidding mountain-tops. The man from Europe is still a foreigner and an alien. And he still hates the man who questioned his path across the continent.

But in the Indian the spirit of the land is still vested; it will be until other men are able to divine and meet its rhythm. Men must be born and reborn to belong. Their bodies must be formed of the dust of their forefathers' bones.

The attempted transformation of the Indian by the white man and the chaos that has resulted are but the fruits of the white man's disobedience of a fundamental and spiritual law. The pressure that has been brought to bear upon the native people, since the cessation of armed conflict, in the attempt to force conformity of custom and habit has caused a reaction more destructive than war, and the injury has not only affected the Indian, but has extended to the white population as well. Tyranny, stupidity, and lack of vision have brought about the situation now alluded to as the 'Indian Problem.'

There is, I insist, no Indian problem as created by the Indian himself. Every problem that exists today in regard to the native population is due to the white man's cast of mind, which is unable, at least reluctant, to seek under- standing and achieve adjustment in a new and a significant environment into which it has so recently come. . . .

After subjugation, after dispossession, there was cast the last abuse upon the people who so entirely resented their wrongs and punishments, and that was the stamping and the labeling of them as savages. To make this label stick has been the task of the white race and the greatest salve that it has been able to apply to its sore and troubled conscience now hardened through the habitual practice of injustice.

But all the years of calling the Indian a savage has never made him one; all the denial of his virtues has never taken them from him; and the very resistance he has made to save the things inalienably his has been his saving strength—that which will stand him in need when justice does make its belated appearance and he undertakes rehabilitation.

All sorts of feeble excuses are heard for the continued subjection of the Indian. One of the most common is that he is not yet ready to accept the society of the white man—that he is not yet ready to mingle as a social entity.

This, I maintain, is beside the question. The matter is not one of making-over the external Indian into the likeness of the white race—a process detrimental to both races. Who can say that the white man's way is better for the Indian? Where resides the human judgment with the competence to weigh and value Indian ideals and spiritual concepts, or substitute for them other values?

Then, has the white man's social order been so harmonious and ideal as to merit the respect of the Indian, and for that matter the thinking class of the white race? Is it wise to urge upon the Indian a foreign social form? Let none but the Indian answer!

Rather, let the white brother face about and cast his mental eye upon a new angle of vision. Let him look upon the Indian world as a human world; then let him see to it that human rights be accorded to the Indians. And this for the purpose of retaining for his own order of society a measure of humanity.

## The Indian School of Thought

I say again that Indians should teach Indians; that Indians should serve Indians, especially on reservations where the older people remain. There is a definite need of the old for the care and sympathy of the young and they are today perishing for the joys that naturally belong to old Indian people. Old Indians are very close to their progeny. It was their delightful duty to care for and instruct the very young, while in turn they looked forward to being cared for by sons and daughters. These were the privileges and blessings of old age. . . .

Why should not America be cognizant of itself; aware of its identity? In short, why should not America be preserved?

There were ideals and practices in the life of my ancestors that have not been improved upon by the present-day civilization; there were in our culture elements of benefit; and there were influences that would broaden any life. But that almost an entire public needs to be enlightened as to this fact need not be discouraging. For many centuries the human mind labored under the delusion that the world was flat; and thousands of men have believed that the heavens were supported by the strength of an Atlas. The human mind is not yet free from fallacious reasoning; it is not yet an open mind and its deepest recesses are not yet swept free of errors.

But it is now time for a destructive order to be reversed, and it is well to inform other races that the aboriginal culture of America was not devoid of beauty. Furthermore, in denying the Indian his ancestral rights and heritages the white race is but robbing itself. But America can be revived, rejuvenated, by recognizing a native school of thought. The Indian can save America.

Regarding the 'civilization' that has been thrust upon me since the days of reservation, it has not added one whit to my sense of justice; to my reverence for the rights of life; to my love for truth, honesty, and generosity; nor to my faith in Wakan Tanka—God of the Lakotas. For after all the great religions have been preached and expounded, or have been revealed by brilliant scholars, or have been written in books and embellished in fine language with finer covers, man—all man—is still confronted with the Great Mystery.

So if today I had a young mind to direct, to start on the journey of life, and I was faced with the duty of choosing between the natural way of my forefathers and that of the white man's present way of civilization, I would, for its welfare, unhesitatingly set that child's feet in the path of my forefathers. I would raise him to be an Indian!

## |Q| uestions for Review and Reflection

1. Why does Luther Standing Bear state that the American Indian is of the soil?
2. What are some of the excuses used for the continued subjugation of the Indians?
3. Luther Standing Bear speaks of the attempted "transformation of the Indian" by white men. What do you think the nature of this transformation was? What was his attitude toward this?
4. Can Luther Standing Bear find anything about the American civilization worth incorporating into his way of life?

# Reading 4

Mike Masaoka, 1942

## Testimony Before Congress

Approximately 120,000 people of Japanese descent were placed in U.S. government–supervised settlements following the Japanese government's attack on the United States at Pearl Harbor, December 7, 1941; they remained interned throughout World War II.

One of the many U.S.-born, Japanese-American citizens interned during World War II, Mike Masaoka (1915–1991) also spent a little time in jail under suspicion of espionage. Despite such treatment, Mr. Masaoka, national secretary for the Japanese American Citizens League, cooperated with and remained loyal to the United States. He encouraged all Japanese Americans to do the same.

His testimony was given to a U.S. congressional committee looking into the proposal for evacuation and internment of Japanese Americans. The government went ahead with the plan because of fear of possible sabotage and disloyalty. In fact, no Japanese American was ever convicted of espionage in the United States during World War II.

Mr. Masaoka was eventually allowed to serve in the military. His 442nd regiment, an all-Japanese combat unit, became the most decorated infantry unit in the war.

On behalf of the 20,000 American citizen members of the 62 chapters of the Japanese American Citizens League in some 300 communities throughout the United States, I wish to thank the Tolan committee for the opportunity given me to appear at this hearing. . . .

We have been invited by you to make clear our stand regarding the proposed evacuation of all Japanese from the West coast. When the President's recent Executive order was issued, we welcomed it as definitely centralizing and coordinating defense efforts relative to the evacuation problem. Later interpretations of the order, however, seem to indicate that it is aimed primarily at the Japanese, American citizens as well as alien nationals. As your committee continues its investigations in this and subsequent hearings, we hope and trust that you will recommend to the proper authorities that no undue discrimination be shown to American citizens of Japanese descent. . . .

If, in the judgment of military and Federal authorities, evacuation of Japanese residents from the West coast is a primary step toward assuring the safety of this Nation, we will have no hesitation in complying with the necessities implicit in that judgment. But, if, on the other hand, such evacuation is primarily a measure whose surface urgency cloaks the desires of political or other pressure groups who want us to leave merely from motives of self-interest, we feel that we have every right to protest and to demand equitable judgment on our merits as American citizens.

## Recommendations

In any case, we feel that the whole problem of evacuation, once its necessity is militarily established, should be met strictly according to that need. Only these areas in which strategic and military considerations make the removal of Japanese residents necessary should be evacuated. . . .

## We Cherish Our American Citizenship

I now make an earnest plea that you seriously consider and recognize our American citizenship status which we have been taught to cherish as our most priceless heritage.

At this hearing, we Americans of Japanese descent have been accused of being disloyal to these United States. As an American citizen, I resent these accusations and deny their validity.

We American-born Japanese are fighting militarist Japan today with our total energies. Four thousand of us are with the armed forces of the United States, the remainder on the home front in the battle of production. We ask a chance to prove to the rest of the American people what we ourselves already know: That we are loyal to the country of our birth and that we will fight to the death to defend it against any and all aggressors.

We think, feel, act like Americans. We, too, remember Pearl Harbor and know that our right to live as free men in a free Nation is in peril as long as the brutal forces of enslavement walk the earth. We know that the Axis aggressors must be crushed and we are anxious to participate fully in that struggle.

The history of our group speaks for itself. It stands favorable comparison with that of any other group of second generation Americans. There is reliable authority to show that the proportion of delinquency and crime within our ranks is negligible. Throughout the long years of the depression, we have been able to stay off the relief rolls better, by far, than any other group. These are but two of the many examples which might be cited as proof of our civic responsibility and pride.

In this emergency, as in the past, we are not asking for special privileges or concessions. We ask only for the opportunity and the right of sharing the common lot of all Americans, whether it be in peace or in war.

This is the American way for which our boys are fighting.


## Questions for Review and Reflection

1. What was the purpose of Mr. Masaoka's testimony?
2. Does Mr. Masaoka support the evacuation and internment of Japanese Americans?
3. Does Mr. Masaoka recommend that Japanese Americans cooperate with the U.S. government?
4. Does Mr. Masaoka rely on someone else's judgment to determine what Japanese Americans ought to do in this set of circumstances?

# Reading 5

Ralph Bunche, 1944

## The Political Status of the Negro after FDR

Throughout the Depression and World War II, African Americans continued to be relegated to a second-class citizenship. Employment was hard to find, and a policy of "last hired, first fired" prevailed. World events made recruitment into the military an employment option, but the armed forces were segregated, with few promotions offered to black men. The Agricultural Adjustment Act of the New Deal disproportionately evicted black tenant farmers through its policy of paying farmers not to plant. As America prepared to enter World War II, blacks urged, "Don't just get rid of Hitler, but Hitlerism," referring to the racism that continued in the United States.

Grandson of a slave, Dr. Ralph Bunche (1904–1971) received his doctorate in political science from Harvard University. He was a respected diplomat and statesman who earned the Nobel Peace Prize in 1950 for his work in the Arab-Israeli conflict.

Dr. Bunche reiterated that the lack of full access to the franchise made a mockery of the guarantees in the Constitution. Bunche prepared a voluminous statistical study to document the need to extend the full measure of the law to African Americans in order to implement the ideals of the Constitution.

The future of the American Negro is a problem of the national society. It is to be solved only through opportunity for development and through assimilation into the political and economic life of the nation. The Negro has for centuries contributed his labor, his intelligence, his blood, and even his life to the development of the country. He asks nothing from American society except that it consider him as a full-fledged citizen, vested with all of the rights and privileges granted to other citizens; that the charter of liberties of the Constitution apply to the black as to all other men. The Negro citizen has long since learned that "special" treatment for him implies differentiation on a racial basis and inevitably connotes inferior status. In a world in which democracy is gravely besieged and its very foundations shaken, the United States must consider seriously the implications of its own failure to extend the democratic process in full to some thirteen million of its citizens whose present status tends to make a mockery of the Constitution. The thinking Negro appreciates fully the difficulties inherent in the American social system. He recognizes that deep-seated social attitudes are not quickly changed. Yet it can be readily understood that, in a world in which dogmas of racial superiority and racial persecution assume an increasingly dominant role, the Negro views with great alarm the stubborn persistence of racial bigotry in America.

The Negro asks only his constitutional right when he demands that the laws of the United States be designed so as to extend their benefits to black as well as to white citizens, and that political parties, governmental agencies, and officials pledge themselves to extend the full measure of law and consti-tution to all men, regardless of race, color, or creed. Never since the Civil War has the Constitution assumed such vital importance in the ordering of the country. The future of the Negro rests with the future of democracy, and Negroes in great numbers now know that every blow struck in behalf of democracy is a blow for the black man's future. . . .

If democracy is to survive the severe trials and buffetings to which it is being subjected in the modern world, it will do so only because it can demonstrate that it is a practical, living philosophy under which all people can live the good life most abundantly. It must prove itself in practice, or be discredited as a theory. Democratic nations such as our own have an obligation to all mankind to prove that democracy, as a form of government, as a practical means of human relationships, is a working and workable concept. This America can do only by abandoning the shallow, vulgar pretense of limited democracy—under which some are free and privileged and others are permanently fettered. The Negro, and especially the Negro in the South, already has had too vivid an experience with embryonic fascism in the very shadow of democracy. Within our own gates are found intense racial hatreds, racial ghettoes, and racial differentials that saturate the political, economic, and social life of the nation. . . .

The Negro should press with all vigor his fight before the courts for the full recognition of his constitutional rights. Court decisions, favorable or unfa-vorable, serve to dramatize the plight of the race more effectively than any other recourse; their propaganda and educative value is great. Certainly appeal to the courts is a useful tactic for an oppressed minority group, and it is fortified by the fact that the Negro cause is honest and just. But the problems of the Negro cannot be solved at the bar. The courts cannot uproot deep-seated social prejudices; they can never bring on a social revolution.

The so-called Negro problem in America is only incidentally a racial one. Many of its roots go deeper than race and are themselves embedded in the fundamental problems of economic conflict and distress which afflict the entire society. The primary interests of the Negro are inextricably tied up with the interests of the masses in the dominant population. Therefore, court decisions such as those upholding the Wagner Act, social security legislation, and minimum wage and hour enactments will in the long run do much to better the condition of the Negro. Every advance made toward lessening the conflict between labor and capital, between laborer and laborer, between white and black workers—in fact, any legislation designed to increase the security of the workingman's present and future—is of the most fundamental significance for the Negro and for all other minority groups in the United States. The courts can never save the Negro from an America torn asunder by industrial conflict and its inevitable by-products, racial intolerance and bigotry. . . .

In the final analysis, however, the political burdens borne by the American Negro cannot be legislated away. The roots of Negro disabilities reach deeply into the economic and political structure of the nation. Negro political ailments are merely symptomatic of more fundamental disorders in the economic system. These disorders cannot be cured by dabbing at the symptoms. The nation's economic house needs to be put in order. In the first place, it is useless to think in terms of full Negro citizenship so long as white and black citizens must engage in daily violent struggle for the wherewithal of life. This is the process that feeds fuel to the fires of race prejudice and perpetuates those mores which stand guard against Negro entrance to the polls. The economy must afford a far larger measure of security for all before the Negro can hope for much greater political advancement. This it can do only as a result of some far-reaching changes in the direction of a socialized economy—at least insofar as the production of the necessities of life is concerned. In the second place, unless the Negro is permitted to share in the fuller fruits of a more liberal and humane economy, political privilege will become sheer mockery. The black vote will never be influential enough to initiate in and of itself any radical changes in the economy. The ballot without bread would be a tragic jest for the Negro.

## Questions for Review and Reflection

1. What does Bunche say is the only real solution to the race problem? How might this assimilation occur? How has "special treatment" established an inferior status for black Americans?
2. What makes a "mockery of the Constitution," according to Bunche?
3. According to Bunche, how are the futures of democracy and of black Americans linked? What is the obligation of all democratic governments?
4. Why do you think that Bunche recommends the courts as the proper arena for the drive for civil rights in America? Do you agree? What might other courses of action be?

# 2

# To Establish Justice

**A**mong the three branches of the federal government, Congress had dominated during the 19th century. National public policy was initiated from the halls of Congress. The 20th century saw a shift of power to the White House.

Article II, Section 2 of the U.S. Constitution states that the president shall report to the Congress "from time to time" on the state of the Union. To determine the state of the Union, presidents can order studies on current issues. President Harry Truman, for example, ordered an accounting from the Commission on Civil Rights. Their report, *To Secure These Rights,* urged federal action to end discrimination in education, employment, and housing. When Truman took those recommendations to Congress, it failed to act. Truman then acted alone and issued Executive Order 9981, which desegregated the armed forces. Presidents have authority to issue such orders that assist the executive branch in carrying out its duties.

Article II, Section 3 of the U.S. Constitution grants the president the power to recommend legislation to the Congress, and President Woodrow Wilson did so as he lobbied for the 19th Amendment, which gives the voting franchise to women. He had opposed the idea but changed his mind, helped to change the votes of some key congressmen, and the long-sought right of women to vote was finally achieved.

Article II, Section 2 of the U.S. Constitution delegates appointment power to the executive. President Franklin D. Roosevelt exercised the authority when he appointed John Collier to head the Bureau of Indian Affairs. With FDR's concept of a *New Deal* for Indians and John Collier's devotion to the Indian struggle for independence, reforms were made including the Indian Reorganization Act which restored at least some Indian sovereignty.

President Dwight Eisenhower exercised his appointment power when he named Earl Warren as chief justice of the Supreme Court. Eisenhower believed that Warren was a moderate, much like himself. To his surprise, Chief Justice Warren turned out to be a judicial activist and a liberal. The first opinion he wrote was the Court's unanimous decision that Warren helped to shape in the 1954 *Brown v. Board of Education* case. The Court heard arguments involving the segregation of African American schoolchildren. "Separate but equal" educational facilities had been the policy in the South since the *Plessy v. Ferguson* decision of 1896. Warren's Court ruled that such a policy violated the 14th Amendment's guarantee of "equal protection," and that it had to end "with all deliberate speed." Much to the chagrin of President Eisenhower, Chief Justice Warren's Court was noted for its liberal decisions.

In the *Hernandez v. Texas* case, the Court expands upon its definition of "equal protection" to assure the rights of Mexican Americans to sit on juries.

Executive Order 9066, issued by President Franklin D. Roosevelt, was the president's attempt to protect national security, but it resulted in the incarceration of over 100,000 Japanese Americans in internment camps during World War II. Following the war, these Asian Americans lobbied Congress for compensation for lost property and other assets. The Evacuation Claims Act was a small step but provided some remuneration.

Presidential power has had mixed results in bringing about more liberty and equality. Sometimes Congress and the courts act in concert with the president and sometimes in spite of him.

## Reading 1

U.S. Congress, 1934

# The Indian Reorganization Act

The Bureau of Indian Affairs (BIA), a federal agency created in the 1830s to oversee Indian public policy, was known to be harsh in its attempts to destroy Indian cultures by limiting the practice of religion, tribal customs, and even the use of Native American language. Native Americans had been dispossessed of their lands because of westward expansion. In the 18th century, the U.S. government placed many tribes onto designated territories "reserved" for them to live in peace. By the 19th century, the government reversed course and introduced a policy of assimilation; that is, a breakup of reservation life through land allotment. It met with little success but contributed to the destruction of lifestyles.

John Collier introduced greater sovereignty in reservation life and employed more Native Americans in the Bureau. A long-time advocate for Indian rights, Collier was appointed by President Franklin D. Roosevelt to take charge of the BIA. He convinced Congress to change its course with the Indian Reorganization Act of 1934. This act provided for the development of Indian lands, purchase of new lands, home rule, economic development, and some self-government. He was instrumental in reestablishing at least a "semisovereign" status for Indian tribes.

## AN ACT

To conserve and develop Indian lands and resources; to extend to Indians the right to form business and other organizations; to establish a credit system for Indians; to grant certain rights of home rule to Indians; to provide for vocational education for Indians; and for other purposes.

*Be it enacted by the Senate and House of Representatives of the United States of America in Congress assembled,* That hereafter no land of any Indian reservation, created or set apart by treaty or agreement with the Indians, Act of Congress, Executive order, purchase, or otherwise, shall be allotted in severalty to any Indian.

SEC. 2. The existing periods of trust placed upon any Indian lands and any restriction on alienation thereof are hereby extended and continued until otherwise directed by Congress.

SEC. 3. The Secretary of the Interior, if he shall find it to be in the public interest, is hereby authorized to restore to tribal ownership the remaining surplus lands of any Indian reservation heretofore opened, or authorized to be opened, to sale, or any other form of disposal by Presidential proclamation, or by any of the public-land laws of the United States: . . .

SEC. 4. Except as herein provided, no sale, devise, gift, exchange or other transfer of restricted Indian lands or of shares in the assets of any Indian tribe or corporation organized hereunder, shall be made or approved: . . .

SEC. 5. . . . Title to any lands or rights acquired pursuant to this Act shall be taken in the name of the United States in trust for the Indian tribe or individual Indian for which the land is acquired, and such lands or rights shall be exempt from State and local taxation. . . .

SEC. 7. The Secretary of the Interior is hereby authorized to proclaim new Indian reservations on lands acquired pursuant to any authority conferred by this Act, or to add such lands to existing reservations: *Provided,* That lands added to existing reservations shall be designated for the exclusive use of Indians entitled by enrollment or by tribal membership to residence at such reservations. . . .

Sᴇᴄ. 16. Any Indian tribe, or tribes, residing on the same reservation, shall have the right to organize for its common welfare, and may adopt an appropriate constitution and bylaws, which shall become effective when ratified by a majority vote of the adult members of the tribe, or of the adult Indians residing on such reservation, as the case may be, at a special election authorized and called by the Secretary of the Interior under such rules and regulations as he may prescribe. Such constitution and bylaws when ratified as aforesaid and approved by the Secretary of the Interior shall be revocable by an election open to the same voters and conducted in the same manner as hereinabove provided. Amendments to the constitution and bylaws may be ratified and approved by the Secretary in the same manner as the original constitution and bylaws.

In addition to all powers vested in any Indian tribe or tribal council by existing law, the constitution adopted by said tribe shall also vest in such tribe or its tribal council the following rights and powers: To employ legal counsel, the choice of counsel and fixing of fees to be subject to the approval of the Secretary of the Interior; to prevent the sale, disposition, lease, or encumbrance of tribal lands, interests in lands, or other tribal assets without the consent of the tribe; and to negotiate with the Federal, State, and local Governments. The Secretary of the Interior shall advise such tribe or its tribal council of all appropriation estimates or Federal projects for the benefit of the tribe prior to the submission of such estimates to the Bureau of the Budget and the Congress. . . .

Sᴇᴄ. 19. The term "Indian" as used in this Act shall include all persons of Indian descent who are members of any recognized Indian tribe now under Federal jurisdiction, and all persons who are descendants of such members who were, on June 1, 1934, residing within the present boundaries of any Indian reservation, and shall further include all other persons of one-half or more Indian blood. For the purposes of this Act, Eskimos and other aboriginal peoples of Alaska shall be considered Indians. The term "tribe" wherever used in this Act shall be construed to refer to any Indian tribe, organized band, pueblo, or the Indians residing on one reservation. The words "adult Indians" wherever used in this Act shall be construed to refer to Indians who have attained the age of twenty-one years.

Approved, June 18, 1934.

# Questions for Review and Reflection

1. What is the purpose of the act?
2. To what use will new Indian lands be put?
3. How does the statute define "Indian"?

# Reading 2

## Executive Order 9981

While entertaining the troops at a USO show during World War II, singer Lena Horne noticed that black troops were seated at the back of the house. She walked through the audience, faced the African-American soldiers with her back to the white audience, and completed her performance. Her statement of opposition represented a growing antipathy among some Americans, black and white, toward racially discriminatory practices.

In World War II, Americans had defeated Nazi Germany and its racist ideology. The sacrifices and contributions of African-American soldiers to that victory were undeniable.

But when an end to segregation in the United States' armed services was proposed after the war, the opposition claimed that integration would harm morale and the cohesiveness of units. In fact, these same arguments are used today against open inclusion of gay men and women in the military.

Nevertheless, President Harry S. Truman (1884–1972), a strong and decisive leader, used the power of his office to end the policy of racial segregation and establish "equality of treatment and opportunity for all persons in the armed services without regard to race, color, religion or national origin."

## Executive Order 9981

**Establishing the President's Committee on Equality of Treatment and Opportunity in the Armed Services**

WHEREAS it is essential that there be maintained in the armed services of the United States the highest standards of democracy, with equality of treatment and opportunity for all those who serve in our country's defense:

NOW, THEREFORE, by virtue of the authority vested in me as President of the United States, by the Constitution and the statutes of the United States, and as Commander in Chief of the armed services, it is hereby ordered as follows:

1. It is hereby declared to be the policy of the President that there shall be equality of treatment and opportunity for all persons in the armed services without regard to race, color, religion or national origin. This policy shall be put into effect as rapidly as possible, having due regard to the time required to effectuate any necessary changes without impairing efficiency or morale.

2. There shall be created in the National Military Establishment an advisory committee to be known as the President's Committee on Equality of Treatment and Opportunity in the Armed Services, which shall be composed of seven members to be designated by the President.

3. The Committee is authorized on behalf of the President to examine into the rules, procedures and practices of the armed services in order to determine in what respect such rules, procedures and practices may be altered or improved with a view to carrying out the policy of this order. The Committee shall confer and advise with the Secretary of Defense, the Secretary of the Army, the Secretary of the Navy, and the Secretary of the Air Force, and shall make such recommendations to the President and to said Secretaries as in the judgment of the Committee will effectuate the policy hereof.

4. All executive departments and agencies of the Federal Government are authorized and directed to cooperate with the Committee in its work, and to furnish the Committee such information or the services of such persons as the Committee may require in the performance of its duties.

# Questions for Review and Reflection

1. Why do you suppose President Truman chose the executive order method of integrating the armed forces instead of congressional legislation? What does his choice reveal about the nature of racism in American society?
2. What was the source of President Truman's authority to unilaterally integrate the armed forces of the United States of America?
3. How did he feel integration of the armed forces would facilitate the highest standards of democracy in the United States? How did Truman's move make the army stronger?
4. What was the President's Committee on Equality of Treatment and Opportunity in the Armed Services? What was the authority of this committee? What was its scope of action?
5. How might the issues surrounding America's involvement in World War II have influenced President Truman's decision to integrate the military? Do you see a similarity between the granting of women's suffrage after World War I and the adoption of desegregation following World War II? Why?

# Reading 3

U.S. Congress, 1948

## The Evacuation Claims Act

With Executive Order 9066, issued by President Franklin D. Roosevelt, over 100,000 Japanese Americans were "relocated" into internment camps for the duration of World War II. (See Chapter 1; Reading 4.) Little notice was given; the interned left behind financial assets that were often confiscated, stolen, or lost. The collective value of this property was over $100 million.

Following the war, there was a short-term effort to compensate some for those losses. The Evacuation Claims Act of 1948 provided relief to those applicants who could demonstrate within an 18-month period their financial loss. The Attorney General was empowered to make payment of awards not exceeding $2500.00. However, it proved to be a highly unsatisfactory compensation plan.

### AN ACT

To authorize the Attorney General to adjudicate certain claims resulting from evacuation of certain persons of Japanese ancestry under military orders.

*Be it enacted by the Senate and House of Representatives of the United States of America in Congress assembled,* That the Attorney General shall have jurisdiction to determine according to law any claim by a person of Japanese ancestry against the United States arising on or after December 7, 1941, when such claim is not compensated for by insurance or otherwise, for damage to or loss of real or personal property (including without limitation as to amount damage to or loss of personal property bailed to or in the custody of the Government or any agent thereof), that is a reasonable and natural consequence of the evacuation or exclusion of such person by the appropriate military commander from a military area in Arizona, California, Oregon, or Washington; or from the Territory of Alaska, or the Territory of Hawaii, under authority of Executive Order Numbered 9066, dated February 19, 1942 (3 CFR, Cum. Supp., 1092), section 67 of the Act of April 30, 1900 (48 U. S. C. 532), or Executive Order Numbered 9489, dated October 18, 1944 (3 CFR, 1944 Supp., 45). As used herein "evacuation" shall include voluntary departure from a military area prior to but in anticipation of an order of exclusion therefrom.

## LIMITATIONS; CLAIMS NOT TO BE CONSIDERED

SEC. 2. (a) The Attorney General shall receive claims for a period of eighteen months from the date of enactment of this Act. All claims not presented within that time shall be forever barred.

(b) The Attorney General shall not consider any claim—

(1) by or on behalf of any person who after December 7, 1941, was voluntarily or involuntarily deported from the United States to Japan or by and on behalf of any alien who on December 7, 1941, was not actually residing in the United States;

(2) for damage or loss arising out of action taken by any Federal agency pursuant to sections 4067, 4068, 4069, and 4070 (relating to alien enemies) of the Revised Statutes, as amended (50 U. S. C. 21–24), or pursuant to the Trading With the Enemy Act, as amended (50 U. S. C. App., and Supp., 1–31, 616);

(3) for damage or loss to any property, or interest therein, vested in the United States pursuant to said Trading With the Enemy Act, as amended;

(4) for damage or loss on account of death or personal injury, personal inconvenience, physical hardship, or mental suffering; and

(5) for loss of anticipated profits or loss of anticipated earnings.

# Ⓠ uestions for Review and Reflection

1. Who will determine the validity of evacuation claims?
2. Why did this act not bring closure to the issue of compensation?

# Reading 4

U.S. Supreme Court, 1954

# *Brown v. Board of Education,* 347 U.S. 483

In the *Plessy v. Ferguson* case, the Supreme Court of the United States in 1896 upheld a Louisiana state law requiring that facilities for blacks and whites be separate in public accommodations such as railroad cars and schools. The Court reasoned that as long as the facilities were equal, a state could keep racial groups apart. This "separate but equal" doctrine legalized segregation in the South for decades afterward.

But in 1954, plaintiffs in the *Brown v. Board of Education* case contended that they were deprived of equal protection of the laws. Lawyers for eight-year-old Linda Brown argued that it was unconstitutional for Topeka, Kansas, to bus Linda five miles to a black school rather than let her attend her neighborhood school. Nor was distance the only issue. As parents were very much aware, schools for African-American students were not only separate but under-equipped and vastly inferior. The Warren Court agreed, reversed *Plessy,* and ordered the integration of schools with all deliberate speed. This case secured the equal right to obtain an education and the equal protections guaranteed in the Fourteenth Amendment. Soon to follow would be a similar demand for equal access to all public facilities, spurred by Montgomery, Alabama, seamstress Rosa Parks, who bravely refused to give up her seat on the bus to a white passenger. In November 1956, the Supreme Court ordered an end to the Montgomery bus segregation.

## Brown v. Board of Education

The plaintiffs contend that segregated public schools are not "equal" and cannot be made equal, and that hence they are deprived of the equal protection of the laws. . . .

Today, education is perhaps the most important function of state and local governments. Compulsory school attendance laws and the great expenditures for education both demonstrate our recognition of the importance of education to our democratic society. It is required in the performance of our most basic public responsibilities, even service in the armed forces. It is the very foundation of good citizenship. Today it is a principal instrument in awakening the child to cultural values, in preparing him for later professional training, and in helping him to adjust normally to his environment. In these days, it is doubtful that any child may reasonably be expected to succeed in life if he is denied the opportunity of an education. Such an opportunity, where the state has undertaken to provide it, is a right which must be made available to all on equal terms.

We come then to the question presented. Does segregation of children in public schools solely on the basis of race, even though the physical facilities and other "tangible" factors may be equal, deprive the children of the minority group equal educational opportunities? We believe that it does.

In *Sweatt v. Painter,* in finding that a segregated law school for Negroes could not provide them equal educational opportunities, this Court relied in large part on "those qualities which are incapable of objective measurement but which make for greatness in a law school." In *McLaurin v. Oklahoma State Regents*, the Court, in requiring that a Negro admitted to a white graduate school be treated like all other students, again resorted to intangible considerations: "his ability to study, to engage in discussions and exchange views with other students, and in general, to learn his profession." Such considerations apply with added force to children in grade and high schools. To separate them from others of similar age and qualifications solely because of their race generates a feeling of inferiority as to their status in the community that may affect their hearts and minds in a way unlikely ever to be undone. . . .

We conclude that in the field of public education the doctrine of "separate but equal" has no place. Separate educational facilities are inherently unequal.

# Questions for Review and Reflection

1. Describe the importance of education as defined by the Supreme Court.
2. What are the "intangible considerations" spelled out by the Court?
3. How does racial separation affect a child, according to this decision?

# Reading 5

U.S. Supreme Court, 1954

## *Hernandez v. Texas*, 347 U.S. 475

The Treaty of Guadalupe Hidalgo that settled the Mexican-American War gave all former citizens of Mexico the rights and privileges of U.S. citizens.

Practically speaking, however, Mexicans who became Americans were given second-class status. Not granted the equal protection of the laws, they were confronted with separate and unequal treatment in public facilities and in education. Sometimes through fraud, sometimes through confiscation, lands that they had owned as Mexicans were taken from them when they became Mexican Americans.

Another practice was to deny Mexican Americans the right to sit on juries, a policy in Texas and in some other southwestern states in the mid-20th century. The case of *Hernandez v. Texas* challenged this practice. Courts had already ruled that it was unconstitutional to single out and discriminate against a distinct class of people based upon race or ethnicity.

In this case, the U.S. Supreme Court ruled against Texas by stating that "the exclusion of otherwise eligible persons from jury service solely because of their ancestry or national origin is discrimination prohibited by the Fourteenth Amendment." Texas had tried to argue that such discrimination applied only to two classes of persons, "white" and "Negro." The Court discarded that notion.

## Hernandez v. Texas

Certiorari to the Court of Criminal Appeals of Texas.

Mr. Chief Justice Warren delivered the opinion of the Court.

The petitioner, Pete Hernandez, was indicted for the murder of one Joe Espinosa by a grand jury in Jackson County, Texas. He was convicted and sentenced to life imprisonment. The Texas Court of Criminal Appeals affirmed the judgment of the trial court.—Tex. Cr. R.—, 251 S.W.2d 531. Prior to the trial, the petitioner, by his counsel, offered timely motions to quash the indictment and the jury panel. He alleged that persons of Mexican descent were systematically excluded from service as jury commissioners, grand jurors, and petit jurors, although there were such persons fully qualified to serve residing in Jackson County. The petitioner asserted that exclusion of this class deprived him, as a member of the class, of the equal protection of the laws guaranteed by the Fourteenth Amendment of the Constitution. . . .

In numerous decisions, this Court has held that it is a denial of the equal protection of the laws to try a defendant of a particular race or color under an indictment issued by a grand jury, or before a petit jury, from which all persons of his race or color have, solely because of that race or color, been excluded by the state, whether acting through its legislature, its courts, or its executive or administrative officers. Although the Court has had little occasion to rule on the question directly, it has been recognized since Strauder v. West Virginia, 100 U.S. 303, that the exclusion of a class of persons from jury service on grounds other than race or color may also deprive a defendant who is a member of that class of the constitutional guarantee of equal protection of the laws. The state of Texas would have us hold that there are only two classes—white and Negro—within the contemplation of the Fourteenth Amendment. The decisions of this Court do not support that view. And, except where the question presented involves the exclusion of persons of Mexican descent from juries, Texas courts have taken a broader view of the scope of the equal protection clause.

Throughout our history differences in race and color have defined easily identifiable groups which have at times required the aid of the courts in securing equal treatment under the laws. But community prejudices are not static, and from time to time other differences from the community norm may define other groups which need the same protection. Whether such a group exists within a community is a question of fact. When the existence of a distinct class is demonstrated, and it is further shown that the laws, as written or as applied, single out that class for different treatment not based on some reasonable classification, the guarantees of the Constitution have been violated. The Fourteenth Amendment is not directed solely against discrimination due to a "two-class theory"—that is, based upon differences between "white" and Negro.

As the petitioner acknowledges, the Texas system of selecting grand and petit jurors by the use of jury commissions is fair on its face and capable of being utilized without discrimination. But as this Court has held, the system is susceptible to abuse and can be employed in a discriminatory manner. The exclusion of otherwise eligible persons from jury service solely because of their ancestry or national origin is discrimination prohibited by the Fourteenth Amendment. The Texas statute makes no such discrimination, but the petitioner alleges that those administering the law do.

The petitioner's initial burden in substantiating his charge of group discrimination was to prove that persons of Mexican descent constitute a separate class in Jackson County, distinct from "whites." One method by which this may be demonstrated is by showing the attitude of the community. Here the testimony of responsible officials and citizens contained the admission that residents of the community distinguished between "white" and "Mexican." The participation of persons of Mexican descent in business and community groups was shown to be slight. Until very recent times, children of Mexican descent were required to attend a segregated school for the first four grades. At least one restaurant in town prominently displayed a sign announcing "no Mexicans served." On the courthouse grounds at the time of the hearing, there were two men's toilets, one unmarked, and the other marked "colored men" and "hombres aqui" ("men here"). No substantial evidence was offered to rebut the logical inference to be drawn from these facts, and it must be concluded that petitioner succeeded in his proof.

Having established the existence of a class, petitioner was then charged with the burden of proving discrimination. To do so, he relied on the pattern of proof established by Norris v. Alabama, 294 U.S. 587. In that case, proof that Negroes constituted a substantial segment of the population of the jurisdiction, that some Negroes were qualified to serve as jurors, and that none had been called for jury service over an extended period of time, was held to constitute prima facie proof of the systematic exclusion of Negroes from jury service. This holding, sometimes called the "rule of exclusion," has been applied in other cases, and it is available in supplying proof of discrimination against any delineated class. . . .

The same reasoning is applicable to these facts.

Circumstances or chance may well dictate that no persons in a certain class will serve on a particular jury or during some particular period. But it taxes our credulity to say that mere chance resulted in there being no members of this class among the over six thousand jurors called in the past 25 years. The result bespeaks discrimination, whether or not it was a conscious decision on the part of any individual jury commissioner. The judgment of conviction must be reversed. . . .

## [Q] uestions for Review and Reflection

1. What U.S. constitutional amendments are at issue in this case?
2. What is the "two-class theory"?
3. What was the petitioner required to present to prove that persons of Mexican descent constitute a separate class?
4. The Supreme Court complained that a fact of the case "taxes our credulity." What was that fact?

# Pursuing the American Dream

In the 1950s an inspired national civil rights movement began. Rosa Parks, a 43-year-old department store worker, went to jail rather than give up her seat to a white person on a Montgomery, Alabama, bus. Her brave stand energized a citywide bus boycott until segregation on the city's transportation system ended.

The 1960s were characterized both by disillusionment with traditional power structures in America and by optimism that unsatisfactory and unfair conditions could be changed. A collection of forces came together to make it a turbulent decade filled with historic moments.

The Reverend Martin Luther King Jr. emerged from the success of the Montgomery bus boycott as leader of an organized program of passive resistance to segregation laws across the South, using the tools of nonviolent protest and peaceful demonstration. In August, 1963, he led over 250,000 people in a march on Washington, D.C., where he spoke of his dream to see America as a truly equal society.

In 1966, Betty Friedan, a major figure in the women's movement, formed the National Organization for Women (NOW), an interest group that worked for equal pay, reproductive rights, and an end to sex discrimination. She spoke on behalf of political, social, and economic equality for all American women. The organization began to recruit female candidates for public office and revitalized the effort to ratify the Equal Rights Amendment.

Cesar Chavez headed the United Farm Workers (UFW) organization, begun in 1962 in California. The UFW is dedicated to the improvement of working conditions and wages for the migrant workers who had long been exploited by giant farming cooperatives.

Latino-American political groups arose throughout the southwest in the 1960s. They worked locally and nationally for bicultural/bilingual education and bilingual balloting.

Native Americans drew energy from the civil rights activism of the 1960s and embarked on their own form of expression. Between 1969 and 1973, members of the activist American Indian Movement (AIM) and other groups occupied three locations as political protests. At the "Rock," Alcatraz Island in California, they hoped to establish a Native-American cultural center. At the Bureau of Indian Affairs in Washington, D.C., they tried to win self-determination and control of the resources of their own lands. At an Indian reservation at Wounded Knee, South Dakota, they demanded redress for the "Trail of Broken Treaties," and took eleven hostages in a 71-day siege there.

Young Asian Americans began to be heard on issues of discrimination, despite their public image as "the model minority," a title they had earned for their ability to enter the mainstream and succeed in American society.

Americans of the 1950s and 1960s, having lived through the Great Depression and World War II, seemed more attuned to the voices of the excluded than they had been in earlier decades. Perhaps their receptivity was partly because television cameras had captured the police dogs and fire hoses used against peaceful, black protesters in Birmingham, Alabama; the migrant workers' fight against agribusiness; and the grim conditions on Indian reservations. Media coverage of stories galvanized support.

The spirit of the 1960s was also fueled by a large population of young "baby boomers," born shortly after World War II. These young optimists heard the challenge in President John F. Kennedy's 1960 Inaugural Address: "Ask not what your country can do for you, but what you can do for your country!" They were inspired to action. Whites joined blacks in "freedom rides" and protests. Men joined women in membership of NOW. Unions asked for public support in their demands for better wages and working conditions and got consumers to join farm workers in their boycott of table grapes.

When Kennedy was assassinated in November 1963, during a motorcade in Dallas, Texas, Vice-President Lyndon Johnson assumed the presidency and continued the programs introduced by the Kennedy administration, with many additions of his own. Americans supported Johnson's use of federal intervention to wage his War on Poverty and to create the Great Society. Congress passed the Head Start program for disadvantaged preschoolers, a Job Corps for training and remedial education, a domestic Peace Corps, a plan for urban renewal, and significant aid programs for elementary and secondary public schools.

Against this backdrop of optimism, the escalating conflict in Vietnam was a persistent source of debate and social confrontation. America had become involved in the affairs of Vietnam while enforcing its policy of containment against communism. The entanglement began slowly but built up over time to a major commitment of over 500,000 troops. The cost in terms of money, equipment, men, and morale was staggering and resulted in the termination of Johnson's political career. The events of 1968 illustrate much of what had gone wrong. Antiwar feeling ran high because of public disillusionment with the war's purpose versus its cost. There was campus unrest among students who questioned the country's moral underpinnings and society's commitment to democratic principles. Race riots had erupted over the previous several years in Watts, a section of Los Angeles, and in Chicago, Detroit, and Cleveland. Muhammad Ali, then heavyweight boxing champion of the world, spoke out against the "white man's war" in Vietnam and refused to be inducted. Some African American groups broke away from Dr. King's message of nonviolence. Malcolm X espoused black nationalism and violence, if necessary, against "Whitey." Violence struck another blow when Martin Luther King Jr. was assassinated. Shortly afterward, John Kennedy's brother, Robert, U.S. senator from New York, was shot and killed while campaigning for the presidential nomination.

Richard Nixon won the presidency in 1968, campaigning on behalf of the "forgotten American," described by Nixon as the hardworking, taxpaying citizen who was part of the "silent majority." He attacked dissenters who spoke against the war, against the country, and against the traditional values of American society. With his election, the burst of enthusiasm and support for economic and social equality sputtered into disillusionment toward the end of the decade. The country underwent a progressive reduction in support for Great Society programs and moved toward moderate government intervention. Desegregation efforts slowed, enforcement of civil rights laws was reduced, and fewer funds were available for welfare assistance.

However, the decade had served to coalesce and organize the groups that had been so long excluded from the system. The sense of their power in numbers and the justice of their cause was not lost, and their fight became a permanent fixture in American politics.

# Reading **1**

Martin Luther King Jr., 1963

# Letter from a Birmingham Jail

Acknowledged leader of the civil rights movement in the 1950s and 1960s and head of the Southern Christian Leadership Conference, the Reverend Martin Luther King Jr. (1929–1968) used a protest march to spotlight the injustice and brutality of the city of Birmingham, Alabama. He was arrested for acting as an "outside agitator" and breaking the law.

An advocate of passive resistance, Dr. King earned the Nobel Peace Prize in 1964. "Nonviolent direct action seeks to create such a crisis and foster such a tension that a community which has constantly refused to negotiate is forced to confront the issue."

King hoped that such action would awaken Americans to "those great wells of democracy which were dug deep by the founding fathers in their formulation of the Constitution and the Declaration of Independence" and which would lead the country toward the practice of democratic principles.

I think I should indicate why I am here in Birmingham, since you have been influenced by the view which argues against "outsiders coming in." I have the honor of serving as president of the Southern Christian Leadership Conference, an organization operating in every southern state, with headquarters in Atlanta, Georgia. We have some eighty-five affiliated organizations across the South, and one of them is the Alabama Christian Movement for Human Rights. Frequently we share staff, educational and financial resources with our affiliates. Several months ago the affiliate here in Birmingham asked us to be on call to engage in a nonviolent direct-action program if such were deemed necessary. We readily consented, and when the hour came we lived up to our promise. So I, along with several members of my staff, am here because I was invited here. I am here because I have organizational ties here. . . .

You deplore the demonstrations taking place in Birmingham. But your statement, I am sorry to say, fails to express a similar concern for the conditions that brought about the demonstrations. I am sure that none of you would want to rest content with the superficial kind of social analysis that deals merely with effects and does not grapple with underlying causes. It is unfortunate that demonstrations are taking place in Birmingham, but it is even more unfortunate that the city's white power structure left the Negro community with no alternative.

In any nonviolent campaign there are four basic steps: collection of the facts to determine whether injustices exist; negotiation; self-purification; and direct action. We have gone through all these steps in Birmingham. There can be no gainsaying the fact that racial injustice engulfs this community. Birmingham is probably the most thoroughly segregated city in the United States. Its ugly record of brutality is widely known. Negroes have experienced grossly unjust treatment in the courts. There have been more unsolved bombings of Negro homes and churches in Birmingham than in any other city in the nation.

These are the hard, brutal facts of the case. On the basis of these conditions, Negro leaders sought to negotiate with the city fathers. But the latter consistently refused to engage in good-faith negotiation. . . .

As in so many past experiences, our hopes had been blasted, and the shadow of deep disappointment settled upon us. We had no alternative except to prepare for direct action, whereby we would present our very bodies as a means of laying our case before the conscience of the local and the national community. Mindful of the difficulties involved, we decided to undertake a process of self-purification. We began a series of workshops on nonviolence, and we repeatedly asked ourselves: "Are you able to accept blows without retaliating?" "Are you able to endure the ordeal of jail?" We decided to schedule our direct-action program for the Easter season, realizing that except for Christmas, this is the main shopping period of the year. Knowing that a strong economic-withdrawal program would be the by-product of direct action, we felt that this would be the best time to bring pressure to bear on the merchants for the needed change.

You may well ask: "Why direct action? Why sit-ins, marches and so forth? Isn't negotiation a better path?" You are quite right in calling for negotiation. Indeed, this is the very purpose of direct action. Nonviolent direct action seeks to create such a crisis and foster such a tension that a community which has constantly refused to negotiate is forced to confront the issue. It seeks so to dramatize the issue that it can no longer be ignored. My citing the creation of tension as part of the work of the nonviolent resister may sound rather shocking. But I must confess that I am not afraid of the word "tension." I have earnestly opposed violent tension, but there is a type of constructive, nonviolent tension which is necessary for growth. Just as Socrates felt that it was necessary to create a tension in the mind so that individuals could rise from the bondage of myths and half-truths to the unfettered realm of creative analysis and objective appraisal, so must we see the need for nonviolent gadflies to create the kind of tension in society that will help men rise from the dark depths of prejudice and racism to the majestic heights of understanding and brotherhood.

The purpose of our direct-action program is to create a situation so crisis-packed that it will inevitably open the door to negotiation. I therefore concur with you in your call for negotiation. Too long has our beloved Southland been bogged down in a tragic effort to live in monologue rather than dialogue. . . .

We know through painful experience that freedom is never voluntarily given by the oppressor; it must be demanded by the oppressed. Frankly, I have yet to engage in a direct-action campaign that was "well timed" in the view of those who have not suffered unduly from the disease of segregation. For years now I have heard the word "Wait!" It rings in the ear of every Negro with piercing familiarity. This "Wait" has almost always meant "Never." We must come to see, with one of our distinguished jurists, that "justice too long delayed is justice denied." . . .

You express a great deal of anxiety over our willingness to break laws. This is certainly a legitimate concern. Since we so diligently urge people to obey the Supreme Court's decision of 1954 outlawing segregation in the public schools, at first glance it may seem rather paradoxical for us consciously to break laws. One may well ask: "How can you advocate breaking some laws and obeying others?" The answer lies in the fact that there are two types of laws: just and unjust. I would be the first to advocate obeying just laws. One has not only a legal but a moral responsibility to obey just laws. Conversely, one has a moral responsibility to disobey unjust laws. I would agree with St. Augustine that "an unjust law is no law at all."

Now, what is the difference between the two? How does one determine whether a law is just or unjust? A just law is a man-made code that squares with the moral law or the law of God. An unjust law is a code that is out of harmony with the moral law. To put it in the terms of St. Thomas Aquinas: An unjust law is a human law that is not rooted in eternal law and natural law. Any law that uplifts human personality is just. Any law that degrades human personality is unjust. All segregation statutes are unjust because segregation distorts the soul and damages the personality. It gives the segregator a false sense of superiority and the segregated a false sense of inferiority. Segregation, to use the terminology of the Jewish philosopher Martin Buber, substitutes an "I-it" relationship for an "I-thou" relationship and ends up relegating persons to the status of things. Hence segregation is not only politically, economically and sociologically unsound, it is morally wrong and sinful. Paul Tillich has said that sin is separation. Is not segregation an existential expression of man's tragic separation, his awful estrangement, his terrible sinfulness? Thus it is that I can urge men to obey the 1954 decision of the Supreme Court, for it is morally right; and I can urge them to disobey segregation ordinances, for they are morally wrong. . . .

I hope you are able to see the distinction I am trying to point out. In no sense do I advocate evading or defying the law, as would the rabid segregationist. That would lead to anarchy. One who breaks an unjust law must do so openly, lovingly, and with a willingness to accept the penalty. I submit that an individual who breaks a law that conscience tells him is unjust, and who willingly accepts the penalty of imprisonment in order to arouse the conscience of the community over its injustice, is in reality expressing the highest respect for law.

Of course, there is nothing new about this kind of civil disobedience. It was evidenced sublimely in the refusal of Shadrach, Meshach and Abednego to obey the laws of Nebuchadnezzar, on the ground that a higher moral law was at stake. It was practiced superbly by the early Christians who were willing to face hungry lions and the excruciating pain of chopping blocks rather than submit to certain unjust laws of the Roman Empire. To a degree, academic freedom is a reality today because Socrates practiced civil disobedience. In our own nation, the Boston Tea Party represented a massive act of civil disobedience. . . .

Before closing I feel impelled to mention one other point in your statement that has troubled me profoundly. You warmly commended the Birmingham police force for keeping "order" and "preventing violence." I doubt that you would have so warmly commended the police force if you had seen its dogs sinking their teeth into unarmed, nonviolent Negroes. I doubt that you would so quickly commend the policemen if you were to observe their ugly and inhumane treatment of Negroes here in the city jail; if you were to watch them push and curse old Negro women and young Negro girls; if you were to see them slap and kick old Negro men and young boys; if you were to observe them, as they did on two occasions, refuse to give us food because we wanted to sing our grace together. I cannot join you in your praise of the Birmingham police department.

It is true that the police have exercised a degree of discipline in handling the demonstrators. In this sense they have conducted themselves rather "nonviolently" in public. But for what purpose? To preserve the evil system of segregation. Over the past few years I have consistently preached that nonviolence demands that the means we use must be as pure as the ends we seek. I have tried to make clear that it is wrong to use immoral means to attain moral ends. But now I must affirm that it is just as wrong, or perhaps even more so, to use moral means to preserve immoral ends. Perhaps Mr. Connor and his policemen have been rather nonviolent in public, as was Chief Pritchett in Albany, Georgia, but they have used the moral means of nonviolence to maintain the immoral end of racial injustice. As T. S. Eliot has said: "The last temptation is the greatest treason: To do the right deed for the wrong reason."

I wish you had commended the Negro sit-inners and demonstrators of Birmingham for their sublime courage, their willingness to suffer and their amazing discipline in the midst of great provocation. One day the South will recognize its real heroes. They will be the James Merediths, with the noble sense of purpose that enables them to face jeering and hostile mobs, and with the agonizing loneliness that characterizes the life of the pioneer. They will be old, oppressed, battered Negro women, symbolized in a seventy-two-year-old woman in Montgomery, Alabama, who rose up with a sense of dignity and with her people decided not to ride segregated buses, and who responded with ungrammatical profundity to one who inquired about her weariness: "My feets is tired, but my soul is at rest." They will be the young high school and college students, the young ministers of the gospel and a host of their elders, courageously and nonviolently sitting in at lunch counters and willingly going to jail for conscience' sake. One day the South will know that when these disinherited children of God sat down at lunch counters, they were in reality standing up for what is best in the American dream and for the most sacred values in our Judaeo-Christian heritage, thereby bringing our nation back to those great wells of democracy which were dug deep by the founding fathers in their formulation of the Constitution and the Declaration of Independence.

# Questions for Review and Reflection

1. According to King, why was he in Birmingham? What were the conditions that brought about the demonstration in the city?
2. King states that they had no alternative but to engage in "direct action." What was the nature of this direct action? Why was it necessary? How did the workshops on nonviolence prepare the protesters for Birmingham? Were they successful?
3. What had history taught King regarding the acquisition of freedom from the oppressors? How did this lesson impact the civil rights movement?
4. What distinction does King draw between laws that should be obeyed and those that should not? Do you agree or disagree? What might lead you to civil disobedience?
5. How did King employ T. S. Eliot's statement, "The last temptation is the greatest treason: To do the right deed for the wrong reason"? Is this an effective argument?

# Reading 2

Betty Friedan, 1963

## *The Feminine Mystique*

Women were accepted into nontraditional fields of work during World War II to replace men lost to the war effort. Women built planes, serviced ships, manufactured weaponry. But when the war was over, they were urged to return to their homes to make room for servicemen coming back. Postwar publicity attempted to glorify the homemaker and her role as wife and mother. Girls were encouraged to marry, have children, and be satisfied with family life. Women who remained at work continued to face legal inequities such as disparate wages and unequal access to job opportunities.

Born in 1921, Betty Friedan was a middle-class housewife who had completed a college degree in psychology, married, and begun to raise a family. She conducted a study from her home in the early '60s by sampling her former fellow college students about the contentment they felt with staying at home. She discovered a "problem that had no name" among the dissatisfied suburban housewives who wanted more out of life.

In 1966 Friedan formed the National Organization for Women, an interest group that advocated absolute political, social, and economic equality. Friedan put forth "a new life plan" for women, which would entitle them to the same rights as men "to compete then, not as a woman, but as a human being."

The problem lay buried, unspoken, for many years in the minds of American women. It was a strange stirring, a sense of dissatisfaction, a yearning that women suffered in the middle of the 20th century in the United States. Each suburban wife struggled with it alone. As she made the beds, shopped for groceries, matched slipcover material, ate peanut butter sandwiches with her children, chauffeured cub scouts and brownies, lay beside her husband at night, she was afraid to ask even of herself the silent question—is this all?

. . . The problem that has no name—which is simply the fact that American women are kept from growing to their full human capacities—is taking a far greater toll on the physical and mental health of our country than any known disease.

. . . These problems cannot be solved by medicine, or even by psychotherapy. We need a drastic reshaping of the cultural image of femininity that will permit women to reach maturity, identity, completeness of self, without conflict with sexual fulfillment. A massive attempt must be made by educators and parents—and ministers, magazine editors, manipulators, guidance counselors—to stop the early-marriage movement, stop girls from growing up wanting to be "just a housewife," stop it by insisting, with the same attention from childhood that parents and educators give to boys, that girls develop the resources of self, goals that will permit them to find their own identity.

. . . It is perhaps beside the point to remark that bowling alleys and supermarkets have nursery facilities, while schools and colleges and scientific laboratories and government offices do not. But it is very much to the point to say that if an able American woman does not use her human energy and ability in some meaningful pursuit . . . she will fritter away her energy in neurotic symptoms, or unproductive exercise, or destructive "love."

It also is time to stop giving lip service to the idea that there are no battles left to be fought for women in America, that women's rights have already been won. It is ridiculous to tell girls to keep quiet when they enter a new field, or an old one, so that men will not notice they are there. In almost every professional field, in business and in the arts and sciences, women are still treated as second-class citizens. It would be a great service to tell girls who plan to work in society to expect this subtle, uncomfortable discrimination—tell them not to be quiet, and hope it will go away, but fight it. A girl should not expect special privileges because of her sex, but neither should she "adjust" to prejudice and discrimination.

She must learn to compete then, not as a woman, but as a human being. Not until a great many women move out of the fringes into the mainstream, will society itself provide the arrangements for their new life plan.

## |Q| uestions for Review and Reflection

1. What is this problem that Friedan claims lay buried, unspoken, for many years? In other words, what is the problem with no name? What is the solution?
2. How might Friedan's suggestion about a "drastic reshaping of the culture" take place? Do you think she is being practical?
3. What does she say is the danger of early marriage for young American women? Do you agree or disagree?
4. What point do you think Friedan was trying to make when she pointed out that bowling alleys and supermarkets have nursery facilities, while schools, colleges, and government buildings do not? How might this point advance her goals?
5. What evidence might Friedan employ to prove her assertion that women in America are still second-class citizens? Do you agree or disagree?

# Reading 3

Martin Luther King Jr., 1963

## "I Have a Dream" Speech

African Americans endured the segregationist policies of the South for decades. Blacks sat in the back of public buses, for example, unless there were unused seats, but had to defer to any white rider. One day in December 1955, Rosa Parks, a black woman, refused to give up her seat to a white person and was arrested. A young minister organized a year-long bus boycott to protest such customs and began the modern civil rights movement.

Dr. Martin Luther King Jr. (1929–1968) was that minister and eventual leader of the Southern Christian Leadership Conference. His was a nonviolent approach. Passive resistance, he said, would eventually bring about the justice so long denied. His oratory rallied not just African Americans but the whole nation, as they watched on television the hatred and brutality that he and the protesters faced day after day. The success of the bus boycott led to a full-scale effort across the South for equal rights through the integration of schools, lunchrooms, and other public facilities.

In August 1963, King led an impressive march on Washington, D.C., where his power and eloquence were spotlighted in this now-famous speech, in which he spoke on behalf of equal rights for all Americans.

I say to you today, my friends, that in spite of the difficulties and frustrations of the moment I still have a dream. It is a dream deeply rooted in the American dream.

I have a dream that one day this nation will rise up and live out the true meaning of its creed: "We hold these truths to be self-evident; that all men are created equal."

I have a dream that one day on the red hills of Georgia the sons of former slaves and the sons of former slaveowners will be able to sit down together at the table of brotherhood.

I have a dream that one day even the state of Mississippi, a desert state sweltering with the heat of injustice and oppression, will be transformed into an oasis of freedom and justice.

I have a dream that my four little children will one day live in a nation where they will not be judged by the color of their skin but by the content of their character.

I have a dream today.

I have a dream that one day the state of Alabama, whose governor's lips are presently dripping with the words of interposition and nullification, will be transformed into a situation where little black boys and black girls will be able to join hands with little white boys and white girls and walk together as sisters and brothers.

I have a dream today.

I have a dream that one day every valley shall be exalted, every hill and mountain shall be made low, the rough places will be made plain, and the crooked places will be made straight, and the glory of the Lord shall be revealed, and all flesh shall see it together.

This is our hope. This is the faith with which I return to the South. With this faith we will be able to hew out of the mountain of despair a stone of hope. With this faith we will be able to transform the jangling discords of our nation into a beautiful symphony of brotherhood.

With this faith we will be able to work together, to pray together, to struggle together, to go to jail together, to stand up for freedom together, knowing that we will be free one day.

This will be the day when all of God's children will be able to sing with new meaning, "My country 'tis of thee, sweet land of liberty, of thee I sing. Land where my fathers died, land of the Pilgrims' pride, from every mountain-side, let freedom ring."

And if America is to be a great nation, this must become true. So let freedom ring from the prodigious hilltops of New Hampshire. Let freedom ring from the mighty mountains of New York. Let freedom ring from the heightening Alleghenies of Pennsylvania!

Let freedom ring from the snowcapped Rockies of Colorado! Let freedom ring from the curvaceous peaks of California! But not only that; let freedom ring from Stone Mountain of Georgia! Let freedom ring from Lookout Mountain of Tennessee!

Let freedom ring from every hill and molehill of Mississippi. From every mountainside, let freedom ring.

When we let freedom ring, when we let it ring from every village and every hamlet, from every state and every city, we will be able to speed up that day when all of God's children, black men and white men, Jews and gentiles, Protestants and Catholics, will be able to join hands and sing in the words of the old Negro spiritual, "Free at last! Free at last! Thank God Almighty, we are free at last!"

## |Q| uestions for Review and Reflection

1. In what way does King draw upon the same natural rights philosophy that the framers of the Constitution did? What are the similarities? What are the differences?
2. Why do you suppose King's emotional appeal struck such a harmonious chord with so many Americans?
3. How do you think King's appeal was received by those who did not agree with his goals?
4. How does King make an appeal to the religious traditions in American history? How effective was this appeal to Christian ideals?
5. In what ways does King both draw upon and challenge traditional American ideals?

# Reading 4

Malcolm X, 1964

## Speech to New York Meeting

So familiar is Malcolm X's name, especially among African Americans, that the shorthand "X" on a cap is enough to evoke it. Born Malcolm Little as one of 11 children, he was a high-school dropout and convicted burglar who joined the Nation of Islam and became a follower of Elijah Mohammed while serving a 10-year prison sentence. He adopted the X, he said, because he became an "ex-smoker, ex-drinker, ex-Christian and ex-slave."

Once out of prison, Malcolm X (1925–1965) became a spokesperson for the Black Muslims to large audiences, both black and white. He was provocative, charismatic, and his words brought him a following. His militant rhetoric advocated black nationalism as the way to achieve full economic and political rights, "by any means necessary," which frightened many white Americans.

Malcolm X eventually broke with Elijah Mohammed and in 1964 went on a pilgrimage to Mecca. There he met white Muslims who were free of prejudice; this experience caused him to reconsider his absolutist position on separatism. Upon returning to America, he formed the Organization of African Unity. He was assassinated following a public speech in 1965, allegedly by jealous partisans of Elijah Mohammed.

Following his trip to Mecca, Malcolm's words continued to have a threatening quality, but his proposals were more conciliatory. The "full use of the ballot in every one of the fifty states," which was essential and fundamental, was the only alternative to a revolution of interracial violence. Those limited choices only underscored the frustration felt by Malcolm X and other black leaders with a system that denied the representation they had been promised since Reconstruction days. He delivered the speech excerpted here to the Militant Labor Forum, a socialist group.

**A**ny kind of racial explosion that takes place in this country today, in 1964, is not a racial explosion that can be confined to the shores of America. It is a racial explosion that can ignite the racial powder keg that exists all over the planet that we call Earth. I think that nobody would disagree that the dark masses of Africa and Asia and Latin America are already seething with bitterness, animosity, hostility, unrest, and impatience with the racial intolerance that they themselves have experienced at the hands of the white West.

And just as they have the ingredients of hostility toward the West in general, here we also have 22 million African-Americans, black, brown, red, and yellow people, in this country who are also seething with bitterness and impatience and hostility and animosity at the racial intolerance not only of the white West but of white America in particular.

And by the hundreds of thousands today we find our own people have become impatient, turning away from your white nationalism, which you call democracy, toward the militant, uncompromising policy of black nationalism. I point out right here that as soon as we announced we were going to start a black nationalist party in this country, we received mail from coast to coast, especially from young people at the college level, the university level, who expressed complete sympathy and support and a desire to take an active part in any kind of political action based on black nationalism, designed to correct or eliminate immediately evils that our people have suffered here for 400 years. . . .

1964 will be America's hottest year, her hottest year yet, a year of much racial violence and much racial bloodshed. But it won't be blood that's going to flow only on one side. The new generation of black people that have grown up in this country during recent years are already forming the opinion, and it's a just opinion, that if there is to be bleeding, it should be reciprocal—bleeding on both sides.

It should also be understood that the racial sparks that are ignited here in America today could easily turn into a flaming fire abroad, which means it could engulf all the people of this earth into a giant race war. You cannot confine it to one little neighborhood, or one little community, or one little country. What happens to a black man in America today happens to the black man in Africa. What happens to a black man in America and Africa happens to the black man in Asia and to the man down in Latin America. What happens to one of us today happens to all of us. And when this is realized, I think that the whites—who are intelligent even if they aren't moral or aren't just or aren't impressed by legalities—those who are intelligent will realize that when they touch this one, they are touching all of them, and this in itself will have a tendency to be a checking factor. . . .

We have to keep in mind at all times that we are not fighting for integration, nor are we fighting for separation. We are fighting for recognition as human beings. We are fighting for the right to live as free humans in this society. In fact, we are actually fighting for rights that are even greater than civil rights and that is human rights. . . .

So in this country you find two different types of Afro-Americans—the type who looks upon himself as a minority and you as the majority, because his scope is limited to the American scene; and then you have the type who looks upon himself as part of the majority and you as part of a microscopic minority. And this one uses a different approach in trying to struggle for his rights. He doesn't beg. He doesn't thank you for what you give him, because you are only giving him what he should have had a hundred years ago. He doesn't think you are doing him any favors.

He doesn't see any progress that he has made since the Civil War. He sees not one iota of progress because, number one, if the Civil War had freed him, he wouldn't need civil-rights legislation today. If the Emancipation Proclamation, issued by that great shining liberal called Lincoln, had freed him, he wouldn't be singing "We Shall Overcome" today. If the amendments to the Constitution had solved his problem, his problem wouldn't still be here today. And if the Supreme Court desegregation decision of 1954 was genuinely and sincerely designed to solve his problem, his problem wouldn't be with us today. . . .

There is no system more corrupt than a system that represents itself as the example of freedom, the example of democracy, and can go all over this earth telling other people how to straighten out their house, when you have citizens of this country who have to use bullets if they want to cast a ballot.

The greatest weapon the colonial powers have used in the past against our people has always been divide and conquer. America is a colonial power. She has colonized 22 million Afro-Americans by depriving us of first-class citizenship, by depriving us of civil rights, actually by depriving us of human rights. She has not only deprived us of the right to be a citizen, she has deprived us of the right to be human beings, the right to be recognized and respected as men and women. In this country the black can be fifty years old and he is still a "boy."

I grew up with white people. I was integrated before they even invented the word and I have never met white people yet—if you are around them long enough—who won't refer to you as a "boy" or a "gal," no matter how old you are or what school you came out of, no matter what your intellectual or professional level is. In this society we remain "boys."

So America's strategy is the same strategy as that which was used in the past by the colonial powers: divide and conquer. She plays one Negro leader against the other. She plays one Negro organization against the other. She makes us think we have different objectives, different goals. As soon as one Negro says something, she runs to this Negro and asks him, "What do you think about what he said?" Why, anybody can see through that today—except some of the Negro leaders.

All of our people have the same goals, the same objective. That objective is freedom, justice, equality. All of us want recognition and respect as human beings. We don't want to be integrationists. Nor do we want to be separationists. We want to be human beings. Integration is only a method that is used by some groups to obtain freedom, justice, equality and respect as human beings. Separation is only a method that is used by other groups to obtain freedom, justice, equality or human dignity.

Our people have made the mistake of confusing the methods with the objectives. As long as we agree on objectives, we should never fall out with each other just because we believe in different methods or tactics or strategy to reach a common objective.

Why is America in a position to bring about a bloodless revolution? Because the Negro in this country holds the balance of power, and if the Negro in this country were given what the Constitution says he is supposed to have, the added power of the Negro in this country would sweep all of the racists and the segregationists out of office. It would change the entire political structure of the country. It would wipe out the Southern segregationism that now controls America's foreign policy, as well as America's domestic policy.

And the only way without bloodshed that this can be brought about is that the black man has to be given full use of the ballot in every one of the fifty states. But if the black man doesn't get the ballot, then you are going to be faced with another man who forgets the ballot and starts using the bullet.

Revolutions are fought to get control of land, to remove the absentee landlord and gain control of the land and the institutions that flow from that land. The black man has been in a very low condition because he has had no control whatsoever over any land. He has been a beggar economically, a beggar politically, a beggar socially, a beggar even when it comes to trying to get some education. The past type of mentality, that was developed in this colonial system among our people, today is being overcome. And as the young ones come up, they know what they want. And as they listen to your beautiful preaching about democracy and all those other flowery words, they know what they're supposed to have.

So you have a people today who not only know what they want, but also know what they are supposed to have. And they themselves are creating another generation that is coming up that not only will know what it wants and know what it should have, but also will be ready and willing to do whatever is necessary to see that what they should have materializes immediately. Thank you.

# [Q] uestions for Review and Reflection

1. How do you think the public at large responded to Malcolm's suggestion that there will be "bleeding on both sides"?
2. In what way does Malcolm see the race problem in global terms?
3. What parallels does Malcolm see between the strategy of the colonial powers and Americans regarding race?
4. Describe the two different kinds of Afro-Americans in this country that Malcolm X sees. How would Malcolm X describe himself?
5. How might Malcolm X's contemporaries see his attitudes as fostering a rebellion?

# Reading 5

National Organization for Women, 1966

## Organizing Statement

Seeking a "full partnership with men," the National Organization for Women (NOW) was founded in order to eliminate all sexual discrimination. The 300 members were mostly professional women who were well educated and politically savvy. They became one of the largest civil rights groups for women in the U.S., with a membership of over 250,000.

NOW sought reforms in employment and educational opportunities, salaries, abortion rights, day-care access, and an end to the discriminatory practices that existed in economic, political, and social life—essentially the same agenda that the organization currently follows.

The organizing statement asserted that these were issues for men and women and that "the power of American law and the protection guaranteed by the U.S. Constitution . . . must be effectively applied and enforced." NOW founders called on the authority of the federal government to assist in such an achievement.

W e, men and women who hereby constitute ourselves as the National Organization for Women, believe that the time has come for a new movement toward true equality for all women in America, and toward a fully equal partnership of the sexes, as part of the worldwide revolution of human rights now taking place within and beyond our national borders.

The purpose of NOW is to take action to bring women into full participation in the mainstream of American society now, exercising all the privileges and responsibilities thereof in truly equal partnership with men.

We believe the time has come to move beyond the abstract argument, discussion and symposia over the status and special nature of women which have raged in America in recent years; the time has come to confront, with concrete action, the conditions that now prevent women from enjoying the equality of opportunity and freedom of choice which is their right, as individual Americans, and as human beings.

NOW is dedicated to the proposition that women, first and foremost, are human beings, who, like all other people in our society, must have the chance to develop their fullest human potential. We believe that women can achieve such equality only by accepting to the full the challenges and responsibilities they share with all other people in our society, as part of the decision-making mainstream of American political, economic, and social life.

We organize to initiate or support action, nationally, or in any part of this nation, by individuals or organizations, to break through the silken curtain of prejudice and discrimination against women in government, industry, the professions, the churches, the political parties, the judiciary, the labor unions, in education, science, medicine, law, religion, and every other field of importance in American society. . . .

WE BELIEVE that the power of American law, and the protection guaranteed by the U.S. Constitution to the civil rights of all individuals, must be effectively applied and enforced to isolate and remove patterns of sex discrimination, to ensure equality of opportunity in employment and education, and equality of civil and political rights and responsibilities on behalf of women, as well as for Negroes and other deprived groups.

We realize that women's problems are linked to many broader questions of social justice; their solution will require concerted action by many groups. Therefore, convinced that human rights for all are indivisible, we expect to give active support to the common cause of equal rights for all those who suffer discrimination and deprivation, and we call upon other organizations committed to such goals to support our efforts toward equality for women.

WE DO NOT ACCEPT the token appointment of a few women to high-level positions in government and industry as a substitute for a serious continuing effort to recruit and advance women according to their individual abilities. To this end, we urge American government and industry to mobilize the same resources of ingenuity and command with which they have solved problems of far greater difficulty than those now impeding the progress of women.

WE BELIEVE that this nation has a capacity at least as great as other nations, to innovate new social institutions which will enable women to enjoy true equality of opportunity and responsibility in society, without conflict with their responsibilities as mothers and homemakers. In such innovations, America does not lead the Western world, but lags by decades behind many European countries. We do not accept the traditional assumption that a woman has to choose between marriage and motherhood, on the one hand, and serious participation in industry or the professions on the other. . . .

WE BELIEVE that it is as essential for every girl to be educated to her full potential of human ability as it is for every boy—with the knowledge that such education is the key to effective participation in today's economy and that, for a girl as for a boy, education can only be serious where there is expectation that it will be used in society. . . .

WE REJECT the current assumptions that a man must carry the sole burden of supporting himself, his wife, and family, and that a woman is automatically entitled to lifelong support by a man upon her marriage, or that marriage, home, and family are primarily woman's world and responsibility—hers to dominate—his to support. We believe that a true partnership between the sexes demands a different concept of marriage, an equitable sharing of the responsibilities of home and children and of the economic burdens of their support. We believe that proper recognition should be given to the economic and social value of homemaking and child care. To these ends, we will seek to open a re-examination of laws and mores governing marriage and divorce, for we believe that the current state of "half-equality" between the sexes discriminates against both men and women, and is the cause of much unnecessary hostility between the sexes.

WE BELIEVE that women must now exercise their political rights and responsibilities as American citizens. They must refuse to be segregated on the basis of sex into separate-and-not-equal ladies' auxiliaries in the political parties, and they must demand representation according to their numbers in the regularly constituted party committees—at local, state, and national levels—and in the informal power structure, participating fully in the selection of candidates and political decision-making, and running for office themselves. . . .

WE BELIEVE that women will do most to create a new image of women by *acting* now, and by speaking out in behalf of their own equality, freedom, and human dignity—not in pleas for special privilege, nor in enmity toward men, who are also victims of the current, half-equality between the sexes—but in an active, self-respecting partnership with men. By so doing, women will develop confidence in their own ability to determine actively, in partnership with men, the conditions of their life, their choices, their future, and their society.

## Questions for Review and Reflection

1. What is the essential goal of the National Organization for Women? What is the purpose of NOW?
2. According to the authors, what are the conditions that bar women from achieving true equality? What kind of "concrete action" do you think will be necessary to change this?
3. How are women's problems linked to the larger problems in society? What are these larger problems?
4. What dangers do the authors see in token appointments of a few women to high governmental and industry positions? Do you agree or disagree?
5. What current assumptions do the authors reject? How are these assumptions about the role of women societal, rather than biological?

# Reading 6

Reies Tijerina, 1969

## Letter from a Santa Fe Jail

In many ways Chicanos' experiences with treaty violations and a gold rush were similar to those of Native Americans. Reies Tijerina was a student of land grants and a Chicano activist of the 1960s who traveled the migrant labor camps as a preacher. He believed that Chicanos had been cheated out of their lands following the Treaty of Guadalupe Hidalgo, which settled the Mexican-American War. Mexico ceded huge territories, and America promised to protect the titles of property holders. Instead, the U.S. government stood by as land speculators spread across the new territories, swindling and defrauding people who did not understand their rights.

Tijerina's message appealed to a number of Mexican Americans who found themselves impoverished and politically powerless. Tijerina and his followers held public demonstrations and called for treaty obligations to be met. One such protest landed him in jail, where he wrote, "I am in jail for defending and fighting for the rights of my people." His group called for the U.S. government to uphold the supremacy of the Treaty of Guadalupe Hidalgo by returning property to the heirs of the original landholders.

From my cell block in this jail I am writing these reflections. I write them to my people, the Indo-Hispanos, to my friends among the Anglos, to the agents of the federal government, the state of New Mexico, the Southwest, and the entire Indo-Hispano world—"Latin America."

I write to you as one of the clearest victims of the madness and racism in the hearts of our present-day politicians and rulers.

At this time, August 17, I have been in jail for 65 days—since June 11, 1969, when my appeal bond from another case was revoked by a federal judge. I am here today because I resisted an assassination attempt led by an agent of the federal government—an agent of all those who do not want anybody to speak out for the poor, all those who do not want Reies Lopez Tijerina to stand in their way as they continue to rob the poor people, all those many rich people from outside the state with their summer homes and ranches here whose pursuit of happiness depends on thievery, all those who have robbed the people of their land and culture for 120 years. . . .

What is my real crime? As I and the poor people see it, especially the Indo-Hispanos, my only crime is UPHOLDING OUR RIGHTS AS PROTECTED BY THE TREATY OF GUADALUPE/HIDALGO which ended the so-called Mexican-American War of 1846–48. My only crime is demanding the respect and protection of our property, which has been confiscated illegally by the federal government. Ever since the treaty was signed in 1848, our people have been asking every elected president of the United States for a redress of grievances. Like the Black people, we too have been criminally ignored. Our right to the Spanish land grant pueblos is the real reason why I am in prison at this moment. . . .

This truth is denied by the conspirators against the poor and by the press which they control. There are also the Silent Contributors. The Jewish people accused the Pope of Rome for keeping silent while Hitler and his machine persecuted the Jews in Germany and other countries. I support the Jews in their right to accuse those who contributed to Hitler's acts by their SILENCE. By the same token, I denounce those in New Mexico who have never opened their mouths at any time to defend or support the thousands who have been killed, robbed, raped of their culture. I don't know of any church or Establishment organization or group of elite intellectuals that has stood up for the Treaty of Guadalupe-Hidalgo. We condemn the silence of these groups and individuals and I am sure that, like the Jewish people, the poor of New Mexico are keeping a record of the Silence which contributes to the criminal conspiracy against the Indo-Hispano in New Mexico. . . .

This government must show its good faith to the Indo-Hispano in respect to the Treaty of Guadalupe-Hidalgo and the land question by forming a presidential committee to investigate and hold open hearings on the land question in the northern part of New Mexico. We challenge our own government to bring forth and put all the facts on the conference table. We have the evidence to prove our claims to property as well as to the cultural rights of which we have been deprived. WE ARE RIGHT—and therefore ready and willing to discuss our problems and rights under the Treaty with the Anglo federal government in New Mexico or Washington, D.C., directly or through agents.

This government must also reform the whole educational structure in the Southwest before it is too late. It should begin in the northern part of New Mexico, where 80% of the population are Indo-Hispanos, as a pilot center. If it works here, then a plan can be developed based on that experience in the rest of the state and wherever the Indo-Hispano population requires it.

Because I know WE ARE RIGHT, I have no regrets as I sit in my jail cell. I feel very, very proud and happy to be in jail for the reason that I am. . . . I am sure that not one of my prison days is lost. Not one day has been in vain. While others are free, building their personal empires, I am in jail for defending and fighting for the rights of my people. Only my Indo-Hispano people have influenced me to be what I am. I am what I am, for my brothers.

**uestions for Review and Reflection**

1. What was Tijerina's "real crime"?
2. What solidarity with the Jewish people does Tijerina articulate in this letter? What similarities does he draw between the Catholic Church's attitude toward the Holocaust and American attitudes toward Mexican Americans? Do you agree?
3. According to Tijerina, how can the federal government redress the Indo-Hispanos' grievances with the American people?

# Reading 7

Delano Grape Workers, 1969

## Delano Grape Workers' Proclamation

Political, social, and economic equality did not exist for the migrant workers of the Southwest any more than it did for the Latino workers in the major cities.

Big-business farming needed cheap migrant labor but offered subsistence wages, substandard living conditions, and a dangerous work environment. Decades of poor wages and working conditions had persisted with little public notice or concern until the 1960s, when the Black Revolution caught the imagination of the Hispanic community. The Chicanos' struggle for equality captured headlines due to a lengthy strike in Delano, California, which eventually led to national boycotts, first of table grapes and later of lettuce.

Educated by the civil rights movement and led by the grape pickers, the field workers of California banded together to proclaim their liberation from their exploitation. They wrote a set of aims which expressed their ambitions for social justice and equal protection of the laws.

**W**e, the striking grape workers of California, join on this International Boycott Day with the consumers across the continent in planning the steps that lie ahead on the road to our liberation. As we plan, we recall the footsteps that brought us to this day and the events of this day. The historic road of our pilgrimage to Sacramento later branched out, spreading like the unpruned vines in struck fields, until it led us to willing exile in cities across this land. There, far from the earth we tilled for generations, we have cultivated the strange soil of public understanding, sowing the seed of our truth and our cause in the minds and hearts of men.

We have been farm workers for hundreds of years and pioneers for seven. Mexicans, Filipinos, Africans and others, our ancestors were among those who founded this land and tamed its natural wilderness. But we are still pilgrims on this land, and we are pioneers who blaze a trail out of the wilderness of hunger and deprivation that we have suffered even as our ancestors did. We are conscious today of the significance of our present quest. If this road we chart leads to the rights and reforms we demand, if it leads to just wages, humane working conditions, protection from the misuse of pesticides, and to the fundamental right of collective bargaining, if it changes the social order that relegates us to the bottom reaches of society, then in our wake will follow thousands of American farm workers. Our example will make them free. But if our road does not bring us to victory and social change, it will not be because our direction is mistaken or our resolve too weak, but only because our bodies are mortal and our journey hard. For we are in the midst of a great social movement, and we will not stop struggling 'til we die, or win!

We have been farm workers for hundreds of years and strikers for four. It was four years ago that we threw down our plowshares and pruning hooks. These Biblical symbols of peace and tranquility to us represent too many lifetimes of unprotesting submission to a degrading social system that allows us no dignity, no comfort, no peace. We mean to have our peace, and to win it without violence, for it is violence we would overcome—the subtle spiritual and mental violence of oppression, the violence subhuman toil does to the human body. So we went and stood tall outside the vineyards where we had stooped for years. But the tailors of national labor legislation had left us naked. Thus exposed, our picket lines were crippled by injunctions and harassed by growers; our strike was broken by imported scabs; our overtures to our employers were ignored. Yet we knew the day must come when they would talk to us, *as equals.*

We have been farm workers for hundreds of years and boycotters for two. We did not choose the grape boycott, but we had chosen to leave our peonage, poverty and despair behind. Though our first bid for freedom, the strike, was weakened, we would not turn back. The boycott was the only way forward the growers left to us. We called upon our fellow men and were answered by consumers who said—as all men of conscience must—that they would no longer allow their tables to be subsidized by our sweat and our sorrow: They shunned the grapes, fruit of our affliction.

We marched alone at the beginning, but today we count men of all creeds, nationalities, and occupations in our number. Between us and the justice we seek now stand the large and powerful grocers who, in continuing to buy table grapes, betray the boycott their own customers have built. These stores treat their patrons' demands to remove the grapes the same way the growers treat our demands for union recognition—by ignoring them. The consumers who rally behind our cause are responding as we do to such treatment—with a boycott! They pledge to withhold their patronage from stores that handle grapes during the boycott, just as we withhold our labor from the growers until our dispute is resolved.

Grapes must remain an unenjoyed luxury for all as long as the barest human needs and basic human rights are still luxuries for farm workers. The grapes grow sweet and heavy on the vines, but they will have to wait while we reach out first for our freedom. The time is ripe for our liberation.

# Questions for Review and Reflection

1. According to the authors, what were the circumstances and conditions that necessitated the boycott? What were the goals of this movement?
2. What reverse biblical symbolism do the authors draw upon when they say that they have thrown down their "plowshares and pruning hooks"? Is this an effective appeal?
3. According to the authors, how would violence detract from the movement's goals? How does this square with the "plowshares" analogy?
4. What do the authors mean by claiming that the "tailors of national labor legislation had left us naked"? To whom do you think that they were referring? Do you agree?

# Reading 8

Theodore H. E. Chen, 1969

# "Silent Minority: The Oriental American's Plight"

This article by Theodore H. E. Chen describes Asian Americans at an early point in the civil rights movement of the 1950s and 1960s. A professor of Education and Asian Studies at the University of Southern California, Dr. Chen laments that industry focused on African Americans and left out Chinese and Japanese

Americans as they implemented the affirmative action policies of hiring, training, and promoting minorities. (See Chapter 4; Reading 7.) Colleges and universities offered Black and Brown Studies but not Asian Studies.

He opines that the older generation of Oriental Americans had not held any vision of equal opportunity and liberty; they had earned their place in the economic and social life of the United States with "dogged individual effort." They accepted the status quo; something, he said, their children could not.

Oriental-American youth were not tied to the Orient, he wrote. They were culturally American, and were not willing to accept such second-class citizenship. Chen warns of a growing generation gap, with young Asian Americans ready to protest and organize. He calls upon Oriental-American adults to provide "constructive leadership" and "not allow their personal success and material comfort to blind them to the injustices . . . that are still prevalent."

In the midst of rapid social change, when ethnic minorities are asserting their rights and raising their position, the Oriental-Americans are unsure of their place in American society. They are not a part of the majority, of course, but are they included in the minorities? Hardly so. When government agencies talk about the ethnic minorities, they think primarily of the blacks and the browns. When industry opens up job opportunities for minority groups, they do not have in mind the Chinese or the Japanese. Some universities that plan ethnic studies provide American-Indian and Asian studies, but the focus is on black and brown studies. . . .

The white majority has made concessions to the blacks and browns, but the benefits are not shared by the Oriental-Americans. Theoretically, the blacks and browns are fighting for all minority groups, but you can't blame them for not sharing the benefits they have won by hard struggle and bitter fight. After all, few Orientals have raised their voice of protest or joined the struggle. Why should they expect to reap the fruits of other people's labor?

The Oriental-Americans are confronted with a dilemma. Many of them are prone to continue their life-long habits of hard work and quiet acceptance of second-rate citizenship. Those who have raised their economic and social position have done so by dogged individual effort, forging ahead in the face of handicaps and various forms of discrimination. . . .

The trouble is that many of the young Oriental-Americans do not share their parents' complacency or acceptance of the status quo. There are signs of restlessness among them. Unlike their parents and grandparents, they have no cultural or emotional ties with the Orient. Their whole life is in America, and they are molded by the forces active in American society. They are sensitive to the cataclysmic changes in American life and inspired by visions of freedom and equal opportunity that their parents dismissed as impossible. . . .

Oriental youth is beginning to question whether the hard-work, long-suffering philosophy of the older generation is adequate today. They are critical of the seeming indifference of their parents to the civil rights movement. They feel disturbed that in the current discussions of the role of ethnic minorities the voice of the Chinese community has not been heard, and that in the gigantic struggle for a better life for minorities the adult Chinese population has, in the main, stood aside as spectators. . . .

. . . [I]t may be possible to narrow the gap if the adult Orientals realize that they have to readjust their life and their thinking in the light of new conditions. They must get out of their little shells of isolated individualism and familialism and show that they are concerned about social issues and that they care about the less fortunate in the Oriental community who have not been able to overcome the obstacles of racial prejudice. They must try to understand and to appreciate the idealism of the young who will not be satisfied with the limited material benefits they get from the affluent society.

The adults of the Oriental community would shudder at the thought of militant action. But by their inaction they are driving the young to extremism. The challenge to them is to explore ways and means of expressing their social concern short of riots and violence. Between inaction and extreme militancy there must be room for many forms of peaceful protests, positive affirmation of rights, and jointly conceived proposals, even aggressive demands, for improving the lot of Oriental-Americans. . . .

The adult Oriental community and the white majority share the opportunity and the responsibility of providing constructive leadership. Those in the Oriental community who are in a position to lead must not allow their personal success and material comfort to blind them to the injustices and discriminatory practices that are still prevalent. . . .

# |Q| uestions for Review and Reflection

1. According to Professor Chen,

    a. which minorities receive benefits from government policies and which do not?
    b. how do young Oriental Americans differ from their parents?
    c. how active and militant are Oriental Americans [at the time of this writing]?

# Reading 9

Citizens' Council on the Status of Women, 1970

## "The Proposed Equal Rights Amendment to the U.S. Constitution —A Memorandum"

By the 1970s the Equal Rights Amendment (ERA) for women had been around for a very long time. It stated simply that "Equality of rights under the law shall not be denied or abridged by the United States or by any state on account of sex." Congress finally took a serious look at the proposal in the 1970s.

This memorandum, entered into the *Congressional Record* in March, 1970, was the result of a needs assessment put together by a group of lawyers known as the Citizens' Advisory Council, and in compliance with Executive Order 11246 (see Chapter 4; Reading 7), which had called for such a study. The report gave a history of the Equal Rights Amendment and a list of continuing gender-based, legal distinctions that existed throughout the country. There were, for example, certain state laws that prohibited women from working in certain occupations or attending certain colleges and universities. After an analysis of how the ERA might change such laws, the report listed a set of objections and the responses to those objections.

Michigan Congresswoman Martha W. Griffiths submitted the memo to the U.S. House of Representatives and endorsed its findings. Congress approved the Equal Rights Amendment on March 22, 1971; however, the ERA failed to achieve ratification by 38 states within seven years, as is prescribed by law and practice.

. . . Numerous distinctions based on sex still exist in the law. For example:

1. State laws placing special restrictions on women with respect to hours of work and weightlifting on the job;
2. State laws prohibiting women from working in certain occupations;
3. Laws and practices operating to exclude women from State colleges and universities (including higher standards required for women applicants to institutions of higher learning and in the administration of scholarship programs);
4. Discrimination in employment by State and local governments;
5. Dual pay schedules for men and women public school teachers;

6. State laws providing for alimony to be awarded, under certain circumstances, to ex-wives but not to ex-husbands;
7. State laws placing special restrictions on the legal capacity of married women or on their right to establish a legal domicile;
8. State laws that require married women but not married men to go through a formal procedure and obtain court approval before they may engage in an independent business;
9. Social Security and other social benefits legislation which give greater benefits to one sex than to the other;
10. Discriminatory preferences, based on sex, in child custody cases;
11. State laws providing that the father is the natural guardian of the minor children;
12. Different ages for males and females in (a) child labor laws, (b) age for marriage, (c) cutoff of the right to parental support, and (d) juvenile court jurisdiction;
13. Exclusion of women from the requirements of the Military Selective Service Act of 1967;
14. Special sex-based exemptions for women in selection of State juries;
15. Heavier criminal penalties for female offenders than for male offenders committing the same crime. . . .

## Questions for Review and Reflection

1. According to the memo,

   a. what is the purpose of the ERA?
   b. how long have proponents been attempting to enact the ERA?
   c. what kinds of laws continue to discriminate against women?
   d. why has the ERA failed?

# Reading 10

National Council on Indian Opportunity, January 26, 1970

## Statement of Indian Members

In response to growing demands from Native Americans for the right to participate in the making of Indian public policy, the federal government established a council in 1968, chaired by the vice president of the United States and made up of Indian representatives and cabinet secretaries. This agency provided the means for Indians and federal officials to communicate directly on decisions affecting Indians' living conditions.

Native Americans utilized this means to submit a very specific agenda that called for programs and funding to provide greater opportunities and civil rights in education, health, welfare, and economic development. Many of their recommendations were directly incorporated into the Nixon administration's policy toward Native Americans, implemented between 1970 and Nixon's resignation in 1974.

Despite this group's progress in framing recommendations, other Native Americans mistrusted the council's ability to represent them adequately. The American Indian Task Force, for example, was among the factions that felt the council lacked real influence and served only as a rubber stamp for the executive branch's initiatives.

## Statement of the Indian Members

- In 1970, when men have landed on the moon, many American Indians still do not have adequate roads to the nearest market.
- In 1970, when almost every American baby can look forward to a life expectancy of 70 years, the Indian infant mortality rate is three times higher than the national average after the first month of life.
- In 1970, when personal income in America is at an unprecedented level, unemployment among American Indians runs as high as 60%.

These are reasons why the National Council on Indian Opportunity—the first agency of the Federal Government where Indian leaders sit as equals with members of the President's Cabinet in overseeing Federal Indian programs and in recommending Federal Indian policy—is of the most vital importance to Indians all across the Nation. Because the essential requirement of any Indian policy must be active and prior Indian consultation and input before major decisions are taken which affect Indian lives, Indian membership on the Council is not only of symbolic importance, but is insurance that such consultation will be sought.

We wonder if the Vice President and the Cabinet Officers fully appreciate the fact of their physical presence here today—the meaning that it has for Indian people? We realize that every group in America would like to have you arrayed before them, commanding your attention.

For the Indian people across the nation to know that at this moment the Vice President and Cabinet Officers are sitting in a working session with Indian leaders is to alleviate some of the cynicism and despair rife among them.

Thus, the Council and the visibility of its Federal members is of great symbolic importance to the Indian people. However, symbolism is not enough.

We must be able to report that we have come away from this meeting with commitments on the part of the Federal members that Indian people and their problems will be considered even out of proportion to their numbers or political impact. Otherwise the distrust, the suspicion on the part of the Indians, which has dogged the Federal Government and has defeated most of its attempts to help the Indian people, will continue.

The National Council has a concern with the well-being of all Indians everywhere—whether they live on the reservations or off; in cities or rural areas; on Federal Indian Reservations or on those established by particular states.

Indian Tribes on Federal reservations have had a very long relationship with the Federal Government. However, in the last decade and a half, long-standing latent suspicion and fear brought about by broken promises, humiliation, and defeat have sharpened into an almost psychological dread of the termination of Federal responsibility. This fear permeates every negotiation, every meeting, every encounter with Indian tribes. Whether this fear can be overcome is debatable, but Federal agencies—especially those represented on this Council—must understand it and be aware of its strangling implications.

Co-existent with this attitude, criticism of the Bureau of Indian Affairs by the Indian people has begun to rise. The criticism has two aspects, the latter of which seems to contradict the opposition to termination.

First, a growing awareness among Indians of how far they have been left behind in achieving the American dream and rising expectations have led to the realization that Bureau services have been grossly inadequate.

Second, a quest for self-determination and control over their own destiny has led to criticism of the paternalistic attitude with which these services have been given in the past. The Indian people are aware that this approach has led to a sense of over-dependency on the Bureau and want to overcome this without losing their special relationship with the Bureau.

In short, the Indian people want more services, more self-determination and relief from the hovering spectre of termination.

The Indian problem has been studied and re-studied, stated and re-stated. There is little need for more study. In 1970, the Indians are entitled to some action, some programs, and some results. To that end we are setting forth a series of specific goals. These goals can and must be met. Such positive federal action will create Indian confidence in the sincerity and capability of the Federal Government. . . .

## Education

It is an appalling fact that between 50 and 60% of all Indian children drop out of school. In some areas the figure is as high as 75%. This stands in sharp contrast to the national average of 23%. The suicide rate among all young Indians is over three times the national average. Estimates place it at five to seven times the national average for boarding school students.

A full generation of Indian adults have been severely damaged by an unresponsive and destructive educational system. At a time when economic survival in society requires increasing comprehension of both general knowledge and technical skills, Indians are lost at the lowest level of achievement of any group within our society. We must not lose this generation of Indian children as well. There is a desperate need for both a massive infusion of funds and complete restructuring of basic educational concepts. . . .

## Health

It is a recognized fact that despite considerable improvement the health status of the American Indian is far below that of the general population of the United States. Indian infant mortality after the first month of life is three times the national average. This means, in plain language, that children are dying needlessly. The average life span of Indians is 44 years, one-third short of the national average of 64 years; in Alaska it is only 36 years. In light of the dire need for all health facilities and health needs, it is criminal to impose a personnel and budget freeze on Indian health programs. Even without a freeze, Indian hospitals are woefully understaffed and undersupplied, even to the extent of lacking basic equipment and medicine. We deplore the budget decisions that have caused this state of inadequacy.

There are a number of specific actions that can be taken now to improve Indian health services:

1. An Indian health aide program has been established. A review should be undertaken of its recruitment, training and assignment policies.
2. The Division of Indian Health and the regular U.S. Public Health Service should establish communication for ascertaining their respective areas of responsibility. There is no excuse for the plight of a sick individual, who also happens to be Indian, to be denied access to health facilities due to jurisdictional conflicts.
3. The establishment of Indian advisory boards at hospitals should be continued and expanded. However, to be meaningful, these boards must be given actual authority in the administrative areas of patient care.
4. The establishment of a program to bring Indian health services into communities rather than simply at the central office location, e.g., traveling clinics.
5. Lastly, the Council goes on record in support of a national health insurance system.

## Welfare

President Nixon's proposal for a Family Assistance Program is a major step toward restoring dignity to the individuals involved. We support the concept of this program and urge its enactment and adequate funding. We also request

Indian input into its planning and delivery, for without a mutual exchange this new, innovative program will not satisfy the unique needs of the Indian people.

We specifically recommend today the following:

1. That an immediate investigation be undertaken of the system whereby many welfare recipients are exploited by trading post and grocery store owners. These trading posts and grocery stores are the mailing address for large numbers of Indian welfare recipients in the surrounding areas. By isolated location, overcharging and credit, and the custom of dependency, the traders and store owners have complete control over the disbursement of the welfare checks;

2. That training programs in the culture and value systems of the Indian populations be required for social workers serving Indian people;

3. That Indian tribes be given the option of contracting with the Federal government for the administration of their own welfare programs.

## Economic Development

Indian people in general have been deprived of the opportunity of obtaining business acumen and have not participated in the benefits of the American free enterprise system. This fact has led to the present economic plight of the first Americans and has been an embarrassment to principles upon which this country was founded. But in recent years, because of a cooperative effort involving government agencies and of the private groups, industrial development on Indian reservations is starting to become a reality. This development is greatly desired by most tribes to improve the economics of the communities and to provide jobs for the individuals of those communities.

However, where large industries have located in Indian communities, the inadequacies of the reservation to accommodate the sudden concentration of employee populations have created serious problems. In most of these new industrial communities there are inadequate schools, too few houses, insufficient hospital and medical capability and generally inadequate community facilities for the population. While Indians desire and deserve job opportunities near their homes, most of the industries thus far attracted to reservations have chiefly employed women. This leaves the male head of the family still unemployed and disrupts the family. Attention of those federal agencies concerned with industrial development should be directed to this problem and they should maximize employment for Indian men.

# Questions for Review and Reflection

1. What is the purpose of the National Council on Indian Affairs?

2. What are some of the agenda items of Native Americans?
3. What would be the role of government vis-à-vis Native Americans if all of these demands were met?
4. What has caused industrial development on tribal lands? What has been the impact of industrial development?

# Reading 11

Armando Rodriguez, 1970

## Testimony to Congress

Armando Rodriguez was director of Spanish-Speaking Affairs for the U.S. Department of Health, Education and Welfare in 1970. His testimony to Congress reported on the second-largest minority group in the United States, which had become 8 percent of the population.

While some Hispanics, particularly in California, were moving toward the middle class, many remained impoverished, with high dropout rates from school.

Some states in the Southwest had segregated Spanish-speaking students in separate schools, while many schools in other states prohibited the use of Spanish. The suppression of language and culture was reminiscent of the Indian assimilation schools that were part of the Dawes Act.

Director Rodriguez made a case for "La Raza," Mexican-Americans who are proud of their culture and want to protect its integrity while being assimilated into American life. He argued that equal opportunity was denied to Latino students when their culture was suppressed and that such a policy held them back rather than advanced them. Rodriguez asked for an equal status for all cultures in America, "where cultural heritage and language assets are prime instruments in the acceptance of human diversity as a major national goal."

We are fast becoming America's most promising human catalyst for the creation of a democratic society where cultural heritage and language assets are prime instruments in the acceptance of human diversity as a major national goal. I refute that television report in April of last year that identified La Raza as "The Invisible Minority." If the producers could sense what I feel and see in my travels, La Raza would be identified as the "dynamic and responsible minority." The old image that the Puerto Rican or the Mexican-American is neither Puerto Rican, Mexican nor American: he is suspended between two cultures, neither of which claims him, is rapidly disappearing. Tomorrow's Puerto Rican and Mexican-American—those forceful, creative, bold youngsters under 25 will be the American citizens who successfully retain and cherish their cultural heritage and simultaneously participate fully in the larger cultural environment of our society. And I suggest that the frontier of this movement will be found in the urban areas of our cities throughout this country. Who is the Puerto Rican or the Mexican-American? He is that unique individual who has suffered from cultural isolation, language rejection, economic and educational inequalities, but who has now begun to take those instruments of oppression and turn them into instruments of change. Bilingual and bicultural education in our public schools will be a reality very shortly. The national moral and legal commitment of our federal government for educational programs that reflect the culture and language of the students will be a common part of curriculums throughout the country. And to a great extent this sweeping movement must be credited to the patience and perseverance of our youth—cultural qualities that for so many years was termed "passivity." . . .

"Who am I?" asks a young Mexican-American high school student. "I am a product of myself. I am a product of you and my ancestors. We came to California long before the Pilgrims landed at Plymouth Rock. We settled California, the Southwestern part of the United States including the states of Arizona, New Mexico, Colorado and Texas. We built the missions, we cultivated the ranches. We were at the Alamo in Texas, both inside and outside. You know we owned California—that is, until gold was found here. Who am I? I'm a human being. I have the same hopes that you do, the same fears, the same drives, same desires, same concerns, same abilities; and I want the same chance that you have to be an individual. Who am I? In reality I am who you want me to be."

# Questions for Review and Reflection

1. In what ways are Latinos suspended between two cultures, according to the author?
2. What is the author's attitude about assimilation into the larger culture? What are the consequences of assimilation?
3. What do the author's concluding remarks reveal about his values and goals?

# Reading 12

Mary Frances Berry, 1971

## *Black Resistance/White Law*

The civil rights movement of the 1950s and 1960s led to momentous changes in the laws of the nation. The 1964 Civil Rights Act brought about integration of public facilities and equal employment protections. The 1965 Voting Rights Act promised federal protection during voter registration and elections. The 1968 Civil Rights Act cemented the guarantees against discrimination and extended fuller opportunities for all minorities in America. But Martin Luther King Jr. was assassinated in 1968, and the momentum was lost. America fell quiet when the Kerner report, commissioned by the federal government, found that the nation was "moving toward two societies, one black, one white, separate and unequal."

The election of Richard Nixon in 1968 and the retirement of Earl Warren in 1969 signaled that perhaps the civil rights efforts had come to an end.

Author and scholar Mary Frances Berry served as an assistant secretary for education and on the U.S. Commission for Civil Rights during this period. She warned in her book that "if real black revolution comes, it will result from this failure of the larger society . . . to use the Constitution to effect needed social, economic, and political reform." She charged that white America used the Constitution to suppress rather than support black achievement.

White oppression and black resistance has been a persistent part of the American scene since the colonial period. The response of the government in its effort to suppress racial disorder has reflected the tension between the lofty ideals expressed in the documents on which constitutional government is based and the tendency of the white majority to desire summary disposition of those they regard as unpopular, unlovely, hateful, or powerless. The predilection of the white majority to suppress efforts by black people to acquire real freedom and equality in America (as black *people*, not as single individuals who may achieve some recognition of the rights), even when white repression means resorting to illegal violence and brutality, has added to that tension. Black people have not been, of course, the only oppressed group in American society—the labor movement, Mexican-Americans, Indians, Mormons, and white radicals have experienced suppression. The black experience is unique because black people have been oppressed from the day they first set foot on English-American soil. The American government and people have persistently defended the repression of blacks in the name of law and order, without admitting that the Constitution was designed and has been interpreted to maintain the racial status quo. Racism, the promotion of white nationalism, is the primary reason why black people have served as the mudsills of American society. The need to respect constitutional government has been so twisted and perverted in the name of this objective that it is no wonder that its victims see beyond the fiction and regard law and order as a mere instrument for their repression.

The reflex action of the national government to black requests for federal action to aid in the improvement of their economic and social condition has always been token measures or assertions that no problem exists. If these tactics failed and black people persisted too vigorously, then force and suppression were used. If the slave experience is any indicator, a serious dislocation of American society might be necessary before the institutional response is changed. Also, if the failure of the economic promises of Reconstruction is relevant, satisfactory improvement in the conditions and status of blacks so as to remove the factors that give rise to riots and rebellion will be a long time in coming.

From 1789 through 1970, governmental action in response to the problem of black-white violence and black rebellion has been slow and uneven until some great cataclysm threatening white people has occurred. While white America and the government generally vacillated on the issue, black advances have been met with repression. And repression has proceeded in the guise of constitutionalism, despite the fact that the Constitution is much more flexible than those who hide behind its provisions will admit. Further, no concerted effort has been made to fully utilize its person-oriented and general welfare provisions to remove the economic and social causes of black rebellion.

Additionally, the government has demonstrated a lack of imagination in eradicating the racial prejudice which undergirds the constitutional suppression of black people. If blacks are to be a part of American society, the removal of racism should have the highest priority. Although racism may not be erased by legislation, educational techniques, even-handed justice, and black self-determination as positive government programs might prove effective. Since Americans are apparently enamored of the profit motive, perhaps a government policy for paying grants or giving tax credits to people and programs designed to end racial antagonism might be useful. Even if these ideas seem utopian, one superficial indicator of prejudice—continued racial violence—is amenable to solution. The enforcement of laws designed to make contact between whites and blacks less abrasive and a willingness on the part of the government to respond as quickly when blacks are the victims as when the persons or property of white people are at stake would be a good beginning.

This study also supports the view that the government allocates military power, as everything else, to defend those who are its friends and to injure those who are its enemies. Unfortunately, blacks in general and militants in particular have always been regarded as enemies. So long as the government possesses a virtual monopoly of military power, is unencumbered by widespread internal disorder, such as that which occurred during the Civil War, and remains able to cope with its enemies at home and abroad, white Americans apparently see no need to deal seriously with the factors which cause black rebellion. If real black revolution comes, it will result from this failure of the larger society to come quickly to an acceptable determination of the status of black people and to use the Constitution to effect needed social, economic, and political reform.

## Questions for Review and Reflection

1. According to Berry, what has been a consistent pattern since colonial days?
2. What recent events have added to the racial tension?
3. In addition to blacks, what other oppressed groups are there in American society?
4. What does Berry see as unique in the black experience among the oppressed groups?
5. How does Berry define "racism"?
6. In what ways are the laws instruments for repression, in Berry's opinion? Do you agree? Why?
7. How did the government respond to black petitions for federal action on their behalf?
8. Berry argues that repression has "proceeded in the guise of constitutionalism." To what is Berry referring? Do you agree? Why?
9. According to Berry, what is necessary for blacks to become part of American society? What methods will accomplish this?
10. What will be the result if Americans do not come to an adequate determination of "the status of black people"? What is this adequate determination?

# Reading 13

James W. Chin, 1971

## "The Subtlety of Prejudice"

The *New York Times* published an article in 1970 that aroused this public retort from James Chin. Fox Butterfield, author of the *Times* article, wrote that prejudice against Asian Americans had subsided, and that they had few complaints about discrimination. Mr. Chin claimed quite the contrary. Prejudice toward Asian Americans was still "ubiquitous."

Chin was critical of Asian Americans for not being sufficiently appreciative of the civil rights legislation that had brought about minority recruitment, training, and promotion programs as well as setting goals and establishing timetables for those goals where "underutilization" existed. He scolded the many Asian Americans who were "not aware of the forces which have opened up the doors to job opportunity." Nevertheless, he dismissed the conclusions advanced by Butterfield and replied that a little investigation would find continuing complaints lodged by Asian Americans all across the nation.

As a matter of fact, Chin declared, because of continued prejudice, Asian Americans had found it necessary to "reject their Oriental identity and heritage . . . a heavy price to pay for admission to a group." And, even with that, "there will always be some Caucasian who will remind us that 'all Orientals look alike.' "

Prejudice against the Orientals in America is no longer gross or blatant as in the past. Nevertheless, it is still ubiquitous although now couched in very sophisticated, subtle forms. Unfortunately, to many observers not sensitive to the new nuances of prejudice, there is the frequent misinterpretation that there is no longer any discrimination against Orientals.

The *New York Times* article of December 13, 1970, by Fox Butterfield, is an example of such misinterpretation. There is no question that the racial milieu was more oppressive in the 1940s and 1950s, when many Chinese-Americans with bachelor's degrees and even advanced university degrees could not find work in white companies, and when they could not purchase homes in the "nicer" residential areas. But this improvement has not been achieved solely by "chance." Due to the civil rights legislation of 1964, reinforced by

Executive Order 11246 of September 25, 1965, companies with government contracts . . . must now pursue an affirmative action program to hire, recruit, train, and promote minority group members. . . .

Younger Asian-Americans—in contrast to their elders who were grateful just to be in America and who were also silent for fear of deportation—expect the full rights and privilege of citizenship, not second-class status. . . .

It is indeed unfortunate that many Orientals, who have been the direct beneficiaries of state-federal programs for equal employment opportunities, are not aware of the forces which have opened up the doors to job opportunity. It is not simply a case of, "If you have ability and can adapt to the American way of speaking, dressing, and doing things, then it doesn't matter any more if you are Chinese." Quite the contrary. Equal Employment Opportunity programs have stressed to corporations the obligation to be more tolerant of the cultural diversity presented by the various ethnic groups and subcultures of the society whether it be a Black with an Afro (hairdo) or an Oriental with an accent. . . . Most importantly, corporations must now set goals and timetables to consciously and deliberately seek out minority group applicants in areas where there is a current underutilization. . . .

The *New York Times* notes that many Chinese may unknowingly perceive a crisis of identity rather than prejudice. In reality, however, the issues of discrimination, identity, and alienation are closely interconnected and in many ways inseparable. Identity crises exist because Orientals are told that if they just act white, they will be treated accordingly, but subconsciously they know that being Chinese still means they will not be allowed to join the Elks Club, "Wellesley Country Club," etc. Even if they should live in a wealthy, exclusive suburb armed with a university degree, professional licence, and great hope, the question persists whether they will be treated and accepted as equals.

We all know of many Orientals who in their quest for acceptance have rejected their Oriental identity and heritage. It is indeed a heavy price to pay for admission to a group that one must reject one's own background since this is a form of self-hatred. Even more vital and critical, Orientals are distinguished by certain physical traits and characteristics unique to Orientals. Even if an Oriental should go to the extreme of changing his name from Wong to Wright, and have surgery performed to make his eyes more oval in conformity to Western ideals of beauty, there will always be some Caucasian who will remind him that "all Orientals look alike."

## Q uestions for Review and Reflection

1. What was the conclusion reached by Fox Butterfield in the *New York Times,* with which the author takes exception?
2. What criticisms does James Chin make toward Asian Americans?

3. James Chin in this article raises a similar complaint toward younger Asian Americans that Theodore Chen raises in his article (Chapter 3; Reading 8). Compare the two readings for their characterization of young Asian Americans.
4. Explain what James Chin means by "identity crisis" and "self-hatred."
5. Does prejudice still exist toward Asian Americans in Chin's view? Explain.

# Reading 14

Cesar Chavez, 1973

## An Interview

Born in 1927, Cesar Chavez grew up in migrant labor camps and knew first-hand the indignities and hardships of Mexican-American second-class citizenship. He attended more than 30 elementary schools as a child. Early on, he served in voter registration drives to earn power for Chicanos, but he became even more active in the issues surrounding workers' rights. In the early 1960s, he founded the United Farm Workers (UFW) organization known as La Causa. Chavez sought economic power through decent wages, labor contracts, and worker education about their rights. He used boycotts as an effective tool to force growers to the bargaining table. He believed that political equality would result from economic strength. "I think that we can develop economic power and put it in the hands of the people . . . and then begin to change the system." Cesar Chavez left behind a membership of about 100,000 in the UFW. His death in 1993 brought renewed interest and support to his cause. An effort to boycott grapes in protest of the use of pesticides is now moving across the state of California.

Once we have reached our goal and have farm workers protected by contracts, we must continue to keep our members involved. The only way is to continue struggling. It's just like plateaus. We get a Union, then we want to struggle for something else. The moment we sit down and rest on our laurels, we're in trouble.

Once we get contracts and good wages, we know the tendency will be for the majority to lose interest, unless the Union is threatened or a contract is being renegotiated. The tendency will be for just a few to remain active and involved, while everybody else just holds out until something very big happens. That's true of other unions that we've seen; that's true of other institutions; that's true of our country.

To avoid that, to keep people's attention and continuing interest, we've got to expand and get them involved in other things. The Union must touch them daily.

Our best education, the most lasting, has been out on the picket line. But when the initial membership gets old and dies off, the new people coming in won't have had the same experience of building a Union. So we must get them involved in other necessary struggles.

Poor people are going to be poor for a long time to come, even though we have contracts, and economic action is an exciting thing for them. If they see an alternative, they will follow it. And we've probably got now the best organization of any poor people in all the country. That's why we can go any place in California where there are farm workers and get a whole group of people together and in action. We are hitting at the real core problems.

After we've got contracts, we have to build more clinics and co-ops, and we've got to resolve the whole question of mechanization. That can become a great issue, not fighting the machines, but working out a program ahead of time so the workers benefit.

Then there's the whole question of political action, so much political work to be done taking care of all the grievances that people have, such as the discrimination their kids face in school, and the whole problem of the police. I don't see why we can't exchange those cops who treat us the way they do for good, decent human beings like farm workers. Or why there couldn't be any farm worker judges.

We have to participate in the governing of towns and school boards. We have to make our influence felt everywhere and anywhere. It's a long struggle that we're just beginning, but it can be done because the people want it.

To get it done, there's a lot of construction work needed with our members. Many are not citizens, and others are not registered to vote. We must work toward the day when the majority of them are citizens with a vote.

But political power alone is not enough. Although I've been at it for some twenty years, all the time and the money and effort haven't brought about any significant change whatsoever. Effective political power is never going to come, particularly to minority groups, unless they have economic power. And however poor they are, even the poor people can organize economic power.

Political power by itself, as we've tried to fathom it and to fashion it, is like having a car that doesn't have any motor in it. It's like striking a match that goes out. Economic power is like having a generator to keep that bulb burning all the time. So we have to develop economic power to assure a continuation of political power.

I'm not advocating black capitalism or brown capitalism. At the worst it gets a black to exploit other blacks, or a brown to exploit others. At the best, it only helps the lives of a few. What I'm suggesting is a cooperative movement.

Power can come from credit in a capitalistic society, and credit in a society like ours means people. As soon as you're born, you're worth so much—not in money, but in the privilege to get in debt. And I think that's a powerful weapon. If you have a lot of people, then you have a lot of credit. The idea is to organize that power and transfer it into something real.

I don't have the answers yet. I'm at the point where I was in 1955 about organizing a farm workers' union. Then I was just talking about ideas and what could be done. A lot of people thought I was crazy. But this is how I learn, by talking and expounding and getting arguments back. That's why we're starting a three-year program to study all of these things. I still know very little about economic theory, but I'm going to learn because the whole fight, if you're poor, and if you're a minority group, is economic power.

As a continuation of our struggle, I think that we can develop economic power and put it into the hands of the people so they can have more control of their own lives, and then begin to change the system. We want radical change. Nothing short of radical change is going to have any impact on our lives or our problems. We want sufficient power to control our own destinies. This is our struggle. It's a lifetime job. The work for social change and against social injustice is never ended.

I know we're not going to see the change, but if we can get an idea and put legs under it, that's all we want. Let it go. Let it start, like the Union.

I guess I have an ideology, but it probably cannot be described in terms of any political or economic system.

Once I was giving a talk in Monterey about the Christian doctrine. When I got through, one man came back and said, "It's very radical, very socialistic."

I didn't say anything, but I was convinced it was very Christian. That's my interpretation. I didn't think it was so much political or economic.

Actually, I can't see where the poor have fared that well under any political or economic system. But I think some power has to come to them so they can manage their lives. I don't care what system it is, it's not going to work if they don't have the power.

That's why if we make democracy work, I'm convinced that's by far the best system. And it will work if people want it to. But to make it work for the poor, we have to work at it full time. And we have to be willing to just give up everything and risk it all.

In the last twenty years, the farm workers' outlook has radically changed, just like day and night. Twenty years ago, to get one person to talk to me about the Union was an effort. They were afraid. Now, we've overcome that.

And the idea of serving without pay—they had never heard about that. Right now we need a good education program, a meaningful education, not just about the Union, but about the whole idea of the Cause, the whole idea of sacrificing for other people.

Fighting for social justice, it seems to me, is one of the profoundest ways in which man can say yes to man's dignity, and that really means sacrifice. There is no way on this earth in which you can say yes to man's dignity and know that you're going to be spared some sacrifice. . . .

I've learned two very big things that I knew and had forgotten. The same methods that we used to build a Union, very effective in the beginning, still apply today and much more so. We thought because we had contracts that there were other things we could do. But I'm convinced we can't. We've got to do exactly what we did back in 1962, 1963, 1964. We must go back to the origins of the Union and do service-center work. The contracts are no substitute for the basic help we provide workers in all aspects of their lives. In some cases we thought that this work didn't deal with what we consider to be trade union business. But they deal very directly with human problems.

The second thing I know from experience is that whenever a critical situation hits us, the best source of power, the best source of hope, is straight from the people. It's happened to me so often.

There's a Mexican dicho [saying] that says there's always a good reason why bad news comes. And I think that in our case probably this will save the Union.

# **Q** uestions for Review and Reflection

1. What does Chavez say happens when the union gets contracts and good wages?
2. What generalization does Chavez make concerning all unions?
3. What role does Chavez see for political action in the union's struggle?
4. Why does Chavez stress economic power over political power? What limitations does he see in exclusive political power?
5. Chavez suggests a "cooperative movement." What does he mean? How would it work?
6. Why do you suppose Chavez believes that his "ideology" cannot be described in terms of any political or economic system?
7. What political system does Chavez believe is the best?
8. According to Chavez, what does fighting for social justice do for the individual?
9. What is the best source of power and the best source for hope in the struggle?

# 4

# The Blessings of Liberty

The American system of government offers opportunities for people to influence public policy. Government responses to the voices raised in the 1960s have policies emanating from a wide range of sources. Power is divided between the national government and state governments. The Constitution defines federal authority, and the Tenth Amendment reserves to the states all power that is neither delegated solely to the national government nor denied to the states. One advantage of such a system is that states can act as laboratories to experiment with new ideas while maintaining their more local approach to matters of public policy. For example, California chose to protect the rights of farm workers to organize unions and to bargain collectively in its California Agricultural Labor Relations Act of 1975.

States can exercise their own power as long as their laws comply with the supreme law of the land, the Constitution of the United States. Idaho state law was struck down in *Reed v. Reed* because it permitted only a father to be executor of a child's estate, violating the equal protection clause of the Fourteenth Amendment.

Congressional law also supersedes state law. When the Voting Rights Act of 1965 was passed, it annulled state laws that denied or abridged the right to vote based on race or color.

Power is allocated at the national level among three branches of government. Congress is granted power over such matters as interstate commerce and defense and is empowered to do whatever is "necessary and proper" to carry out those delegated powers. Congress exercised its power over interstate commerce when it found it necessary and proper to pass the Civil Rights Act of 1964. Immigration policy also belongs to the Congress per the Constitution. The 1965 Immigration and Nationality Act dropped the old quota system; other criteria were established for entry into the United States.

The Senate's rule allowing unlimited debate enabled the opposition to conduct a filibuster (a tactic to stall a vote from taking place through endless debate on the floor of the Senate) over civil rights in 1964. History was made when, for the first time, "talking a bill to death" was halted by a cloture vote (forcing an end to debate), and the landmark 1964 Civil Rights Act was passed.

Various departments and agencies are created to administer the law. The Equal Employment Opportunity Commission came into being in order to enforce civil rights legislation. Presidential leadership is often required for effective administration of the law. In a public address at Howard University, President Lyndon Johnson exercised his own brand of leadership as he outlined what he insisted was necessary to accomplish equal rights and opportunities for all Americans.

Supreme Court justices interpret the laws of the country. Such was the case in *Roe v. Wade.* The state of Texas asserted that abortion was a matter best left to the state legislature. The Supreme Court disagreed. It recognized instead a right to privacy "broad enough to encompass a woman's decision" about whether or not to terminate a pregnancy.

The president recommends and the Congress acts. This was the case when President Richard Nixon recommended and Congress enacted an Indian self-determination policy in the 1970s.

Once Congress has enacted law, the president can issue orders to assist in its enforcement. President Johnson issued Executive Order 11246 following passage of the 1964 Civil Rights Act. His order went even further than the law by requiring federal agencies to take "affirmative steps" to end discrimination by "recruiting, hiring, training, and promoting without regard to race, creed, color, or national origin."

All levels of power were active during the 1960s, producing a stream of action in response to calls for justice by the voices of the excluded. The results were rapid and encompassing.

# Reading **1**

U.S. Supreme Court, 1964

## *Reynolds v. Sims,* 377 U.S. 533

Registered voters and taxpayers of Alabama brought suit against their state over district apportionment. At issue was the unequal representation that existed between geographic areas due to differences in population density. Some representatives to the upper house of the Alabama state legislature had constituencies of 15,000, while others had over 10 times that number. Despite Alabama's argument that United States senators represent unequal numbers of people, the Supreme Court found that counties are unlike states. The Court concluded that "the right of suffrage can be denied by a debasement of suffrage or dilution of the weight of a citizen's vote just as effectively as by wholly prohibiting the free exercise of the franchise." When the Court ordered reapportionment based on population, the one-person, one-vote rule was affirmed, based on the equal protection clause of the Fourteenth Amendment. This key decision helped future groups to challenge other forms of discriminatory election structures.

Legislators represent people, not trees or acres. Legislators are elected by voters, not farms or cities or economic interests. As long as ours is a representative form of government, and our legislatures are those instruments of government elected directly by and directly representative of the people, the right to elect legislators in a free and unimpaired fashion is a bedrock of our political system. It could hardly be gainsaid that a constitutional claim had been asserted by an allegation that certain otherwise qualified voters had been entirely prohibited from voting for members of their state legislature. And, if a State should provide that the votes of citizens in one part of the State should be given two times, or five times, or 10 times the weight of votes of citizens in another part of the State, it could hardly be contended that the right to vote of those residing in the disfavored areas had not been effectively diluted. It would appear extraordinary to suggest that a State could be constitutionally permitted to enact a law providing that certain of the State's voters could vote two, five, or 10 times for their legislative representatives, while voters living elsewhere could vote only once. And it is inconceivable that a state law to the effect that, in counting votes for legislators, the votes of citizens in one part of the State would be multiplied by two, five, or 10, while the votes of persons in another area would be counted only at face value, could be constitutionally sustainable. . . .

Overweighting and overvaluation of the votes of those living here has the certain effect of dilution and undervaluation of the votes of those living there. The resulting discrimination against those individual voters living in disfavored areas is easily demonstrable mathematically. Their right to vote is simply not the same right to vote as that of those living in a favored part of the State. Two, five, or 10 of them must vote before the effect of their voting is equivalent to that of their favored neighbor. Weighting the votes of citizens differently, by any method or means, merely because of where they happen to reside, hardly seems justifiable. One must be ever aware that the Constitution forbids "sophisticated as well as simple-minded modes of discrimination." . . . As we stated in Wesberry v Sanders, supra:

"We do not believe that the Framers of the Constitution intended to permit the same vote-diluting discrimination to be accomplished through the device of districts containing widely varied numbers of inhabitants." . . .

State legislatures are, historically, the fountainhead of representative government in this country. A number of them have their roots in colonial times, and substantially antedate the creation of our nation and our federal government. In fact, the first formal stirrings of American political independence are to be found, in large part, in the views and actions of several of the colonial legislative bodies. . . .

But representative government is in essence self-government through the medium of elected representatives of the people, and each and every citizen has an inalienable right to full and effective participation in the political processes of his State's legislative bodies. Most citizens can achieve this participation only as qualified voters through the election of legislators to represent them. Full and effective participation by all citizens in state government requires, therefore, that each citizen have an equally effective voice in the election of members of his state legislature. Modern and viable state government needs, and the Constitution demands, no less. . . .

To conclude differently, and to sanction minority control of state legislative bodies, would appear to deny majority rights that might otherwise be thought to result. Since legislatures are responsible for enacting laws by which all citizens are to be governed, they should be bodies which are collectively responsive to the popular will. And the concept of equal protection has been traditionally viewed as requiring the uniform treatment of persons standing in the same relation to the governmental action questioned or challenged. With respect to the allocation of legislative representation, all voters, as citizens of a State, stand in the same relation regardless of where they live. . . .

# [Q] uestions for Review and Reflection

1. In the case at issue here, how is a vote multiplied in force as a result of geographic location?
2. What is the "fountainhead" of republican government?
3. Can you see that this concept of "one-person, one-vote" could be applied to factors other than geography?
4. Could a vote be diluted by where it is placed within a district?

# Reading 2

U.S. Congress, 1964

## The Civil Rights Act

The 1964 Civil Rights Act was a landmark piece of legislation that resulted from the civil rights movement of the 1950s and 1960s. Congress enacted the law by exercising its authority to regulate the nation's commerce. The new law prohibited discrimination on the basis of race, color, religion, or national origin in places of public accommodation and employment, and it established the Equal Employment Opportunity Commission to investigate complaints. Other acts followed, such as the Age Discrimination in Employment Act of 1967, the Fair Housing Act of 1968, and Title IX of the Education Act of 1972 that banned gender discrimination in education programs. With these decisions, lawmakers brought the full force of the federal government to bear on the issue of equal protection before the law. The Civil Rights Act had been proposed during John F. Kennedy's administration, but it was enacted after his death. It was the first of many steps to achieve what Kennedy's successor, Lyndon Johnson, called the Great Society.

### Subchapter II—Public Accommodations

#### § 2000a. Prohibition against discrimination or segregation in places of public accommodation

**Equal Access**
(a) All persons shall be entitled to the full and equal enjoyment of the goods, services, facilities, privileges, advantages, and accommodations of any place of public accommodation, as defined in this section, without discrimination or segregation on the ground of race, color, religion, or national origin.

> **Establishments affecting interstate commerce or supported in their activities by State action as places of public accommodation; lodgings; facilities principally engaged in selling food for consumption on the premises; gasoline stations; places of exhibition or entertainment; other covered establishments**

(b) Each of the following establishments which serves the public is a place of public accommodation within the meaning of this subchapter if its operations affect commerce, or if discrimination or segregation by it is supported by State action:

(1) any inn, hotel, motel, or other establishment which provides lodging to transient guests, other than an establishment located within a building which contains not more than five rooms for rent or hire and which is actually occupied by the proprietor of such establishment as his residence;

(2) any restaurant, cafeteria, lunchroom, lunch counter, soda fountain, or other facility principally engaged in selling food for consumption on the premises, including, but not limited to, any such facility located on the premises of any retail establishment; or any gasoline station;

(3) any motion picture house, theater, concert hall, sports arena, stadium or other place of exhibition or entertainment; and

(4) any establishment (A)(i) which is physically located within the premises of any establishment otherwise covered by this subsection, or (ii) within the premises of which is physically located any such covered establishment, and (B) which holds itself out as serving patrons of such covered establishment. . . .

## Historical Note

**Short Title of 1972 Amendment.** Pub.L. 92–261, § 1, Mar. 24, 1972, 86 Stat. 103, provided: "That this Act [which enacted sections 2000e–16 and 2000e–17 of this title, amended sections 5108 and 5314 to 5316 of Title 5, Government Organization and Employees, and sections 2000e to 2000e–6, 2000e–8, 2000e–9, 2000e–13, and 2000e–14 of this title, and enacted provisions set out as a note under section 2000e–5 of this title] may be cited as the 'Equal Employment Opportunity Act of 1972'."

**Short Title.** Section 1 of Pub.L. 88–352 provided: "That this Act [which enacted subchapters II to IX of this chapter, amended sections 2204 and 2205 of former Title 5, Executive Departments and Government Officers and Employees, section 1447(d) of Title 28, Judiciary and Judicial Procedure, and sections 1971 and 1975a to 1975d of this title, and enacted provisions set out as a note under section 2000e of this title] may be cited as the 'Civil Rights Act of 1964'."

**Legislative History.** For legislative history and purpose of Pub.L. 88–352, see 1964 U.S. Code Cong. and Adm. News, p. 2355.

## § 2000e–2. Unlawful employment practices

### Employer Practices

(a) It shall be an unlawful employment practice for an employer—

(1) to fail or refuse to hire or to discharge any individual, or otherwise to discriminate against any individual with respect to his compensation, terms,

conditions, or privileges of employment, because of such individual's race, color, religion, sex, or national origin; or

(2) to limit, segregate, or classify his employees or applicants for employment in any way which would deprive or tend to deprive any individual of employment opportunities or otherwise adversely affect his status as an employee, because of such individual's race, color, religion, sex, or national origin.

### Employment Agency Practices

(b) It shall be an unlawful employment practice for an employment agency to fail or refuse to refer for employment, or otherwise to discriminate against, any individual because of his race, color, religion, sex, or national origin, or to classify or refer for employment any individual on the basis of his race, color, religion, sex, or national origin.

### Labor Organization Practices

(c) It shall be an unlawful employment practice for a labor organization—

(1) to exclude or to expel from its membership, or otherwise to discriminate against, any individual because of his race, color, religion, sex, or national origin;

(2) to limit, segregate, or classify its membership or applicants for membership, or to classify or fail or refuse to refer for employment any individual, in any way which would deprive or tend to deprive any individual of employment opportunities, or would limit such employment opportunities or otherwise adversely affect his status as an employee or as an applicant for employment, because of such individual's race, color, religion, sex, or national origin; or

(3) to cause or attempt to cause an employer to discriminate against an individual in violation of this section.

### Training Programs

(d) It shall be an unlawful employment practice for any employer, labor organization, or joint labor-management committee controlling apprenticeship or other training or retraining, including on-the-job training programs to discriminate against any individual because of his race, color, religion, sex, or national origin in admission to, or employment in, any program established to provide apprenticeship or other training.

# |Q| uestions for Review and Reflection

After reading this section of the *U.S. Code Annotated:*

1. Distinguish between 2000a and 2000e–2 in terms of who is protected and from what.
2. Identify what is defined as a "public accommodation."
3. What kinds of exceptions are noted and why?

# Reading **3**

U.S. Congress, 1965

## The Voting Rights Act

Despite its intent, the Fifteenth Amendment did not result in full voting rights for African Americans. For nearly a century, effective barriers continued to stand between these citizens and the polling booths. A "grandfather clause" exempted white voters from tests and taxes by enfranchising those whose grandfathers had had the vote. Literacy tests and poll taxes were placed on every "newer" citizen. From Reconstruction forward, the South was remarkably successful in shutting down the black vote. The exemptions of grandfather clauses were found unconstitutional in 1915, but literacy tests, character tests, property requirements, and polling taxes continued.

In 1965, Congress passed the Voting Rights Act to provide a series of remedies to Southern roadblocks. Federal agents were sent into districts where less than 50 percent of the population was registered to vote. At long last, literacy and other qualifying tests were outlawed; poll taxes had been eliminated with the passage of the Twenty-fourth Amendment in 1964. Any procedures that had the effect of denying the right to vote based on color or race were interdicted. The Voting Rights Act of 1965 had a dramatic impact on the number of American voters. It was a major step in making political equality a reality, and it was the second building block in Johnson's Great Society.

### 1971. Sec. Voting rights.

(a) Race, color, or previous condition not to affect right to vote; uniform standards for voting qualification; errors or omissions from papers; literacy tests; agreements between Attorney General and State or local authorities; definitions.

(b) Intimidation, threats, or coercion.

(c) Prevention relief; injunction; rebuttable literacy presumption; liability of United States for costs; State as party defendant.

(d) jurisdiction; exhaustion of other remedies.

(e) Order qualifying person to vote; application; hearing; voting referees; transmittal of report and order; certification of qualification; definitions.

(f) Contempt; assignment of counsel; witnesses.

(g) Three-judge district court: hearing, determination, expedition of action, review by Supreme Court; single-judge district court: hearing, determination, expedition of action.

## 1972. Interference with freedom of elections.

## Subchapter I-A—Enforcement of Voting Rights

**1973.** Denial or abridgement of right to vote on account of race or color through voting qualifications or prerequisites.

**1973a.** Proceeding to enforce right to vote.

(a) Authorization by court for appointment of federal examiners.

(b) Suspension of use of tests and devices which deny or abridge right to vote.

(c) Retention of jurisdiction to prevent commencement of new devices to deny or abridge right to vote.

**1973b.** Suspension of use of tests or devices in determining eligibility to vote.

(a) Action by State or political subdivision for declaratory judgment of no denial or abridgement; three-judge district court; appeal to Supreme Court; retention of jurisdiction by three-judge court.

(b) Required factual determinations necessary to allow suspension of compliance with tests and devices; publication in Federal Register.

(c) Definition of test or device.

(d) Required frequency, continuation and probable recurrence of incidents of denial or abridgement to constitute forbidden use of tests or devices.

(e) Completion of requisite grade level of education in American-flag schools in which predominant classroom language was other than English.

(f) Congressional findings of voting discrimination against language minorities; prohibition of English-only elections; other remedial measures.

**1973c.** Alteration of voting qualifications and procedures; action by State or political subdivision for declaratory judgment of no denial or abridgement of voting rights; three-judge district court; appeal to Supreme Court.

**1973d.** Federal voting examiners; appointment.

**1973e.** Examination of applicants for registration.

(a) Form of application; requisite allegation of non-registration.

(b) Placement of eligible voters on official lists; transmittal of lists.

(c) Certificate of eligibility.

(d) Removal of names from list by examiners.

**1973f.** Observers at elections; assignment; duties; reports.

**1973g.** Challenges to eligibility listings.

(a) Filing of challenge; supplementary affidavits; service upon person challenged; hearing; review.

(b) Rules and regulations by Director of Office of Personnel Management.

(c) Subpoena power of Director of Office of Personnel Management; contempt.

**1973h.**    Poll taxes.

(a) Congressional finding and declaration of policy against enforced payment of poll taxes as device to impair voting rights.

(b) Authority of Attorney General to institute actions for relief against enforcement of poll tax requirement.

(c) Jurisdiction of three-judge district courts; appeal to Supreme Court.

**1973i.**    Prohibited acts.

(a) Failure or refusal to permit casting or tabulation of vote.

(b) Intimidation, threats, or coercion.

# |Q| uestions for Review and Reflection

According to the Voting Rights Act in the *United States Code Annotated:*

1. What practices are not allowed when carrying out the vote?
2. Can education be a prerequisite for voting?
3. Can certificates of eligibility be required?
4. Does it appear that intimidation had been used as a tactic to deny the right to vote?

# Reading 4

Hubert Humphrey, 1965

# Civil Rights Commission Report

The Civil Rights Act was an omnibus law that spawned many more decisions supporting, strengthening, and enhancing the initial legislation. The Civil Rights Act of 1968 prohibited discrimination in the sale or rental of housing. The 1972 Equal Employment Opportunity Act broadened opportunities for the disadvantaged. The 1972 Education Amendment prohibited sex discrimination in school programs and activities.

Long an advocate on behalf of minorities, Vice President Hubert Humphrey (1911–1978) was assigned by Lyndon Johnson to assist in the implementation of the civil rights legislation. This report reflects the number of agencies and commissions involved and the scope of the commitment to exercise federal authority to enforce constitutional principles.

## A. Department of Justice.

The Department, through civil law suits and criminal prosecutions, acts to protect certain rights guaranteed by Federal law. Prior to 1964, its major statutory responsibilities involved protection of voting rights, enforcement of the Civil Rights Acts of 1957 and 1960 and prior civil rights statutes, representation of other Federal agencies in law suits, and assistance in enforcement of court orders. In addition, the Attorney General serves as chief legal advisor to the President on civil rights as well as other matters.

The 1964 Civil Rights Act added the following responsibilities: initiation of suits to require desegregation of governmentally owned or operated facilities and public schools, upon complaint of individuals who themselves are unable to sue, initiation of suits to end discrimination in public accommodations or in employment, where such discrimination is part of a pattern or practice; intervention in private law suits involving discrimination in places of public accommodation and in employment, or in suits alleging denial of equal protection of the laws.

## B. U.S. Commission on Civil Rights.

Established by the Civil Rights Act of 1957, the Commission investigates denials of the right to vote, studies legal developments, and appraises Federal policies relating to the equal protection of the laws in such areas as education, housing, employment, the administration of justice, use of public facilities, and transportation. It makes recommendations to the President and Congress and serves as a national clearing house for civil rights information.

## C. Community Relations Service.

The Service was established by the Civil Rights Act of 1964 as a unit of the Department of Commerce to assist communities in resolving disputes arising from discriminatory practices which impair rights guaranteed by Federal law or which affect interstate commerce. It conciliates complaints referred by Federal courts in law suits to desegregate public accommodations and seeks, through conferences, publications, and technical assistance, to aid communities in developing plans to improve racial relations and understanding.

### D. Equal Employment Opportunity Commission.

Established by the Civil Rights Act of 1964, the Commission will investigate charges of discrimination and through conciliation seek to resolve disputes involving discrimination by employers, unions and employment agencies covered by Title VII of the 1964 Act. It will carry out technical studies, make assistance available to persons subject to the Act, and may refer matters for action by the Department of Justice.

### E. President's Committee on Equal Employment Opportunity.

This Committee, established by Executive Order 10925, enforces the requirements of the Order and of Executive Order 11114 that there be equal job opportunities in Federal employment, in work performed under government contract, and in all Federally-assisted construction projects. It supervises the compliance activities of each Federal contracting agency subject to the Orders.

### F. Housing and Home Finance Agency.

The Agency is responsible for securing compliance with Executive Order 11063 and other Federal laws which require nondiscrimination in the sale and rental of Federal and Federally-assisted housing, including public housing, urban renewal, college housing, FHA-insured homes, and community facilities. It also has responsibility for insuring non-discrimination in employment under Executive Order 11114 in Federal and Federally-assisted housing construction projects.

### G. President's Committee on Equal Opportunity in Housing.

Established by Executive Order 11063, the Committee coordinates the activities of departments and agencies in preventing discrimination in housing and also conducts educational programs designed to foster acceptance of the Federal policy of equal opportunity in housing.

### H. Department of Health, Education, and Welfare.

Several constituent units of the Department have civil rights responsibilities.

The Office of Education is charged by the 1964 Civil Rights Act to conduct a survey on the availability of equal educational opportunity and to provide technical and financial assistance to school boards in carrying out plans for the desegregation of public schools and for assisting in resolution of problems incident to desegregation. The Office is also responsible for assuring non-discrimination in Federal aid-to-education programs including aid to colleges and universities, elementary and secondary schools, and libraries.

The Public Health and the Welfare Administrations are responsible under Title VI of the 1964 Civil Rights Act for assuring non-discrimination in Federally-assisted health and welfare programs, including aid to hospitals, State and county welfare departments, health clinics, and community mental health centers.

## I. Department of Defense.

The Department implements programs requiring equal opportunity in the recruitment, training, and promotion of military personnel in the Armed Forces, the Reserves, and the National Guard. The Department also carries out, through base-community relations committees, programs designed to secure equal treatment for military personnel and their families in such off-base facilities as public schools, housing, and public accommodations. Because of its volume of expenditures, the Department has substantial responsibility for implementing Executive Order 10925 requiring non-discrimination in employment by Government contractors, and is responsible for assuring that grants and loans made by the Department to colleges, universities, and other institutions are administered without discrimination. The President's Committee on Equal Opportunity in the Armed Forces has submitted reports on efforts to eliminate discrimination against members of the uniformed services and their dependents.

## J. Office of Economic Opportunity.

Established in 1964 to administer anti-poverty programs under the Economic Opportunity Act, the Office is directly responsible for operating the Job Corps, the Community Action Program, and the VISTA volunteers program. It also supervises a number of delegated programs, including the Neighborhood Youth Corps, college work-study, adult literacy, rural loans, small business loans, and work-experience programs.

Activities of the Office are significant in the civil rights field not only because they will be administered on a completely non-segregated basis, but also because they seek to involve the disadvantaged in the planning and administration of the anti-poverty programs. With more than half of all Negro, Spanish-speaking and Puerto Rican families afflicted with poverty, this emphasis is likely to produce significant benefits in bringing these groups more into local community life.

## K. Other Agencies with Civil Rights Responsibilities.

**Education.** In addition to the Department of Health, Education and Welfare, the Department of Defense, and the Housing and Home Finance Agency, several other agencies are responsible for assuring non-discrimination in college and university programs for which they provide Federal financial assistance. These include the Atomic Energy Commission, the National Science Foundation, the

National Aeronautics and Space Administration, and the Departments of Agriculture and Interior.

**Employment.**    In addition to the President's Committee on Equal Employment Opportunity and the Equal Employment Opportunity Commission, other agencies having civil rights responsibilities in employment include:

— the Department of Labor, which is responsible for securing non-discrimination in Federally-financed recruitment, training, referral, employment service and apprenticeship programs;

— the National Labor Relations Board, which has held certain racially discriminatory practices to be unfair labor practices;

— the Department of Commerce which offers technical assistance to business through its Task Force on Equal Employment Opportunities and which has major responsibilities under Executive Order 11114 and Title VI of the 1964 Civil Rights Act through the Bureau of Public Roads, the Area Redevelopment Administration, and other programs;

— the U.S. Civil Service Commission, which carries out certain responsibilities for the President's Committee on Equal Employment Opportunity to eliminate discrimination within the Federal service;

— the General Services Administration which, through its letting of contracts for government buildings and facilities, is involved in implementation of Executive Order 11114 barring discrimination in employment by government contractors.

**Federal Financial Assistance.**    Of course, all Federal agencies are responsible under Title VI of the 1964 Act for assuring nondiscrimination in Federally-financed programs administered by them. Some have already been mentioned. Others include:

— the Department of Agriculture, which helps finance State Extension Services, and other agricultural programs;

— the General Services Administration, which is responsible for the disposal of surplus government property;

— the Federal Aviation Agency, which assists in the construction and maintenance of airport terminal facilities.

In addition, the Small Business Administration operates a program of special services aimed at expanding business opportunities among minority groups.

# Q uestions for Review and Reflection

1. In this report, distinguish between existing agencies and new bureaucratic agencies created to enforce the law.
2. What specific responsibilities are outlined for the new agencies created?

3. What does all this additional federal protection say about the federal government's role in civil rights?

# Reading 5

U.S. Congress, 1965

## Immigration and Nationality Act

Until 1965, laws restricting Asian-American immigration had existed since the 19th century. An actual ban on immigrants from Asia was enacted in the national Origins Act of 1924. Some barriers were eased in 1952, but it was not until the Immigration and Nationality Act of 1965 that all restrictions were lifted. "No person shall receive any preference or priority or be discriminated against the issuance of an immigrant visa because of his race, sex, nationality, place of birth." Preferences were given for family members and for certain job skills. As a result, by 1990, the U.S. population contained over 7 million people from Asian countries, mostly China, Japan, and Korea. Included in that number was an influx of Southeast Asians, primarily Vietnamese refugees, who came to the United States after the Vietnam War.

Public Law 89-236

### AN ACT

To amend the Immigration and Nationality Act, and for other purposes.

*Be it enacted by the Senate and House of Representatives of the United States of America in Congress assembled,* that section 201 of the Immigration and Nationality Act (66 Stat. 175; U.S.C. 1151) be amended to read as follows:

"SEC 201. (a) Exclusive of special immigrants defined in section 101(a) (27), and of the immediate relatives of United States citizens specified in subsection (b) of this section, the number of aliens who may be issued immigrant visas or who may otherwise acquire the status of an alien lawfully admitted to the United States for permanent residence, or who may, pursuant to section 203(a) (7) enter conditionally, (i) shall not in any of the first three quarters of any fiscal year exceed a total of 45,000 and (ii) shall not in any fiscal year exceed a total of 170,000.

"(b) The 'immediate relatives' referred to in subsection (a) of this section shall mean the children, spouses, and parents of a citizen of the United States: *Provided,* That in the case of parents, such citizen must be at least twenty-one years of age. the immediate relatives specified in this subsection who are otherwise qualified for admission as immigrants shall be admitted as such, without regard to the numerical limitations in this Act. . . .

SEC. 2. . . .

"(a) No person shall receive any preference or priority or be discriminated against the issuance of an immigrant visa because of his race, sex, nationality, place of birth, or place of residence, except as specifically provided in section 101(a) (27), section 201(b), and section 203: *Provided,* That the total number of immigrants visas and the number of conditional entries made available to natives of any single foreign state under paragraphs (1) through (8) of section 203(a) shall not exceed 20,000 in any fiscal year: *Provided further,* That the foregoing proviso shall not operate to reduce the number of immigrants who may be admitted under the quota of any quota area before June 30, 1968. . . .

SEC. Section 203 of the Immigration and Nationality Act (66 Stat. 175; 8 U.S.C. 1153) is amended to read as follows:

"SEC 203. (a) Aliens who are subject to the numerical limitations specified in section 201(a) shall be allotted visas or their conditional entry authorized, as the case may be as follows:

"(1) Visas shall be first made available, in a number not to exceed 20 per centum of the number specified in section 201(a) (ii), to qualified immigrants who are the unmarried sons or daughters of citizens of the United States.

"(2) Visas shall next be made available, in a number not to exceed 20 per centum of the number specified in section 201(a) (ii), plus any visas not required for the classes specified in paragraph (1), to qualified immigrants who are the spouses, unmarried sons and unmarried daughters of an alien lawfully admitted for permanent residence.

"(3) Visas shall next be made available, in a number not to exceed 10 per centum of the number specified in section 201(a) (ii), to qualified immigrants who are members of the professions, or who because of their exceptional ability in the sciences or the arts will substantially benefit prospectively the national economy, cultural interests, or welfare of the United States.

"(4) Visas shall next be made available, in a number not to exceed 10 per centum of the number specified in section 201(a) (ii), plus any visas not required for the classes specified in paragraphs (1) through (3), to qualified immigrants who are the married sons or the married daughters of citizens of the United States.

"(5) Visas shall next be made available, in a number not to exceed 24 per centum of the number specified in section 201(a) (ii), plus any visas not required for the classes specified in paragraphs (1) through (4), to qualified immigrants who are the brothers or sisters of citizens of the United States.

"(6) Visas shall next be made available, in a number not to exceed 10 per centum of the number specified in section 201(a) (ii), to qualified immigrants who are capable of performing specified skilled or unskilled labor, not of a temporary or seasonal nature, for which a shortage of employable and willing persons exists in the United States. . . .

 **uestions for Review and Reflection**

1. According to the act,

   a. Who are "immediate relatives"?
   b. How does the old quota system change?
   c. How does this new law benefit Asian Americans?
   d. How are "professionals" treated?

## Reading 6

Lyndon B. Johnson, 1965

# Howard University Speech

Lyndon B. Johnson (1908–1973) took over the presidency of the United States following the assassination of President John F. Kennedy in 1963. Johnson was elected into office in 1964, and during his tenure he put forward the Great Society, a government program to combat poverty and assume a much greater role in assisting all citizens to achieve the American dream.

In Johnson's view, government's obligation began with ensuring political and legal equality for all, but it did not end there. "We seek not just legal equity but human ability, not just equality as a right and a theory but equality as a fact and equality as a result." Jobs, homes, and social welfare programs were part of the equation. Using the Civil Rights Act as a foundation, Johnson built a series of laws and programs to fulfill this broad interpretation of government's role.

In far too many ways American Negroes have been another nation; deprived of freedom, crippled by hatred, the doors of opportunity closed to hope.

In our time change has come to this nation. The American Negro, acting with impressive restraint, has peacefully protested and marched, entered the courtrooms and the seats of government, demanding a justice that has long been denied. The voice of the Negro was the call to action. But it is a tribute to America that, once aroused, the courts and the Congress, the President and most of the people, have been the allies of progress.

The voting rights bill will be the latest, and among the most important, in a long series of victories. But this victory—as Winston Churchill said of another triumph for freedom—"is not the end. It is not even the beginning of the end. But it is, perhaps, the end of the beginning."

That beginning is freedom; and the barriers to that freedom are tumbling down. Freedom is the right to share, share fully and equally, in American society—to vote, to hold a job, to enter a public place, to go to school. It is the right to be treated in every part of our national life as a person equal in dignity and promise to all others.

But freedom is not enough. You do not wipe away the scars of centuries by saying: Now you are free to go where you want, and do as you desire, and choose the leaders you please.

You do not take a person who for years has been hobbled by chains and liberate him, bring him up to the starting line of a race and then say, "you are free to compete with all the others," and still justly believe that you have been completely fair.

Thus it is not enough just to open the gates of opportunity. All our citizens must have the ability to walk through those gates.

This is the next and the more profound stage of the battle for civil rights. We seek not just freedom but opportunity. We seek not just legal equity but human ability, not just equality as a right and a theory but equality as a fact and equality as a result. . . .

Of course Negro Americans as well as white Americans have shared in our rising national abundance. But the harsh fact of the matter is that in the battle for true equality too many—far too many—are losing ground every day.

We are not completely sure why this is. We know the causes are complex and subtle. But we do know the two broad basic reasons. And we do know that we have to act.

First, Negroes are trapped—as many whites are trapped—in inherited, gateless poverty. They lack training and skills. They are shut in, in slums, without decent medical care. Private and public poverty combine to cripple their capacities.

We are trying to attack these evils through our poverty program, through our education program, through our medical care and our other health programs, and a dozen more of the Great Society programs that are aimed at the root causes of this poverty.

We will increase, and we will accelerate, and we will broaden this attack in years to come until this most enduring of foes finally yields to our unyielding will.

But there is a second cause—much more difficult to explain, more deeply grounded, more desperate in its force. It is the devastating heritage of long years of slavery; and a century of oppression, hatred, and injustice.

For Negro poverty is not white poverty. Many of its causes and many of its cures are the same. But there are differences—deep, corrosive, obstinate differences—radiating painful roots into the community, and into the family, and the nature of the individual.

These differences are not racial differences. They are solely and simply the consequence of ancient brutality, past injustice, and present prejudice. They are anguishing to observe. For the Negro they are a constant reminder of oppression. For the white they are a constant reminder of guilt. But they must be faced and they must be dealt with and they must be overcome, if we are ever to reach the time when the only difference between Negroes and whites is the color of their skin.

Nor can we find a complete answer in the experience of other American minorities. They made a valiant and a largely successful effort to emerge from poverty and prejudice.

The Negro, like these others, will have to rely mostly upon his own efforts. But he just cannot do it alone. For they did not have the heritage of centuries to overcome, and they did not have a cultural tradition which had been twisted and battered by endless years of hatred and hopelessness, nor were they excluded—these others—because of race or color—a feeling whose dark intensity is matched by no other prejudice in our society.

Nor can these differences be understood as isolated infirmities. They are a seamless web. They cause each other. They result from each other. They reinforce each other.

Much of the Negro community is buried under a blanket of history and circumstance. It is not a lasting solution to lift just one corner of that blanket. We must stand on all sides and we must raise the entire cover if we are to liberate our fellow citizens. . . .

There is no single easy answer to all of these problems.

Jobs are part of the answer. They bring the income which permits a man to provide for his family.

Decent homes in decent surroundings and a chance to learn—an equal chance to learn—are part of the answer.

Welfare and social programs better designed to hold families together are part of the answer.

Care for the sick is part of the answer.

An understanding heart by all Americans is another big part of the answer.

And to all of these fronts—and a dozen more—I will dedicate the expanding efforts of the Johnson Administration.

# Q uestions for Review and Reflection

1. To whom does President Johnson attribute the advancement in black Americans' civil rights? Who deserves the credit?
2. Why does Johnson employ Winston Churchill's statement that this victory is "not the end, not the beginning, but the end of the beginning"? What does Johnson mean by the statement "freedom is not enough"? Do you agree?
3. Although poor blacks and poor whites both bear the devastation of poverty, what special burden does Johnson see causing even more hardship on America's black population? How might wealthy blacks respond to this aspect of the black experience?
4. How does the special burden experienced by American blacks inhibit them from fully taking part in American society? Can this ever be overcome?
5. According to Johnson, what extra burden does the disintegration of the Negro family structure place upon the black family? How would his administration's programs help in this area?

# Reading 7

Lyndon B. Johnson, 1965

# Executive Order 11246

"It is the policy of the Government of the United States to provide equal opportunity in Federal employment for all qualified persons, to prohibit discrimination in employment because of race, creed, color, or national origin. . . ."

With these words, President Lyndon Johnson (1908–1973), author of the Great Society, began a program of affirmative action in which government contractors were required to take steps not only to employ people but also to recruit, train, and promote them without engaging in any discriminatory practices.

Government was no longer neutral in its handling of the principle of equality. A ban on discrimination had not achieved the desired results of integration in the workplace, so government undertook the new responsibility of affirming equality of opportunity through action.

In addition to the Civil Rights and Voting Rights Acts, other parts of Johnson's ambitious social program were the Office of Economic Opportunity, Project Head Start, the Job Corps, and Medicaid and Medicare.

## Equal Employment Opportunity

Under and by virtue of the authority vested in me as President of the United States by the Constitution and statutes of the United States, it is ordered as follows:

### Part I—Nondiscrimination in Government Employment

Section 101. It is the policy of the Government of the United States to provide equal opportunity in Federal employment for all qualified persons, to prohibit discrimination in employment because of race, creed, color, or national origin, and to promote the full realization of equal employment opportunity through a positive, continuing program in each executive department or agency. The policy of equal opportunity applies to every aspect of Federal employment policy and practice.

Sec. 102. The head of each executive department and agency shall establish and maintain a positive program of equal employment opportunity for all civilian employees and applicants for employment within his jurisdiction in accordance with the policy set forth in Section 101.

Sec. 103. The Civil Service Commission shall supervise and provide leadership and guidance in the conduct of equal employment opportunity programs for civilian employees and of applications for employment within the executive departments and agencies and shall review agency program accomplishments periodically. In order to facilitate the achievement of a model program for equal employment opportunity in the Federal service, the Commission may consult from time to time with such individuals, groups, or organizations as may be of assistance in improving the Federal program and realizing the objectives of this Part.

Sec. 104. The Civil Service Commission shall provide for the prompt, fair, and impartial consideration of all complaints of discrimination in Federal employment on the basis of race, creed, color, or national origin. Procedures for the consideration of complaints shall include at least one impartial review within the executive department or agency and shall provide for appeal to the Civil Service Commission.

Sec. 105. The Civil Service Commission shall issue such regulations, orders, and instructions as it deems necessary and appropriate to carry out its responsibilities under this Part, and the head of each executive department and agency shall comply with the regulations, orders, and instructions issued by the Commission under this Part.

## Part II—Nondiscrimination in Employment by Government Contractors and Subcontractors

**Subpart A—Duties of the Secretary of Labor**     Sec. 201. The Secretary of Labor shall be responsible for the administration of Parts II and III of this Order and shall adopt such rules and regulations and issue such orders as he deems necessary and appropriate to achieve the purposes thereof.

**Subpart B—Contractors' Agreements**     Sec. 202. Except in contracts exempted in accordance with Section 204 of this Order, all Government contracting agencies shall include in every Government contract hereafter entered into the following provisions:

"During the performance of this contract, the contractor agrees as follows:

"(1) The Contractor will not discriminate against any employee or applicant for employment because of race, creed, color, or national origin. The contractor will take affirmative action to ensure that applicants are employed, and that employees are treated during employment, without regard to their race, creed, color, or national origin. Such action shall include, but not be limited to the following: employment, upgrading, demotion, or transfer; recruitment or recruitment advertising; layoff or termination; rates of pay or other forms of compensation; and selection for training, including apprenticeship. The contractor agrees to post in conspicuous places, available to employees and applicants for employment, notices to be provided by the contracting officer setting forth the provisions for this nondiscrimination clause.

"(2) The Contractor will, in all solicitations or advertisements for employees placed by or on behalf of the contractor, state that all qualified applicants will receive consideration for employment without regard to race, creed, color, or national origin."

# Q uestions for Review and Reflection

1. Compare and contrast this executive order with the executive order issued by President Truman to integrate the military (Chapter 2, Reading 2). What was the goal of each order?
2. What was the scope of this executive order? Were there any areas of the federal bureaucracy that were not covered by this order?
3. What role does the Civil Service Commission have in the implementation of President Johnson's executive order? Can you think of another appropriate agency to oversee the policies established by this order?
4. By what authority did President Johnson seek to require private contractors to abide by the terms and conditions of this executive order? What groups might be exempted by this executive order?

5. Are there any differences between the requirements placed by this executive order on federal agencies and those for private contractors?

# Reading 8

Richard M. Nixon, 1970

## Message to Congress

Native Americans had spent the 1960s asking for more self-determination. President Richard Nixon (1913–1994) responded to that call in his 1970 recommendations to Congress regarding Indian-American relations. His comments reflected a sensitivity to the issues and concerns so long communicated by the many Indian organizations. His message abandoned government's historic policy of trying to assimilate the tribes, replacing it with one that sought a new sovereignty for Native Americans.

The Nixon administration worked with Indian groups to formulate a series of bills, which were then submitted to the Congress. The resulting legislation helped to bring about a new self-governing authority for the Native American tribes in the United States. "It is a new and balanced relationship between the United States Government and the first Americans that is at the heart of our approach to Indian problems." A framework was established for respectful coexistence, rather than the subjugation Native Americans had suffered for so long.

### To the Congress of the United States:

The first Americans—the Indians—are the most deprived and most isolated minority group in our nation. On virtually every scale of measurement—employment, income, education, health—the condition of the Indian people ranks at the bottom.

This condition is the heritage of centuries of injustice. From the time of their first contact with European settlers, the American Indians have been oppressed and brutalized, deprived of their ancestral lands and denied the opportunity to control their own destiny. Even the Federal programs which are intended to meet their needs have frequently proven to be ineffective and demeaning.

But the story of the Indian in America is something more than the record of the white man's frequent aggression, broken agreements, intermittent remorse and prolonged failure. It is a record also of endurance, of survival, of adaptation and creativity in the face of overwhelming obstacles. It is a record of enormous contributions to this country—to its art and culture, to its strength and spirit, to its sense of history and its sense of purpose.

It is long past time that the Indian policies of the Federal government began to recognize and build upon the capacities and insights of the Indian people. Both as a matter of justice and as a matter of enlightened social policy, we must begin to act on the basis of what the Indians themselves have long been telling us. The time has come to break decisively with the past and to create the conditions for a new era in which the Indian future is determined by Indian acts and Indian decisions.

## Self-Determination Without Termination

The first and most basic question that must be answered with respect to Indian policy concerns the historic and legal relationship between the Federal government and Indian communities. In the past, this relationship has oscillated between two equally harsh and unacceptable extremes.

On the one hand, it has—at various times during previous Administrations—been the stated policy objective of both the Executive and Legislative branches of the Federal government eventually to terminate the trusteeship relationship between the Federal government and the Indian people. As recently as August of 1953, in House Concurrent Resolution 108, the Congress declared that termination was the long-range goal of its Indian policies. This would mean that Indian tribes would eventually lose any special standing they had under Federal law; the tax exempt status of their lands would be discontinued; Federal responsibility for their economic and social well-being would be repudiated; and the tribes themselves would be effectively dismantled. Tribal property would be divided among individual members who would then be assimilated into the society at large.

This policy of forced termination is wrong, in my judgment, for a number of reasons. First, the premises on which it rests are wrong. Termination implies that the Federal government has taken on a trusteeship responsibility for Indian communities as an act of generosity toward a disadvantaged people and that it can therefore discontinue this responsibility on a unilateral basis whenever it sees fit. But the unique status of Indian tribes does not rest on any premise such as this. The special relationship between Indians and the Federal government is the result instead of solemn obligations which have been entered into by the United States Government. Down through the years, through written treaties and through formal and informal agreements, our government has made specific commitments to the Indian people. For their part, the Indians have often surrendered claims to vast tracts of land and have accepted life on government reservations. In exchange, the government has agreed to provide community services such as health, education and public safety, services which would presumably allow Indian communities to enjoy a standard of living comparable to that of other Americans.

This goal, of course, has never been achieved. But the special relationship between the Indian tribes and the Federal government which arises from these agreements continues to carry immense moral and legal force. To terminate this relationship would be no more appropriate than to terminate the citizenship rights of any other American.

The second reason for rejecting forced termination is that the practical results have been clearly harmful in the few instances in which termination actually has been tried. The removal of Federal trusteeship responsibility has produced considerable disorientation among the affected Indians and has left them unable to relate to a myriad of Federal, State and local assistance efforts. Their economic and social condition has often been worse after termination than it was before.

The third argument I would make against forced termination concerns the effect it has had upon the overwhelming majority of tribes which still enjoy a special relationship with the Federal government. The very threat that this relationship may someday be ended has created a great deal of apprehension among Indian groups and this apprehension, in turn, has had a blighting effect on tribal progress. Any step that might result in greater social, economic or political autonomy is regarded with suspicion by many Indians who fear that it will only bring them closer to the day when the Federal government will disavow its responsibility and cut them adrift. . . .

I believe that both of these policy extremes are wrong. Federal termination errs in one direction, Federal paternalism errs in the other. Only by clearly rejecting both of these extremes can we achieve a policy which truly serves the best interests of the Indian people. Self-determination among the Indian people can and must be encouraged without the threat of eventual termination. In my view, in fact, that is the only way that self-determination can effectively be fostered.

This, then, must be the goal of any new national policy toward the Indian people: to strengthen the Indian's sense of autonomy without threatening his sense of community. We must assure the Indian that he can assume control of his own life without being separated involuntarily from the tribal group. And we must make it clear that Indians can become independent of Federal control without being cut off from Federal concern and Federal support. My specific recommendations to the Congress are designed to carry out this policy.

### Rejecting Termination

Because termination is morally and legally unacceptable, because it produces bad practical results, and because the mere threat of termination tends to discourage greater self-sufficiency among Indian groups, I am asking the Congress to pass a new Concurrent Resolution which would expressly renounce, repudiate and repeal the termination policy as expressed in House Concurrent Resolution 108 of the 83rd Congress. This resolution would explicitly affirm the integrity and right to continued existence of all Indian tribes and Alaska native governments, recognizing that cultural pluralism is a source of national strength. . . .

For years we have talked about encouraging Indians to exercise greater self-determination, but our progress has never been commensurate with our promises. Part of the reason for this situation has been the threat of termination. But another reason is the fact that when a decision is made as to whether a Federal program will be turned over to Indian administration, it is the Federal authorities and not the Indian people who finally make that decision.

This situation should be reversed. In my judgment, it should be up to the Indian tribe to determine whether it is willing and able to assume administrative responsibility for a service program which is presently administered by a Federal agency. To this end, I am proposing legislation which would empower a tribe or a group of tribes or any other Indian community to take over the control or operation of Federally-funded and administered programs in the Department of the Interior and the Department of Health, Education and Welfare whenever the tribal council or comparable community governing group voted to do so. . . .

Consistent with our policy that the Indian community should have the right to take over the control and operation of federally funded programs, we believe every Indian community wishing to do so should be able to control its own Indian schools. This control would be exercised by school boards selected by Indians and functioning much like other school boards throughout the nation. To assure that this goal is achieved, I am asking the Vice President, acting in his role as Chairman of the National Council on Indian Opportunity, to establish a Special Education Subcommittee of that Council. The members of that Subcommittee should be Indian educators who are selected by the Council's Indian members. . . .

Economic deprivation is among the most serious of Indian problems. Unemployment among Indians is ten times the national average; the unemployment rate runs as high as 80 percent on some of the poorest reservations. Eighty percent of reservation Indians have an income which falls below the poverty line; the average annual income for such families is only $1,500. As I said in September of 1968, it is critically important that the Federal government support and encourage efforts which help Indians develop their own economic infrastructure. To that end, I am proposing the "Indian Financing Act of 1970."

This act would do two things:

1. It would broaden the existing Revolving Loan Fund, which loans money for Indian economic development projects. I am asking that the authorization for this fund be increased from approximately $25 million to $75 million.

2. It would provide additional incentives in the form of loan guarantees, loan insurance and interest subsidies to encourage *private* lenders to loan more money for Indian economic projects. An aggregate amount of $200 million would be authorized for loan guarantee and loan insurance purposes. . . .

The Indians of America need Federal assistance—this much has long been clear. What has not always been clear, however, is that the Federal government needs Indian energies and Indian leadership if its assistance is to be effective in improving the conditions of Indian life. It is a new and balanced relationship between the United States Government and the first Americans that is at the heart of our approach to Indian problems. And that is why we now approach these problems with new confidence that they will successfully be overcome.

# |Q| uestions for Review and Reflection

1. How does Nixon describe the American Indian?
2. What is the most basic issue, according to Nixon, with regard to Indian rights?
3. What are some of the specific problems addressed by President Nixon?
4. Does Nixon's policy respond to the Indian demands made earlier?

# Reading 9

U.S. Supreme Court, 1971

## *Reed v. Reed,* 404 U.S. 71

Sex discrimination was a major agenda item for the women's movement of the 1960s and 1970s. Under the Constitution, state and federal laws could differentiate people according to gender, but only on a reasonable and relevant basis. Increasingly, women took their cases to court, charging violations of their constitutional guarantee of equal protection.

In the *Reed* case, Mr. and Mrs. Reed both applied to become the administrator of their son's estate. Idaho law required the probate court, when hearing several claims for the position of administrator, to favor male over female applications. Mrs. Reed challenged the law on the grounds that it violated her right to equal protection.

The Court, in a unanimous decision, agreed that a law that arbitrarily based its decision solely on gender was unconstitutional. "By providing dissimilar treatment for men and women who are thus similarly situated, the challenged section violates the Equal Protection Clause." This was the first time the standard of rationality was applied to laws involving gender-based differential treatment. In subsequent cases, a Florida law exempting widows, but not widowers, from property taxes was upheld; a Utah law requiring divorced fathers to support daughters to age 18 but sons to age 21 was struck down.

Richard Lynn Reed, a minor, died intestate in Ada County, Idaho, on March 29, 1967. His adoptive parents, who had separated sometime prior to his death, are the parties to this appeal. Approximately seven months after Richard's death, his mother, appellant Sally Reed, filed a petition in the Probate Court of Ada County, seeking appointment as administratrix of her son's estate. Prior to the date set for a hearing on the mother's petition, appellee Cecil Reed, the father of the decedent, filed a competing petition seeking to have himself appointed administrator of the son's estate. The probate court held a joint hearing on the two petitions and thereafter ordered that letters of administration be issued to appellee Cecil Reed upon his taking the oath and filing the bond required by law. The court treated §§ 15–312 and 15–314 of the Idaho Code as the controlling statutes and read those sections as compelling a preference for Cecil Reed because he was a male. . . .

Sally Reed appealed from the probate court order, and her appeal was treated by the District Court of the Fourth Judicial District of Idaho as a constitutional attack on §15–314. In dealing with the attack, that court held that the challenged section violated the Equal Protection Clause of the Fourteenth Amendment and was, therefore void; the matter was ordered "returned to the Probate Court for its determination of which of the two parties" was better qualified to administer the estate.

This order was never carried out, however, for Cecil Reed took a further appeal to the Idaho Supreme Court, which reversed the District Court and reinstated the original order naming the father administrator of the estate. In reaching this result, the Idaho Supreme Court first dealt with the governing statutory law and held that under § 15–312 "a father and mother are 'equally entitled' to letters of administration," but the preference given to males by § 15–314 is "mandatory" and leaves no room for the exercise of a probate court's discretion in the appointment of administrators. Having thus definitively and authoritatively interpreted the statutory provisions involved, the Idaho Supreme Court then proceeded to examine, and reject, Sally Reed's contention that § 15–314 violates the Equal Protection Clause by giving a mandatory preference to males over females, without regard to their individual qualifications as potential estate administrators. . . .

Sally Reed thereupon appealed for review by this court. . . . Having examined the record and considered the briefs and oral arguments of the parties, we have concluded that the arbitrary preference established in favor of males by § 15–314 of the Idaho Code cannot stand in the face of the Fourteenth Amendment's command that no State deny the equal protection of the laws to any person within its jurisdiction. . . .

In applying that clause, this Court has consistently recognized that the Fourteenth Amendment does not deny to States the power to treat different classes of persons in different ways. . . . The Equal Protection clause of that amendment does, however, deny to States the power to legislate that different treatment be accorded to persons placed by a statute into different classes on the basis of criteria wholly unrelated to the objective of that statute. A classification "must be reasonable, not arbitrary, and must rest upon some ground of difference having a fair and substantial relation to the object of the legislation, so that all persons similarly circumstanced shall be treated alike." *Royster Guano Co. v. Virginia*, 253 U.S. 412, 415 (1920). The question presented by this case, then, is whether a difference in the sex of competing applicants for letters of administration bears a rational relationship to a state objective that is sought to be advanced by the operation of §§ 15–312 and 15–314. . . .

We note finally that if § 15–314 is viewed merely as a modifying appendage to § 15–312 and as aimed at the same objective, its constitutionality is not thereby saved. The objective of § 15–312 clearly is to establish degrees of entitlement of various classes of persons in accordance with their varying degrees and kinds of relationship to the intestate. Regardless of their sex, persons within any one of the enumerated classes of that section are similarly situated with respect to that objective. By providing dissimilar treatment for men and women who are thus similarly situated, the challenged section violates the Equal Protection Clause.

# Questions for Review and Reflection

1. What was the probate court policy regarding assigning an administrator to a child's estate?
2. Why did the Idaho Supreme Court reverse the district court's decision?
3. What does the Fourteenth Amendment provide that is violated by the Idaho Supreme Court?
4. When can a law treat people differently?

# Reading 10

U.S. Supreme Court, 1973

## *Roe v. Wade*, 410 U.S. 113

In the 1870s the Comstock Laws were passed, banning distribution of all "obscene, lewd, lascivious, filthy, indecent" materials, including those that contained contraception information. Under these federal laws, birth control clinics like the one established by Margaret Sanger in 1914 were shut down, and Sanger and other practitioners were arrested.

State governments extended the restrictions by outlawing abortion toward the end of the nineteenth century. Their goal was to discourage illicit sexual conduct as well as to protect prenatal life.

Nearly a century later, a Texas statute of this type was challenged in the Supreme Court. The Court, in an opinion written by Associate Justice Harry Blackmun, acknowledged a right to privacy that extended to control over one's own body, at least during the first trimester of pregnancy. In this decision, which remains controversial, women won additional rights over their reproductive systems and a measure of freedom from government control over their childbearing decisions. The Supreme Court in 1993 refused to overturn *Roe v. Wade*, but its provisions will probably continue to be hotly contested for some time.

## Excerpts from *Roe v. Wade*

Mr. Justice BLACKMUN delivered the opinion of the Court. . . .

### II

Jane Roe, a single woman who was residing in Dallas County, Texas, instituted this federal action in March 1970 against the District Attorney of the county. She sought a declaratory judgment that the Texas criminal abortion statutes were unconstitutional on their face, and an injunction restraining the defendant from enforcing the statutes.

Roe alleged that she was unmarried and pregnant; that she wished to terminate her pregnancy by an abortion "performed by a competent, licensed physician, under safe, clinical conditions"; that she was unable to get a "legal" abortion in Texas because her life did not appear to be threatened by the continuation of her pregnancy; and that she could not afford to travel to another jurisdiction in order to secure a legal abortion under safe conditions. She claimed that the Texas statutes were unconstitutionally vague and that they abridged her right of personal privacy, protected by the First, Fourth, Fifth, Ninth and Fourteenth Amendments. . . .

### V

The principal thrust of appellant's attack on the Texas statutes is that they improperly invade a right, said to be possessed by the pregnant woman, to choose to terminate her pregnancy. Appellant would discover this right in the concept of personal "liberty" embodied in the Fourteenth Amendment's Due Process Clause. . . .

## VII

Three reasons have been advanced to explain historically the enactment of criminal abortion laws in the 19th century and to justify their continued existence.

It has been argued occasionally that these laws were the product of a Victorian social concern to discourage illicit sexual conduct. Texas, however, does not advance this justification in the present case, and it appears that no court or commentator has taken the argument seriously. The appellants and *amici* contend, moreover, that this is not a proper state purpose at all and suggest that if it were, the Texas statutes are overbroad in protecting it since the law fails to distinguish between married and unwed mothers.

A second reason is concerned with abortion as a medical procedure. When most criminal abortion laws were first enacted, the procedure was a hazardous one for the woman. This was particularly true prior to the development of antisepsis. Antiseptic techniques, of course, were based on discoveries by Lister, Pasteur, and others first announced in 1867, but were not generally accepted and employed until about the turn of the century. Abortion mortality was high, even after 1900, and perhaps until as late as the development of antibiotics in the 1940's, standard modern techniques such as dilation and curettage were not nearly so safe as they are today. Thus, it has been argued that a State's real concern in enacting a criminal abortion law was to protect the pregnant woman, that is, to restrain her from submitting to a procedure that placed her life in serious jeopardy.

Modern medical techniques have altered this situation. . . .

The third reason is the State's interest—some phrase it in terms of duty—in protecting prenatal life. Some of the argument for this justification rests on the theory that a new human life is present from the moment of conception. The State's interest and general obligation to protect life then extends, it is argued, to prenatal life. Only when the life of the pregnant mother herself is at stake, balanced against the life she carries within her, should the interest of the embryo or fetus not prevail. Logically, of course, a legitimate state interest in this area need not stand or fall on acceptance of the belief that life begins at conception or at some other point prior to live birth. In assessing the State's interest, recognition may be given to the less rigid claim that as long as at least *potential* life is involved, the State may assert interests beyond the protection of the pregnant woman alone. . . .

It is with these interests, and the weight attached to them, that this case is concerned.

## VIII

The constitution does not explicitly mention any right of privacy. In a line of decisions, however, going back perhaps as far as *Union Pacific R. Co. v. Botsford,* 141 U.S. 250, 251, 11 S.Ct. 1000, 1001, the Court has recognized that a right of personal privacy, or a guarantee of certain areas or zones of privacy, does exist, under the Constitution. . . .

This right of privacy, whether it be founded in the Fourteenth Amendment's concept of personal liberty and restrictions upon state action, as we feel it is, or, as the District Court determined, in the Ninth Amendment's reservation of rights of people, is broad enough to encompass a woman's decision whether or not to terminate her pregnancy. . . . The Court's decisions recognizing a right of privacy also acknowledge that some state regulation in areas protected by that right is appropriate. As noted above, a State may properly assert important interests in safeguarding health, in maintaining medical standards, and in protecting *potential* life. At some point in pregnancy, these respective interests become sufficiently compelling to sustain regulation of the factors that govern the abortion decision. The privacy right involved, therefore, cannot be said to be absolute. In fact, it is not clear to us that the claim asserted by some *amici* that one has an unlimited right to do with one's body as one pleases bears a close relationship to the right of privacy previously articulated in the Court's decision. The Court has refused to recognize an unlimited right of this kind in the past. . . .

We, therefore, conclude that the right to personal privacy includes the abortion decision, but that this right is not unqualified and must be considered against important state interests in regulation. . . .

## XI

. . . To summarize and to repeat

1. A state criminal abortion statute of the current Texas type, that excepts from criminality only a *life*-saving procedure on behalf of the mother, without regard to pregnancy stage and without recognition of the other interests involved, is violative of the Due Process Clause of the Fourteenth Amendment.

(a) For the stage prior to approximately the end of the first trimester, the abortion decision and its effectuation must be left to the medical judgment of the pregnant woman's attending physician.

(b) For the stage subsequent to approximately the end of the first trimester, the State, in promoting its interest in the health of the mother, may, if it chooses, regulate the abortion procedure in ways that are reasonably related to maternal health.

(c) For the stage subsequent to viability, the State in promoting its interest in the potentiality of human life may, if it chooses, regulate, and even proscribe, abortion except where it is necessary, in appropriate medical judgment, for the preservation of the life, or health of the mother. . . .

## XII

Our conclusion that Art. 1196 is unconstitutional means, of course, that the Texas abortion statutes, as a unit, must fall.

. . . In all other respects, the judgment of the District Court is affirmed. Costs are allowed to the appellee.

It is so ordered. Affirmed in part and reversed in part.

# Q uestions for Review and Reflection

1. What were the conditions under which Jane Roe sought an abortion?
2. What were the three reasons offered for making abortion a criminal offense?
3. What new right was established as a result of this decision?
4. What are the rights of the unborn, according to this decision?

# Reading 11

U.S. Congress, 1975

# The Indian Self-Determination and Assistance Act

Spurred by President Richard Nixon's leadership and advocacy, the federal government undertook major reforms in its relationship with Native Americans. Congress concluded that "the prolonged Federal domination of Indian service programs has served to retard rather than enhance the progress of Indian people." In 1975, members enacted the legislation excerpted here to ensure "maximum Indian participation" in federal services. While it led to increased Indian sovereignty, some Native Americans criticized the law as a perpetuation of the "domestic dependent" status for Indians, on the basis that the federal government retained its "unique and continuing relationship with and responsibility to the Indian people." The statute resulted in greater freedom from government control for the tribes, while it perpetuated the federal government's role in Native American affairs.

## Pub.L. 93–638, Jan. 4, 1975.

### § 450. Congressional statement of findings

(a) The Congress, after careful review of the Federal government's historical and special legal relationship with, and resulting responsibilities to, American Indian people, finds that—

(1) the prolonged Federal domination of Indian service programs has served to retard rather than enhance the progress of Indian people and their

communities by depriving Indians of the full opportunity to develop leadership skills crucial to the realization of self-government, and has denied to the Indian people an effective voice in the planning and implementation of programs for the benefit of Indians which are responsive to the true needs of Indian communities; and

(2) the Indian people will never surrender their desire to control their relationships both among themselves and with non-Indian governments, organizations, and persons.

**(b)** The Congress further finds that—

(1) true self-determination in any society of people is dependent upon an educational process which will insure the development of qualified people to fulfill meaningful leadership roles;

(2) the Federal responsibility for and assistance to education of Indian children has not effected the desired level of educational achievement or created the diverse opportunities and personal satisfaction which education can and should provide; and

(3) parental and community control of the educational process is of crucial importance to the Indian people.

### § 450a. Congressional declaration of policy

**(a)** The Congress hereby recognizes the obligation of the United States to respond to the strong expression of the Indian people for self-determination by assuring maximum Indian participation in the direction of educational as well as other Federal services to Indian communities so as to render such services more responsive to the needs and desires of those communities.

**(b)** The Congress declares its commitment to the maintenance of the Federal Government's unique and continuing relationship with and responsibility to the Indian people through the establishment of a meaningful Indian self-determination policy which will permit an orderly transition from Federal domination of programs for and services to Indians to effective and meaningful participation by the Indian people in the planning, conduct, and administration of those programs and services.

**(c)** The Congress declares that a major national goal of the United States is to provide the quantity and quality of educational services and opportunities which will permit Indian children to compete and excel in the life areas of their choice, and to achieve the measure of self-determination essential to their social and economic well-being. . . .

### § 450b. Definitions

For the purposes of this Act, the term—

**(a)** "Indian" means a person who is a member of an Indian tribe;

**(b)** "Indian tribe" means any Indian tribe, band, nation, or other organized group or community, including any Alaska Native village or regional or village corporation as defined in or established pursuant to the Alaska Native Claims Settlement Act [43 U.S.C.A. § 1601 et seq.] which is recognized as eligible for the special programs and services provided by the United States to Indians because of their status as Indians;

(c) "Tribal organization" means the recognized governing body of any Indian tribe; any legally established organization of Indians which is controlled, sanctioned, or chartered by such governing body or which is democratically elected by the adult members of the Indian community to be served by such organization and which includes the maximum participation of Indians in all phases of its activities: *Provided,* That in any case where a contract is let or grant made to an organization to perform services benefitting more than one Indian tribe, the approval of each such Indian tribe shall be a prerequisite to the letting or making of such contract or grant;

(d) "Secretary", unless otherwise designated, means the Secretary of the Interior;

(e) "State education agency" means the State board of education or other agency or officer primarily responsible for supervision by the State of public elementary and secondary schools, or, if there is no such officer or agency, an officer or agency designated by the Governor or by State law.

# |Q| uestions for Review and Reflection

According to the Indian Self-Determination Act:

1. How does Congress define the relationship between the federal government and the Indians?
2. How is self-determination accomplished?
3. What does the federal government owe the Indian people?
4. What is the definition of an Indian?
5. What is the definition of a tribal organization?

# Reading 12

State of California, 1975

# The California Agricultural Labor Relations Act

The Chicano farm workers of California eventually won the right to organize and bargain, to have secret ballot elections, and to be free from "restraint" or "coercion." After many years of strikes and boycotts, agribusiness and field-workers declared a truce through the California Agricultural Labor Relations Act of 1975, which attempted to address many of the issues raised by the United Farm Workers (UFW) in earlier decades. The law also created the Agricultural Labor Relations Board, whose functions are to investigate unfair labor practices, to mediate disputes, and to supervise elections.

Implementation of the law under Governor Jerry Brown seemed to favor the interests of farm workers. However, new appointments to the board by subsequent governors have led to UFW charges that the law and its board are now pro-farmer. Although the Chicano workers' struggle is far from over, this state legislation remains a potentially useful tool. It also set a precedent for legislation elsewhere in the nation, paving the way for the 1983 federal Migrant and Seasonal Agricultural Workers Act, which mandates health and safety standards, timely payment of wages, posting of hours and wages, and much more.

## § 1140.2. State policy

It is hereby stated to be the policy of the State of California to encourage and protect the right of agricultural employees to full freedom of association, self-organization, and designation of representatives of their own choosing, to negotiate the terms and conditions of their employment, and to be free from the interference, restraint, or coercion of employers of labor, or their agents, in the designation of such representatives or in self-organization or in other concerted activities for the purpose of collective bargaining or other mutual aid or protection. For this purpose this part is adopted to provide for collective-bargaining rights for agricultural employees.

## § 1141. Creation; membership; appointment; tenure; vacancies; removal

(a) There is hereby created in state government the Agricultural Labor Relations Board, which shall consist of five members.

(b) The members of the board shall be appointed by the Governor with the advice and consent of the Senate. The term of office of the members shall be five years, and the terms shall be staggered at one-year intervals. Upon the initial appointment, one member shall be appointed for a term ending January 1, 1977, one member shall be appointed for a term ending January 1, 1978, one member shall be appointed for a term ending January 1, 1979, one member shall be appointed for a term ending January 1, 1980, and one member shall be appointed for a term ending January 1, 1981. Any individual appointed to fill a vacancy of any member shall be appointed only for the unexpired term of the member to whose term he is succeeding. The Governor shall designate one member to serve as chairperson of the board. Any member of the board may be removed by the Governor, upon notice and hearing, for neglect of duty or malfeasance in office, but for no other cause. . . .

### § 1142. Principal office; regional offices; delegation of powers; review by board

(a) The principal office of the board shall be in Sacramento, but it may meet and exercise any or all of its power at any other place in California.

(b) Besides the principal office in Sacramento, as provided in subdivision (a), the board may establish offices in such other cities as it shall deem necessary. The board may delegate to the personnel of these offices such powers as it deems appropriate to determine the unit appropriate for the purpose of collective bargaining, to investigate and provide for hearings, to determine whether a question of representation exists, to direct an election by a secret ballot pursuant to the provisions of Chapter 5 (commencing with Section 1156), and to certify the results of such election, and to investigate, conduct hearings and make determinations relating to unfair labor practices. The board may review any action taken pursuant to the authority delegated under this section upon a request for a review of such action filed with the board by an interested party. Any such review made by the board shall not, unless specifically ordered by the board, operate as a stay of any action taken. The entire record considered by the board in considering or acting upon any such request or review shall be made available to all parties prior to such consideration or action, and the board's findings and action thereon shall be published as a decision of the board.

## |Q| uestions for Review and Reflection

According to the Agricultural Labor Relations Act:

1. What rights do agricultural employees enjoy?
2. What is the role of the Agricultural Labor Relations Board?
3. Who should serve on the board?
4. How should elections take place?

# 5

# Redefining Democracy

The unity that existed among diverse groups during the era of the civil rights movement gave way to a "me decade" by the 1980s, a period when people were looking out for themselves first; gains in civil rights and opportunities for minorities made in prior decades sustained some backlash.

Ronald Reagan's conservative agenda won public favor, and he was inaugurated as president in 1981. He had campaigned on a platform that touted the theory of "supply side economics." It relied on a giant tax cut to reinvigorate investment, and required a decrease in government spending. The conservative backlash was evident in a reduction in discretionary programs, such as food stamps, welfare benefits, and subsidized programs for education and housing. This reversal of public policy was supported by a political bloc of traditionalists and neoconservatives, coupled with the "religious right," a coalition of evangelical Christian organizations who perceived an erosion of traditional family values. They fought the Equal Rights Amendment, as well as the right to abortion, and challenged the "new feminism" as an offense against the family.

Susan Faludi wrote a book entitled *Backlash*, and charged that a counterassault was being waged just as women were winning a more level playing field.

Women were divided among themselves on women's rights versus women's role in society. A backlash came from those who feared that any new legal status of equality could deprive a woman of respect for her roles as wife and mother. Phyllis Schlafly was a premier spokeswoman for the conservatives, critical of affirmative action and favorable toward a more traditional role for women. The Equal Rights Amendment failed, three votes short of ratification, in part because of those who believed that it could force women into the military and out of such gender-separate facilities as toilets or dormitories. By the early 1990s, research challenged Schlafly's ideas of gender separation. Preliminary findings concluded that men and women could operate on a much more co-equal basis at home and at work.

Women also found themselves on opposite sides of the abortion issue. The controversial *Roe v. Wade* (see Chapter 4; Reading 10) decision in 1973 that legalized abortion created considerable backlash; intense lobbying efforts arose to deny public funding for abortion and to restrain access to the procedure through state government regulation. Some state legislatures passed laws that required a waiting period or counseling. Other states raised issues of parental notification or spousal consent.

Although the Supreme Court continued to uphold the right to abortion, the justices also upheld state laws that restricted access, so long as the statutes didn't place an "undue burden" on the mother.

The repercussions also affected affirmative action programs that had begun in the 1960s. (See Chapter 4; Reading 7.) Whites charged that requiring employers to hire and schools to admit a "quota" of minorities and women in order to comply with the law resulted in numbers games. This "preferential treatment," some people alleged, led to "reverse discrimination" and denied equal opportunities to white men. The backlash manifested itself in a series of challenges not only in the courts but also in Congress, on the meaning of a "color blind" Constitution.

Minority communities became divided over the effectiveness and desirability of affirmative action. Clarence Thomas, justice of the Supreme Court and an African American, defended the notion of self-reliance and individual responsibility for making one's own opportunities. Another African American and scholar, Shelby Steele, believed that Blacks were stigmatized by affirmative action. Instead, they were left with little self-esteem and the conviction that they could compete and win only with some form of preferential treatment. And still another scholar and African American, Herbert Hill, insisted that race-based hiring, promotion, and admissions policies were the only way to end blatant, long-standing, and pervasive discrimination.

These reactions caused anger, frustration, and impatience. Supreme Court Justice Thurgood Marshall, the first African American to sit on this bench, reminded Americans during the nation's Constitutional Bicentennial that inequality was a system by design of the framers.

Linda Chavez defended assimilation as the quickest path to equal opportunity. John Mohawk and Vine Deloria Jr., two Native Americans, rejected the "melting pot," demanding cultural recognition and independence rather than absorption.

As immigration, both legal and illegal, rose significantly between 1960 and 1990, Latinos became a potentially powerful voting bloc. A reaction against such power was attacked by Joaquin Avila in the courts. He successfully challenged the "at-large" election system, arguing that it was an effort to minimize minority voting power.

A new mix of diverse needs and views was changing the face of American society, forcing a reexamination of U.S. politics and a reappraisal of democracy. Learning to live with America's diversity had become a major challenge.

# Reading 1

Phyllis Schlafly, 1977

## *The Power of the Positive Woman*

Following the publication of *The Feminine Mystique* in the 1960s, a new women's movement got under way. The National Organization for Women (NOW) was founded, called for an equal rights amendment to the Constitution, and wrote a NOW bill of rights that included women's rights to maternity leave from work, social security benefits, tax deductions for child-care expenses, equal job training, and other equal opportunities.

Journalist, attorney, and author Phyllis Schlafly became a spokesperson for traditional family values. Her book, the source of this reading, criticized the positions of NOW and the women's "liberation" movement.

Schlafly objected to identical treatment for men and women, rejected the "gender-free" approach to public policy, and accepted some sex-based differences. Equal opportunity should be offered to each individual rather than to groups, she proposed.

Equal opportunity included the right to employment and education without regard to sex, she maintained, but it also included the right of employers to give job preference to a wage earner who was supporting dependents. Women's rights included the right of a woman to stay home, be wife and mother, and protect the institution of the family.

Schlafly can be seen as speaking for women who defeated the ERA because they did not support the level of equality it would have afforded them.

## The Five Principles

When the women's liberationists enter the political arena to promote legislation and litigation in pursuit of their goals, their specific demands are based on five principles.

(1) They demand that a "gender-free" rule be applied to every federal and state law, bureaucratic regulation, educational institution, and expenditure of public funds. Based on their dogma that there is no real difference between men and women (except in sex organs), they demand that males and females have identical treatment always. Thus, if fathers are not expected to stay home and care for their infant children, then neither should mothers be expected to do so; and, therefore, it becomes the duty of the government to provide kiddy-care centers to relieve mothers of that unfair and unequal burden.

The women's lib dogma demands that the courts treat sex as a "suspect" classification—just as race is now treated—so that no difference of treatment or separation between the sexes will ever be permitted, no matter how reasonable or how much it is desired by reasonable people. . . .

The Positive Woman rejects the "gender-free" approach. She knows that there are many differences between male and female and that we are entitled to have our laws, regulations, schools, and courts reflect these differences and allow for reasonable differences in treatment and separations of activities that reasonable men and women want.

The Positive Woman also rejects the argument that sex discrimination should be treated the same as race discrimination. There is vastly more difference between a man and a woman than there is between a black and a white, and it is nonsense to adopt a legal and bureaucratic attitude that pretends that those differences do not exist. Even the United States Supreme Court has, in recent and relevant cases, upheld "reasonable" sex-based differences of treatment by legislatures and by the military.

(2) The women's lib legislative goals seek an irrational mandate of "equality" at the expense of justice. The fact is that equality cannot always be equated with justice, and may sometimes even be highly unjustified if we had absolutely equal treatment in regard to taxes, then everyone would pay the same income tax, or perhaps the same rate of income tax, regardless of the size of the income.

If we had absolutely equal treatment in regard to federal spending programs, we would have to eliminate welfare, low-income housing benefits, food stamps, government scholarships, and many other programs designed to benefit low-income citizens. If we had absolutely equal treatment in regard to age, then seventeen-year-olds, or even ten-year-olds, would be permitted to vote, and we would have to eliminate Social Security unless all persons received the same benefits that only those over sixty-two receive now.

Our legislatures, our administrative departments, and our courts have always had and still retain the discretion to make reasonable differences in treatment based on age, income, or economic situation. The Positive Woman believes that it makes no sense to deprive us of the ability to make reasonable distinctions based on sex that reasonable men and women want.

(3) The women's liberation movement demands that women be given the benefit of "reverse discrimination." The Positive Woman recognizes that this is mutually exclusive with the principle of equal opportunity for all. Reverse discrimination is based on the theory that "group rights" take precedence over individual rights, and that "reverse discrimination" (variously called "preferential treatment," "remedial action," or "affirmative action") should be imposed in order to compensate some women today for alleged past discriminations against other women. The word "quotas" is usually avoided, but it amounts to the same thing.

The fallacy of reverse discrimination has been aptly exposed by Professor Sidney Hook. No one would argue, he wrote, that because many years ago blacks and women were denied the right to vote, we should now compensate by giving them an extra vote or two, or by barring white men from voting at all.

The Positive Woman supports equal opportunity for individuals of both sexes, as well as of all faiths and races. She rejects the theories of reverse discrimination and "group rights." It does no good for the woman who may have been discriminated against twenty-five years ago to know that an unqualified woman today receives preferential treatment at the expense of a qualified man. Only the vindictive radical would support such a policy of revenge.

(4) The women's liberation movement is based on the unproven theory that uniformity should replace diversity—or, in simpler language, the federalization of all remaining aspects of our life. The militant women demand that *all* educational institutions conform to federally determined rules about sex discrimination.

There is absolutely no evidence that HEW bureaucrats can do a better or fairer job of regulating our schools and colleges than local officials. Nor is there any evidence that individuals, or women, or society as a whole, would be better off under a uniform system enforced by the full power of the federal government than they would be under a free and competitive system, under local control, using diverse methods and regulations. It is hard to see why anyone would want to put more power into the hands of federal bureaucrats who cannot cope with the problems they already have.

The militant women demand that HEW regulations enforce a strict gender-free uniformity on all schools and colleges. Everything from sports to glee clubs must be coed, regardless of local customs or wishes. The militants deplore the differences from state to state in the laws governing marriage and divorce. Yet does anyone think our nation would be improved if we were made subject to a national divorce law devised by HEW?

The Positive Woman rejects the theory that Washington, D.C., is the fountainhead of all wisdom and professional skill. She supports the principle of leaving all possible control and discretion in the hands of local school and college officials and their elected boards.

(5) The women's liberation movement pushes its proposals on the premise that everything must be neutral as between morality and immorality, and as

between the institution of the family and alternate lifestyles: for example, that homosexuals and lesbians should have just as much right to teach in the schools and to adopt children as anyone else; and that illegitimate babies and abortions by married or single mothers should be accepted as normal behavior for teachers—and funded by public money. . . .

The Positive Woman believes that our educational institutions have not only the right, but the obligation, to set minimum standards of moral conduct at the local level. She believes that schools and colleges have no right to use our public money to promote conduct that is offensive to the religious and moral values of parents and taxpayers. . . .

Here is a starting checklist of goals that can be restored to America if Positive Women will apply their dedicated efforts:

(1) The right of a woman to be a full-time wife and mother and to have this right recognized by laws that obligate her husband to provide the primary financial support and a home for her and their children.

(2) The responsibility of parents (not the government) for the care of preschool children.

(3) The right of parents to insist that the schools:

    a. permit voluntary prayer,

    b. teach the "fourth R," right and wrong, according to the precepts of Holy Scriptures,

    c. use textbooks that do not offend the religious and moral values of the parents,

    d. use textbooks that honor the family, monogamous marriage, woman's role as wife and mother, and man's role as provider and protector,

    e. teach such basic educational skills as reading and arithmetic before time and money are spent on frills,

    f. permit children to attend school in their own neighborhood, and

    g. separate the sexes for gym classes, athletic practice and competition, and academic and vocational classes, if so desired.

(4) The right of employers to give job preference (where qualifications are equal) to a wage earner supporting dependents.

(5) The right of a woman engaged in physical-labor employment to be protected by laws and regulations that respect the physical differences and different family obligations of men and women.

(6) The right to equal opportunity in employment and education for all persons regardless of race, creed, sex, or national origin.

(7) The right to have local governments prevent the display of printed or pictorial materials that degrade women in a pornographic, perverted, or sadistic manner.

(8) The right to defend the institution of the family by according certain rights to husbands and wives that are not given to those choosing immoral lifestyles.

(9) The right to life of all innocent persons from conception to natural death.

(10) The right of citizens to live in a community where state and local government and judges maintain law and order by a system of justice under due process and punishment that is swift and certain.

(11) The right of society to protect itself by designating different roles for men and women in the armed forces and police and fire departments, where necessary.

(12) The right of citizens to have the federal government adequately provide for the common defense against aggression by any other nation.

## Questions for Review and Reflection

1. Why do you think Schlafly claims that the real goal of the women's movement is an "irrational mandate of 'equality' "?
2. Why does Schlafly argue that racial discrimination is nothing like gender discrimination? Do you agree? Why?
3. Describe Schlafly's "Positive Woman." Do you find Schlafly's arguments reasonable? Somewhat reasonable? Absurd? Why?
4. Schlafly argues that the women's liberation movement is based on the "unproven" theory that "uniformity should replace diversity." Is this an accurate assessment of the movement, in your opinion?
5. On which points in Schlafly's "checklist of goals" for the Positive Woman do you think feminists would agree? On which might they disagree? Are there more areas of agreement or disagreement between these two positions?

## Reading 2

Clarence Thomas, 1987

## "No Room at the Inn—The Loneliness of the Black Conservative"

Supreme Court Justice Clarence Thomas is only the second African American to serve on the U.S. Supreme Court bench. After graduating from Yale Law School, he became chairman of the Equal Employment Opportunity Commission from 1982 to 1989.

He then was appointed to the U.S. Court of Appeals for the District of Columbia before he went on to the U.S. Supreme Court.

In his remarks to the Heritage Foundation, Thomas portrays the African-American community as diverse, not monolithic as some had characterized, in views on race, equality, and affirmative action.

Justice Thomas describes his own experience growing up with segregation. There was no government help, he states, only the "common sense" of a family who valued individual responsibility. Their advice to him was simply to stand on his "own two feet." Conservative ideals such as individualism and self-help were principles with which he and many black Americans were raised, declares Thomas.

African Americans have been reluctant to sign on to the conservative agenda because conservatives are viewed by Blacks as "anti-civil rights," claims Thomas. A welcoming message must be delivered to the African-American community that stipulates "the principled approach . . . that protect[s] all individuals, including blacks," and "aggressive enforcement of civil rights laws and equal employment opportunity laws designed to protect individual rights . . . the hallmark of conservatism."

**M**uch has been said about blacks and conservatism. Those on the Left smugly assume blacks are monolithic and will by force of circumstances always huddle to the left of the political spectrum. The political Right watches this herd mentality in action, concedes that blacks are monolithic, picks up a few dissidents, and wistfully shrugs at the seemingly unbreakable hold of the liberal Left on black Americans. . . .

Many pundits have come along in recent years, who claim an understanding of why so many blacks think right and vote left. They offer "the answer" to the problem of blacks failing to respond favorably to conservatism. I, for one, am not certain there is such a thing as "the answer." And, even if there is, I assure you I do not have it.

I have only my experiences and modest observations to offer. First, I may be somewhat of an oddity. I grew up under state-enforced segregation, which is as close to totalitarianism as I would like to get. My household, notwithstanding the myth fabricated by experts, was strong, stable, and conservative. In fact, it was far more conservative than many who fashion themselves conservatives today. God was central. School, discipline, hard work, and knowing right from wrong were of the highest priority. Crime, welfare, slothfulness, and alcohol were enemies. But these were not issues to be debated by keen intellectuals, bellowed about by rousing orators, or dissected by pollsters and researchers. They were a way of life; they marked the path of survival and the escape route from squalor.

## My Grandparents' Family Policy

Unlike today, we debated no one about our way of life—we lived it. I must add that my grandparents enforced the no-debate rule. There were a number of concerns I wanted to express. In fact, I did on a number of occasions at a great price. But then, I have always found a way to get in my two cents.

Of course, I thought my grandparents were too rigid and their expectations were too high. I also thought they were mean at times. But one of their often-stated goals was to raise us so that we could "do for ourselves," so that we could stand on our "own two feet." This was not their social policy, it was their family policy—for their family, not those nameless families that politicians love to whine about. The most compassionate thing they did for us was to teach us to fend for ourselves and to do that in an openly hostile environment. In fact, the hostility made learning the lesson that much more urgent. It made the difference between freedom and incarceration; life and death; alcoholism and sobriety. The evidence of those who failed abounded, and casualties lay everywhere. But there were also many examples of success—all of whom, according to my grandfather, followed the straight and narrow path. I was raised to survive under the totalitarianism of segregation, not only without the active assistance of government but with its active opposition. We were raised to survive in spite of the dark oppressive cloud of governmentally sanctioned bigotry. Self-sufficiency and spiritual and emotional security were tools to carve out and secure freedom. Those who attempt to capture the daily counseling, oversight, common sense, and vision of my grandparents in a governmental program are engaging in sheer folly. Government cannot develop individual responsibility, but it certainly can refrain from preventing or hindering the development of this responsibility. . . .

I am of the view that black Americans will move inexorably and naturally toward conservatism when we stop discouraging them; when they are treated as a diverse group with differing interests; and when conservatives stand up for what they believe in rather than stand against blacks. . . .

It appears that we are welcomed by those who dangle the lure of the wrong approach and we are discouraged by those who, in my view, have the right approach. But conservatives must open the door and lay out the welcome mat if there is ever going to be a chance of attracting black Americans. There need be no ideological concessions, just a major attitudinal change. Conservatives must show that they care. By caring I do not suggest or mean the phony caring and tearjerking compassion being bandied out today. I, for one, do not see how the government can be compassionate; only people can be compassionate and then only with their own money, their own property, or their own effort, not that of others. Conservatives must understand that it is not enough just to be right. . . .

Equality of rights, not of possessions or entitlements, offered the opportunity to be free and self-governing. . . .

This approach allows us to reassert the primacy of the individual, and establishes our inherent equality as a God-given right. This inherent equality is the basis for aggressive enforcement of civil rights laws and equal employment opportunity laws designed to protect individual rights. Indeed, defending the individual under these laws should be the hallmark of conservatism rather than its Achilles' heel. And in no way should this be the issue of those who are antagonistic to individual rights and the proponents of a bigger, more intrusive government. Indeed, conservatives should be as adamant about freedom here at home as we are about freedom abroad. We should be at least as incensed about the totalitarianism of drug traffickers and criminals in poor neighborhoods as we are about totalitarianism in Eastern bloc countries. The primacy of individual rights demands that conservatives be the first to protect them. . . .

But with the benefits of freedom come responsibilities. Conservatives should be no more timid about asserting the responsibilities of the individual than they should be about protecting individual rights.

The principled approach would, in my view, make it clear to blacks that conservatives are not hostile to their interests but aggressively supportive. This is particularly true to the extent that conservatives are now perceived as anti-civil rights. Unless it is clear that conservative principles protect all individuals, including blacks, there are no programs or arguments, no matter how brilliant, sensible, or logical, that will attract blacks to the conservative ranks. They may take the idea and run, but they will not stay and fraternize without a clear, principled message that they are welcome and well protected.

# |Q| uestions for Review and Reflection

1. According to Justice Clarence Thomas:

   a. What are the basic tenets of conservatism?
   b. What is the Republican failure?
   c. Define what is meant by "equality of rights."
   d. Without affirmative action, how will equal protection of the laws be achieved?

# Reading 3

Thurgood Marshall, 1987

## Speech on the Bicentennial of the Constitution

Justice Thurgood Marshall (1908–1993) was the first black judge ever to be appointed to the Supreme Court. Earlier in his career, Marshall had argued the landmark case of *Brown v. Board of Education* before the Supreme Court; he won the decision that stated that separate is inherently unequal, which forced the integration of public schools.

A champion of minority rights, Justice Marshall cautioned Americans to be aware of the "evolving nature of the Constitution." He reminded people in a speech during the bicentennial of the Constitution that when the framers wrote, "We the People," that "they did not have in mind the majority of America's citizens."

He challenged his audience to see the "defects" of the Constitution, which were only overcome through the persistent courage of many different groups. It was their struggle that brought about the amendments incorporating and extending many democratic principles, which have made the Constitution of the United States as relevant to our lives today as it was to those of eighteenth-century Americans.

1987 marks the 200th anniversary of the United States Constitution. A Commission has been established to coordinate the celebration. The official meetings, essay contests, and festivities have begun.

The planned commemoration will span three years, and I am told 1987 is "dedicated to the memory of the Founders and the document they drafted in Philadelphia." We are to "recall the achievements of our Founders and the knowledge and experience that inspired them, the nature of the government they established, its origins, its character, and its ends, and the rights and privileges of citizenship, as well as its attendant responsibilities."

Like many anniversary celebrations, the plan for 1987 takes particular events and holds them up as the source of all the very best that has followed. Patriotic feelings will surely swell, prompting proud proclamations of the wisdom, foresight, and sense of justice shared by the Framers and reflected in a written document now yellowed with age. This is unfortunate—not the patriotism itself, but the tendency for the celebration to oversimplify, and overlook the many other events that have been instrumental to our achievements as a nation. The focus of this celebration invites a complacent belief that the vision of those who debated and compromised in Philadelphia yielded the "more perfect Union" it is said we now enjoy.

I cannot accept this invitation, for I do not believe that the meaning of the Constitution was forever "fixed" at the Philadelphia Convention. Nor do I find the wisdom, foresight, and sense of justice exhibited by the Framers particularly profound. To the contrary, the government they devised was defective from the start, requiring several amendments, a civil war, a momentous social transformation to attain the system of constitutional government, and its respect for the individual freedoms and human rights, we hold as fundamental today. When contemporary Americans cite "The Constitution," they invoke a concept that is vastly different from what the Framers barely began to construct two centuries ago.

For a sense of the evolving nature of the Constitution we need look no further than the first three words of the document's preamble: "We the People." When the founding Fathers used this phrase in 1787, they did not have in mind the majority of America's citizens. "We the People" included, in the words of the Framers, "the whole Number of free Persons." On a matter so basic as the right to vote, for example, Negro slaves were excluded, although they were counted for representational purposes—at three-fifths each. Women did not gain the right to vote for over a hundred and thirty years.

These omissions were intentional. The record of the Framers' debates on the slave question is especially clear: the Southern States acceded to the demands of the New England States for giving Congress broad power to regulate commerce, in exchange for the right to continue the slave trade. The economic interests of the regions coalesced: New Englanders engaged in the "carrying trade" would profit from transporting slaves from Africa as well as goods produced in America by slave labor. The perpetuation of slavery ensured the primary source of wealth in the Southern States.

Despite this clear understanding of the role slavery would play in the new republic, use of the words "slaves" and "slavery" was carefully avoided in the original document. Political representation in the lower House of Congress was to be based on the population of "free Persons" in each State, plus three-fifths of all "other Persons." Moral principles against slavery, for those who had them, were compromised, with no explanation of the conflicting principles for which the American Revolutionary War had ostensibly been fought: the self-evident truths "that all men are created equal, that they are endowed by their Creator with certain unalienable Rights, that among these are Life, Liberty and the pursuit of Happiness."

It was not the first such compromise. Even these ringing phrases from the Declaration of Independence are filled with irony, for an early draft of what became that Declaration assailed the King of England for suppressing legislative attempts to end the slave trade and for encouraging slave rebellions. The final draft adopted in 1776 did not contain this criticism. And so again at the Constitutional Convention eloquent objections to the institution of slavery went unheeded, and its opponents eventually consented to a document which laid a foundation for the tragic events that were to follow. . . .

No doubt it will be said, when the unpleasant truth of the history of slavery in America is mentioned during this bicentennial year, that the Constitution was a product of its times, and embodied a compromise which, under other circumstances, would not have been made. But the effects of the Framers' compromise have remained for generations. They arose from the contradiction between guaranteeing liberty and justice to all, and denying both to Negroes. . . .

While the Union survived the Civil War, the Constitution did not. In its place arose a new, more promising basis for justice and equality, the 14th Amendment, ensuring protection of the life, liberty, and property of *all* persons against deprivations without due process, and guaranteeing equal protection of the laws. And yet almost another century would pass before any significant recognition was obtained of the rights of black Americans to share equally even in such basic opportunities as education, housing, and employment, and to have their votes counted, and counted equally. In the meantime, blacks joined America's military to fight its wars and invested untold hours working in its factories and on its farms, contributing to the development of this country's magnificent wealth and waiting to share in its prosperity.

What is striking is the role legal principles have played throughout America's history in determining the condition of Negroes. They were enslaved by law, emancipated by law, disenfranchised and segregated by law; and finally, they have begun to win equality by law. Along the way, new constitutional principles have emerged to meet the challenges of a changing society. The progress has been dramatic, and it will continue.

The men who gathered in Philadelphia in 1787 could not have envisioned these changes. They could not have imagined, nor would they have accepted, that the document they were drafting would one day be construed by a Supreme Court to which had been appointed a woman and the descendent of an African slave. "We the People" no longer enslave, but the credit does not belong to the Framers. It belongs to those who refused to acquiesce in outdated notions of "liberty," "justice," and "equality," and who strived to better them.

And so we must be careful, when focusing on the events which took place in Philadelphia two centuries ago, that we not overlook the momentous events which followed, and thereby lose our proper sense of perspective. Otherwise, the odds are that for many Americans the bicentennial celebration will be little more than a blind pilgrimage to the shrine of the original document now stored in a vault in the National Archives. If we seek, instead, a sensitive understanding of the Constitution's inherent defects, and its promising evolution through 200 years of history, the celebration of the "Miracle at Philadelphia" will, in my view, be a far more meaningful and humbling experience. We will see that the true miracle was not the birth of the Constitution, but its life, a life nurtured through two turbulent centuries of our own making, and a life embodying much good fortune that was not.

Thus, in this bicentennial year, we may not all participate in the festivities with flag-waving fervor. Some may more quietly commemorate the suffering, struggle, and sacrifice that has triumphed over much of what was wrong with the original document, and observe the anniversary with hopes not realized and promises not fulfilled. I plan to celebrate the bicentennial of the Constitution as a living document, including the Bill of Rights and the other amendments protecting individual freedoms and human rights.

# Questions for Review and Reflection

1. Why does Marshall believe it is "unfortunate" that the planned celebration for the birth of the U.S. Constitution is concentrating exclusively on positive elements?
2. What is this compromise in Philadelphia to which Marshall speaks?
3. Why does Marshall refuse to accept the invitation to celebrate the Constitution?
4. What were some of the faults in the Founders' document that required adjustment over the years?
5. Who did the Founding Fathers include in "We the People"?
6. What was exchanged for the right to continue with the slave trade?
7. What two words were carefully avoided in the Constitution? What words were used in their place?
8. What were the lasting effects of the Framers' compromise?
9. How does Marshall plan to celebrate the bicentennial of the Constitution? How is the Constitution a living document?

# Reading 4

Herbert Hill, 1988

## "Race, Affirmative Action, and the Constitution"

Despite government's reinvigorated effort to guarantee equal protection and freedom from discrimination, imbalances continued in education, employment, and job training for women and minorities. Past practices had left them lagging behind other groups, unable to compete on an equal playing field. Government responded by ordering that affirmative action steps be taken to make up for the past.

Affirmative action programs were widely supported by black organizations to promote economic and educational opportunities for African Americans. Recruiting efforts, special training programs, and numerically based goals that took race and ethnicity into account were seen as one way to open doors so long closed.

Professor of African-American Studies at the University of Wisconsin and author of many writings on race, Dr. Herbert Hill presented his views on affirmative action in a lecture at the City College of New York. He concluded that such programs "can become a major instrument for social change."

1988 begins the third century of the United States Constitution and having survived the ritual celebration of the 1987 bicentennial, it is appropriate that we take a fresh critical look at that document and its legacy. As we examine the historical circumstances in which the Constitution emerged, we must acknowledge the continuing centrality of race in the evolution of the Constitution and of this nation.

Under the original Constitution, a system of slavery based on race existed for many generations, a system that legally defined black people as property and declared them to be less than human. Under its authority an extensive web of racist statutes and judicial decisions emerged over a long period. The Naturalization Law of 1790 explicitly limited citizenship to "white persons," the Fugitive Slave Acts of 1793 and 1850 made a travesty of law and dehumanized the nation, and the Dred Scott Decision of 1857, where Chief Justice Taney declared that blacks were not people but "articles of merchandise," are but a few of the legal monuments grounded on the assumption that this was meant to be a white man's country and that all others had no rights in the law.

With the ratification of the 13th, 14th, and 15th Amendments in 1865, 1868 and 1870 respectively and the adoption of the Civil Rights Acts of 1866, 1870 and 1875, a profoundly different set of values was asserted. This new body of law affirmed that justice and equal treatment were not for white persons exclusively, and that black people, now citizens of the nation, also were entitled to "the equal protection of the laws."

The Civil Rights Amendments and the three related Acts proclaim a very different concept of the social order than that implicit in the "three-fifths" clause contained in Section 2 of Article 1 of the Constitution. A concept that required the reconstruction of American society so that it could be free of slavery, free of a racism that was to have such terrible long-term consequences for the entire society.

The struggle to realize the great potential of the Reconstruction amendments to the Constitution, the struggle to create a just, decent and compassionate society free of racist oppression, is a continuing struggle that has taken many different forms in each era since the Reconstruction Period and one that continues today. In our own time the old conflict between those interests intent on perpetuating racist patterns rooted in the past and the forces that struggle for a society free of racism and its legacy continues in the raging battle for and against affirmative action.

During the late 1950's and early 1960's, as a result of direct confrontation with the system of state imposed segregation, together with the emergence of a new body of constitutional law on race, a hope was born that the legacy of centuries of slavery and racism would finally come to an end. But the hope was not yet to be realized. The high moral indignation of the 1960's was evidently but a passing spasm which was quickly forgotten.

A major manifestation of the sharp turning away from the goals of justice and equality is to be found in the shrill and paranoid attacks against affirmative action. The effort to eliminate the present effects of past discrimination, to correct the wrongs of many generations was barely underway when it came under powerful attack. And now, even the very modest gains made by racial minorities through affirmative action are being erased, as powerful institutions try to turn the clock of history back to the dark and dismal days of a separate and unequal status for black Americans.

Judging by the vast outcry, it might be assumed that the remedy of affirmative action to eliminate racist and sexist patterns has become as widespread and destructive as discrimination itself. And once again, the defenders of the racial *status quo* have succeeded in confusing the remedy with the original evil. The term "reverse discrimination," for example, has become another code word for resisting the elimination of prevailing patterns of discrimination.

The historic dissent of Justice John Marshall Harlan in the 1883 decision of the Supreme Court in the Civil Rights Cases defines the constitutional principle requiring the obligation of the government to remove all the "badges and incidents" of slavery. Although initially rejected, the rationale of Harlan's position was of course vindicated in later Supreme Court decisions, as in *Brown v. Board of Education* in 1954 and *Jones v. Mayer* in 1968, among others.

The adoption by Congress of the Civil Rights Act of 1964 further confirmed this constitutional perception of the equal protection clause of the 14th Amendment and reinforced the legal principle that for every right there is a remedy. I believe that what Justice Harlan called the "badges and incidents" of slavery include every manifestation of racial discrimination, not against black people alone, but also against other people of color who were engulfed by the heritage of racism that developed out of slavery.

In this respect, I believe that an interpretation of the law consistent with the meaning of the 13th and 14th Amendments to the Constitution holds that affirmative action programs carry forth the contemporary legal obligation to eradicate the consequences of slavery and racism. In order to do that, it is necessary to confront the present effects of past discrimination and the most effective remedy to achieve that goal is affirmative action. Mr. Justice Blackmun in his opinion in *Bakke* wrote, " . . . in order to get beyond racism, we must first take account of race. There is no other way."

By now it should be very clear, that the opposition to affirmative action is based on perceived group interest rather than on abstract philosophical differences about "quotas," "reverse discrimination," "preferential treatment" and the other catch-phrases commonly raised in public debate. After all the pious rhetoric equating affirmative action with "reverse discrimination" is stripped away, it is evident that the opposition to affirmative action is in fact the effort to perpetuate the privileged position of white males in American society.

In his dissent in *Bakke,* Justice Thurgood Marshall wrote, "The experience of Negroes in America has been different in kind, not just in degree, from that of other ethnic groups. It is not merely the history of slavery alone but also that a whole people were marked as inferior by the law. And that mark has endured. The dream of America as the great melting pot has not been realized for the Negro; because of his skin color he never even made it into the pot." . . .

Before the emergence of affirmative action remedies, the legal prohibitions against job discrimination were for the most part declarations of abstract morality that rarely resulted in any change. Pronouncements of public policy such as state and municipal fair employment practice laws were mainly symbolic, and the patterns of job discrimination remained intact. Because affirmative action programs go beyond individual relief to attack long-established patterns of discrimination and, if vigorously enforced by government agencies over a sustained period can become a major instrument for social change, they have come under powerful and repeated attack.

As long as Title VII litigation was concerned largely with procedural and conceptual issues, only limited attention was given to the consequences of remedies. However, once affirmative action was widely applied and the focus of litigation shifted to the adoption of affirmative action plans, entrenched interests were threatened. And as the gains of the 1960's are eroded, the nation becomes even more mean-spirited and self-deceiving.

Racism in the history of the United States has not been an aberration. It has been systematized and structured into the functioning of the society's most important institutions. In the present as in the past, it is widely accepted as a basis for promoting the interests of whites. For many generations the assumptions of white supremacy were codified in the law, imposed by custom and often enforced by violence. While the forms have changed, the legacy of white supremacy is expressed in the continuing patterns of racial discrimination, and for the vast majority of black and other non-white people, race and racism remain the decisive factors in their lives.

The current conflict over affirmative action is not simply an argument about abstract rights or ethnic bigotry. In the final analysis it is an argument between those who insist upon the substance of a long-postponed break with the traditions of American racism, and those groups that insist upon maintaining the valuable privileges and benefits they now enjoy as a consequence of that dismal history.

# Questions for Review and Reflection

1. According to the author, is racism in America an aberration, or is it part of the permanent fabric of American culture?
2. What is the author's attitude toward the concept of government-sponsored affirmative action? Do you agree with his position? Why? What have the defenders of the *status quo* managed to do with their charges of "reverse discrimination" in America?
3. What does the term "badge of slavery" mean? Which Supreme Court decision recognized the truth and reality of this concept?
4. According to Hill, what is the basis for the opposition to affirmative action? How might this opposition be overcome?
5. What distinctions does Justice Thurgood Marshall see between black Americans and other minorities in the United States? Do you agree with his assessment? Why?

# Reading 5

Joaquin Avila, 1988

## *Latino Political Empowerment*

A graduate of Harvard Law School, Joaquin Avila has served as counsel for the Mexican-American Legal Defense and Education Fund. He used litigation to challenge "discriminatory election systems," and his lawsuits brought an end to some redistricting plans and at-large elections that diluted minority voices in California and Texas. Now in private law practice in

California, Avila continues to challenge districts where minority votes are not afforded sufficient weight, so that true equality in the voting booth can be achieved. He says in this essay published in 1988, "Presently, the Latino community is engaged in a struggle for political equality . . . evidenced by aggressive litigation to enforce the Voting Rights Act, and by legislative and community political advocacy to secure the implementation of non-discriminatory election systems."

Latinos in California are not politically integrated. Although permitted to vote, their voting power in many communities is ineffective.

This ineffective voting power is due to discriminatory election structures. These election structures deny Latinos their right to effective participation in the political process.

This denial of effective political participation serves only to contribute to the growing alienation experienced by the Latino community. California cannot afford to have this alienation, especially from a growing Latino community. This alienation is not conducive toward the creation of a cohesive society.

The ability of California to achieve a more cohesive society is inextricably tied to the well-being of the Latino community. A characteristic of such a healthy community is the presence of political activity. Political participation contributes to the cohesiveness of the body politic.

Active political participation can only be achieved by the removal of discriminatory election systems.

Presently the Latino community is engaged in a struggle for political equality. This struggle is evidenced by aggressive litigation to enforce the Voting Rights Act, and by legislative and community political advocacy to secure the implementation of non-discriminatory election systems.

The timing of this political struggle is critical. The changing of boundaries for congressional, state legislative, and local governmental districts through the redistricting process will occur in 1991. The Latino community must be prepared to participate in these redistrictings. These redistrictings are important since this redistribution of political power occurs only once every ten years.

These efforts to eliminate discriminatory election systems should not be viewed simply as another minority issue. All racial and ethnic groups have a vested interest in having an active political community. Such a community will create leadership and community institutions at the local level.

The issue of voting rights for the Latino community is not simply another equity issue to resolve. Rather, the key to the advancement of the Latino community will be dependent upon the community's degree of integration into the political process. Thus, for Latinos, successful resolution of the voting rights issue will determine the political survival of our community.

The purpose of this essay is to emphasize the importance of Latino voting rights. This emphasis hopefully will play a role in convincing key decision makers of the importance of eliminating discriminatory election systems.

The time for action is now. These key decision makers cannot continue to ignore our problems. We simply do not have the luxury of waiting any longer. . . .

## Political Empowerment

The quality of representation is an issue which will eventually have to be addressed by Latino communities. A non-discriminatory election system will provide the minority community with an opportunity for holding elected officials accountable. This accountability in turn will result in more responsive officials.

More responsive elected officials will aggressively seek to improve the community's quality of life standards. Basic employment and educational needs will be addressed. These officials and community leaders can create opportunities for small businesses to provide more employment opportunities and to support educational programs. The first priority of any educational program should be to address the high dropout rates within urban and barrio schools.

For the moment, the issue of the quality of representation for many communities must be subordinated to the basic issue of securing access to the political process. Such access will only be accomplished if discriminatory election systems are eliminated.

## Conclusion

The issue of political integration is not just a minority issue. A state such as California can not continue to have a growing population which is under-educated, unemployed, and not involved in the political process. Maintenance of the status quo is a recipe for disaster. To change this status quo, the Latino community and its leadership must seize the initiative of aggressively pursuing litigative, legislative, and other advocacy strategies to remove discriminatory election systems. This aggressive promotion must be premised upon the notion that every vote counts. . . .

The Latino community cannot afford to wait for responsive governmental actions to accomplish the task. The initiative and perseverance must come from within. And action from the Latino community must begin now.

The first step is the investment: registering to vote and participating in elections. The second step is to support and become involved in the advocacy strategies to enforce the Voting Rights Act. These two steps are critical for the political survival of the Latino community and for the future of California.

The agenda has been established; and the call to action has been announced. It's our future; let us take charge.

# Questions for Review and Reflection

1. Why do you suppose Avila believes that Latino voting power in many communities is ineffective? What are his suggestions to make it more effective?
2. What is the effect of the denial of effective political participation of the Latino community? What will be the result in the Latino community if this is reversed?
3. How is the issue of Latino voting different from other issues of equity that need to be solved?
4. According to the author, how might "accountability" be instilled in the political process if a system of non-discriminatory elections is established in America? Why is the issue of political integration not just another minority issue?

# Reading 6

Shelby Steele, 1991

## The Content of Our Character

Some black leaders opposed what was called "preferential treatment," calling it social engineering that demoralized rather than uplifted blacks. These critics contended that entitlements were based on victim status rather than on true merit. Shelby Steele, an outspoken critic, termed such programs "manufacturing parity."

Steele, a professor of English at California State University at San Jose, has written several essays on the subject of race for *Harper's* magazine, one of which was included in *The Best American Essays of 1989*. He followed these writings with the book from which this reading was taken, a critical examination of the whole policy of affirmative action. He writes, "Under affirmative action the quality that earns us preferential treatment is an implied inferiority." Steele argues that government should use its vast power to offer preferential treatment based on disadvantage regardless of race, while imposing severe sanctions for discrimination. This dilemma over the proper exercise of government authority to guarantee opportunity remains a nagging question in making public policy.

So, in theory, affirmative action certainly has all the moral symmetry that fairness requires—the injustice of historical and even contemporary white advantage is offset with black advantage; preference replaces prejudice, inclusion answers exclusion. It is reformist and corrective, even repentant and redemptive. And I would never sneer at these good intentions. . . .

Yet good intentions, because of the opportunity for innocence they offer us, are very seductive and can blind us to the effects they generate when implemented. In our society, affirmative action is, among other things, a testament to white goodwill and to black power, and in the midst of these heavy investments, its effects can be hard to see. But after twenty years of implementation, I think affirmative action has shown itself to be more bad than good and that blacks—whom I will focus on in this essay—now stand to lose more from it than they gain.

In talking with affirmative action administrators and with blacks and whites in general, it is clear that supporters of affirmative action focus on its good intentions while detractors emphasize its negative effects. Proponents talk about "diversity" and "pluralism"; opponents speak of "reverse discrimination," the unfairness of quotas and set-asides. It was virtually impossible to find people outside either camp. The closest I came was a white male manager at a large computer company who said, "I think it amounts to reverse discrimination, but I'll put up with a little of that for a little more diversity." I'll live with a little of the effect to gain a little of the intention, he seemed to be saying. But this only makes him a halfhearted supporter of affirmative action. I think many people who don't really like affirmative action support it to one degree or another anyway. . . .

I think that one of the most troubling effects of racial preferences for blacks is a kind of demoralization, or put another way, an enlargement of self-doubt. Under affirmative action the quality that earns us preferential treatment is an implied inferiority. However this inferiority is explained—and it is easily enough explained by the myriad deprivations that grew out of our oppression—it is still inferiority. . . .

The effects of this may be a subject for another essay. The point here is that the implication of inferiority that racial preferences engender in both the white and black mind expands rather than contracts this doubt. . . .

Preferential treatment, no matter how it is justified in the light of day, subjects blacks to a midnight of self-doubt, and so often transforms their advantage into a revolving door.

Another liability of affirmative action comes from the fact that it indirectly encourages blacks to exploit their own past victimization as a source of power and privilege. Victimization, like implied inferiority, is what justifies preference, so that to receive the benefits of preferential treatment one must, to some extent, become invested in the view of one's self as a victim. In this way, affirmative action nurtures a victim-focused identity in blacks. The obvious irony here is that we become inadvertently invested in the very condition we are trying to overcome. Racial preferences send us the message that there is more power in our past suffering than our present achievements—none of which could bring us a *preference* over others.

When power itself grows out of suffering, then blacks are encouraged to expand the boundaries of what qualifies as racial oppression, a situation that can lead us to paint our victimization in vivid colors, even as we receive the benefits of preference. The same corporations and institutions that give us preference are also seen as our oppressors. At Stanford University minority students—some of whom enjoy as much as $15,000 a year in financial aid—recently took over the president's office demanding, among other things, more financial aid. The power to be found in victimization, like any power, is intoxicating and can lend itself to the creation of a new class of super-victims who can feel the pea of victimization under twenty mattresses. Preferential treatment rewards us for being underdogs rather than for moving beyond that status—a displacement of incentives that, along with its deepening of our doubt, is more a yoke than a spur.

But, I think, one of the worst prices that blacks pay for preference has to do with an illusion. I saw this illusion at work recently in the mother of a middle-class black student who was going off to his first semester of college. "They owe us this, so don't think for a minute that you don't belong there." This is the logic by which many blacks, and some whites, justify affirmative action—it is something "owed," a form of reparation. But this logic overlooks a much harder and less digestible reality, that it is impossible to repay blacks living today for the historic suffering of the race. If all blacks were given a million dollars tomorrow morning it would not amount to a dime on the dollar of three centuries of oppression, nor would it obviate the residues of that oppression that we still carry today. The concept of historic reparation grows out of man's need to impose a degree of justice on the world that simply does not exist. Suffering can be endured and overcome, it cannot be repaid. Blacks cannot be repaid for the injustice done to the race, but we can be corrupted by society's guilty gestures of repayment.

Affirmative action is such a gesture. It tells us that racial preferences can do for us what we cannot do for ourselves. The corruption here is in the hidden incentive *not* to do what we believe preferences will do. This is an incentive to be reliant on others just as we are struggling for self-reliance. And it keeps alive the illusion that we can find some deliverance in repayment. The hardest thing for any sufferer to accept is that his suffering excuses him from very little and never has enough currency to restore him. To think otherwise is to prolong the suffering. . . .

I believe affirmative action is problematic in our society because it tries to function like a social program. Rather than ask it to ensure equal opportunity we have demanded that it create parity between the races. But preferential treatment does not teach skills, or educate, or instill motivation. It only passes out entitlement by color, a situation that in my profession has created an unrealistically high demand for black professors. The social engineer's assumption is that this high demand will inspire more blacks to earn Ph.D.'s and join the profession. In fact, the number of blacks earning Ph.D.'s has declined in recent years. A Ph.D. must be developed from preschool on. He requires family and community support. He must acquire an entire system of values that enables him to work hard while delaying gratification. There are social programs, I believe, that can (and should) help blacks develop in all these areas, but entitlement by color is not a social program; it is a dubious reward for being black. . . .

But if not preferences, then what? I think we need social policies that are committed to two goals: the educational and economic development of disadvantaged people, regardless of race, and the eradication from our society—through close monitoring and severe sanctions—of racial, ethnic, or gender discrimination. Preferences will not deliver us to either of these goals, since they tend to benefit those who are not disadvantaged—middle-class white women and middle-class blacks—and attack one form of discrimination with another. Preferences are inexpensive and carry the glamour of good intentions—change the numbers and the good deed is done. To be against them is to be unkind. But I think the unkindest cut is to bestow on children like my own an undeserved advantage while neglecting the development of those disadvantaged children on the East Side of my city who will likely never be in a position to benefit from a preference. Give my children fairness; give disadvantaged children a better shot at development—better elementary and secondary schools, job training, safer neighborhoods, better financial assistance for college, and so on.

 **uestions for Review and Reflection**

1. To what famous speech does the title of Steele's book allude? Why do you suppose he chose this particular sentiment to entitle his work?
2. According to the author, what does the existence of an affirmative action policy reveal about the nature of American society? Do you agree?
3. What is the author's position on affirmative action? What are some of its positive elements, according to Steele?

4. The author refers to the concept of victimization in this selection and suggests that it is intoxicating. What is victimization, and how is it intoxicating?
5. If the policy of affirmative action is unwise for the nation, what two social policies does the author recommend instead?

# Reading 7

Linda Chavez, 1991

## *Out of the Barrio*

Linda Chavez served as a public official in a variety of federal posts during the 1980s and was one of the first women appointed to the Civil Rights Commission. She has edited *American Educator* magazine and has written many articles as well as the book from which this reading was taken.

In this study of Hispanics in American society, Chavez objects to abandoning the "melting pot" approach to assimilation and defends its successful incorporation of an ethnically diverse population during the nineteenth and twentieth centuries.

The role of government, according to Chavez, is to promote the common culture and language. The protection and advancement of native cultures should be accomplished by the communities themselves. Chavez points to Chinese, Jewish, and other groups who "have long established after-school and weekend programs to teach [their own] language and culture to children from these groups."

She credits both education and politics as great "equalizers" and encourages assimilation in politics by reaching out to broadly based constituencies and community issues. She is describing a pluralist system with a sense of community for all Americans.

**A**ssimilation has become a dirty word in American politics. It invokes images of people, cultures, and traditions forged into a colorless alloy in an indifferent melting pot. But, in fact, assimilation, as it has taken place in the United States, is a far more gentle process, by which people from outside the community gradually became part of the community itself. Descendants of the German, Irish, Italian, Polish, Greek, and other immigrants who came to the United States bear little resemblance to the descendants of the country-men their forebears left behind. America changed its immigrant groups—and was changed by them. Some groups were accepted more reluctantly than others—the Chinese, for example—and some with great struggle. Blacks, whose ancestors were forced to come here, have only lately won their legal right to full participation in this society; and even then civil rights gains have not been sufficiently translated into economic gains. Until quite recently, however, there was no question but that each group desired admittance to the mainstream. No more. Now ethnic leaders demand that their groups remain separate, that their native culture and language be preserved intact, and that whatever accommodation takes place be on the part of the receiving society. . . .

The government should not be obliged to preserve any group's distinctive language or culture. Public schools should make sure that all children can speak, read, and write English well. When teaching children from non-English-speaking backgrounds, they should use methods that will achieve English proficiency quickly and should not allow political pressure to interfere with meeting the academic needs of students. No children in an American school are helped by being held back in their native language when they could be learning the language that will enable them to get a decent job or pursue higher education. More than twenty years of experience with native-language instruction fails to show that children in these programs learn English more quickly or perform better academically than children in programs that emphasize English acquisition.

If Hispanic parents want their children to be able to speak Spanish and know about their distinctive culture, they must take the responsibility to teach their children these things. Government simply cannot—and should not—be charged with this responsibility. Government bureaucracies given the authority to create bicultural teaching materials homogenize the myths, customs, and history of the Hispanic peoples of this hemisphere, who, after all, are not a single group but many groups. It is only in the United States that "Hispanics" exist; a Cakchiquel Indian in Guatemala would find it remarkable that anyone could consider his culture to be the same as a Spanish Argentinean's. The best way for Hispanics to learn about their native culture is in their own commu-nities. Chinese, Jewish, Greek, and other ethnic communities have long estab-lished after-school and weekend programs to teach language and culture to children from these groups. . . .

The real barriers to Hispanic political power are apathy and alienage. Too few native-born Hispanics register and vote; too few Hispanic immigrants become citizens. The way to increase real political power is not to gerrymander districts to create safe seats for Hispanic elected officials or treat illegal aliens and other immigrants as if their status were unimportant to their political representation; yet those are precisely the tactics Hispanic organizations have urged lately. Ethnic politics is an old and honored tradition in the United States. . . .

Politics has traditionally been a great equalizer. One person's vote was as good as another's, regardless of whether the one was rich and the other poor. But politics requires that people participate. The great civil rights struggles of the 1960s were fought in large part to guarantee the right to vote. Hispanic leaders demand representation but do not insist that individual Hispanics participate in the process. The emphasis is always on rights, never on obligations. Hispanic voter organizations devote most of their efforts toward making the process easier—election law reform, postcard registration, election materials in Spanish—to little avail; voter turnout is still lower among Hispanics than among blacks and white. Spanish posters urge Hispanics to vote because it will mean more and better jobs and social programs, but I've never seen one that mentions good citizenship. Hispanics (and others) need to be reminded that if they want the freedom and opportunity democracy offers, the least they can do is take the time to register and vote. These are the lessons with which earlier immigrants were imbued, and they bear reviving. . . .

The government can do only so much in promoting higher education for Hispanics or any group. It is substantially easier today for a Hispanic student to go to college than it was even twenty or thirty years ago, yet the proportion of Mexican Americans who are graduating from college today is unchanged from what it was forty years ago. When the former secretary of education Lauro Cavazos, the first Hispanic ever to serve in the Cabinet, criticized Hispanic parents for the low educational attainment of their children, he was roundly attacked for blaming the victim. But Cavazos's point was that Hispanic parents must encourage their children's educational aspirations and that, too often, they don't. Those groups that have made the most spectacular socioeconomic gains—Jews and Chinese, for example—have done so because their families placed great emphasis on education.

Hispanics cannot have it both ways. If they want to earn as much as non-Hispanic whites, they have to invest the same number of years in schooling as these do. The earnings gap will not close until the education gap does. Native-born Hispanics are already enjoying earnings comparable to those of non-Hispanic whites, once educational differences are factored in. If they want to earn more, they must become better educated. But education requires sacrifices, especially for persons from lower-income families. Poverty, which was both more pervasive and severe earlier in this century, did not prevent Jews or Chinese from helping their children get a better education. These families were willing to forgo immediate pleasures, even necessities, in order to send their children to school. Hispanics must be willing to do the same—or else be satisfied with lower socioeconomic status. The status of second- and third-generation Hispanics will probably continue to rise even without big gains in college graduation; but the rise will be slow. Only a substantial commitment to the education of their children on the part of this generation of Hispanic parents will increase the speed with which Hispanics improve their social and economic status. . . .

Affirmative action politics treats race and ethnicity as if they were synonymous with disadvantage. The son of a Mexican American doctor or lawyer is treated as if he suffered the same disadvantage as the child of a Mexican farm worker; and both are given preference over poor, non-Hispanic whites in admission to most colleges or affirmative action employment programs. Most people think this is unfair, especially white ethnics whose own parents and grandparents also faced discrimination in this society but never became eligible for the entitlements of the civil rights era. It is inherently patronizing to assume that all Hispanics are deprived and grossly unjust to give those who aren't preference on the basis of disadvantages they don't experience. Whether stated or not, the essence of affirmative action is the belief that Hispanics—or any of the other eligible groups—are not capable of measuring up to the standards applied to whites. This is a pernicious idea.

Ultimately, entitlements based on their status as "victims" rob Hispanics of real power. The history of American ethnic groups is one of overcoming disadvantage, of competing with those who were already here and proving themselves as competent as any who came before. Their fight was always to be treated the same as other Americans, never to be treated as special, certainly not to turn the temporary disadvantages they suffered into the basis for permanent entitlement. Anyone who thinks this fight was easier in the early part of this century when it was waged by other ethnic groups does not know history. Hispanics have not always had an easy time of it in the United States. Even though discrimination against Mexican Americans and Puerto Ricans was not as severe as it was against blacks, acceptance has come only with struggle, and some prejudices still exist. Discrimination against Hispanics, or any other group, should be fought, and there are laws and a massive administrative apparatus to do so. But the way to eliminate such discrimination is not to classify all Hispanics as victims and treat them as if they could not succeed by their own efforts. Hispanics can and will prosper in the United States by following the example of the millions before them.

# |Q| uestions for Review and Reflection

1. According to Chavez:

    a. Why is assimilation a dirty word?
    b. What is the role of government vis-à-vis culture and language?
    c. How can culture be preserved?
    d. What are the real barriers to Hispanic political power?
    e. What is the great equalizer? Explain why this is so.

# Reading 8

Susan Faludi, 1991

## *Backlash: The Undeclared War against American Women*

Harvard graduate and Pulitzer Prize–winning journalist Susan Faludi wrote an award-winning book in which she exposed what she saw as a diminution of the women's rights movement since the 1980s. Faludi disputed "conventional wisdom," which said that women were achieving full equality. Instead, she charged that a "powerful counter-assault" had been waged to halt the progress that women had made. Faludi declared that equal opportunities for women had regressed due to this backlash. "Just when women's quest for equal rights seemed closest to achieving its objectives, the backlash struck it down." She produced an itemized agenda of what must be achieved in employment, education, and reproductive rights in order to remedy discrimination and win back all that had been lost.

The backlash decade produced one long, painful, and unremitting campaign to thwart women's progress. And yet, for all the forces the backlash mustered—the blistering denunciations from the New Right, the legal setbacks of the Reagan years, the powerful resistance of corporate America, the self-perpetuating myth machines of the media and Hollywood, the "neotraditional" marketing drive of Madison Avenue—women never really surrendered. The federal government may have crippled equal employment enforcement and the courts may have undermined twenty-five years of antidiscrimination law—yet women continued to enter the work force in growing numbers each year. Newsstands and airwaves may have been awash with frightening misinformation on spinster booms, birth dearths, and deadly day care—yet women continued to postpone their wedding dates, limit their family size, and combine work with having children. Television sets and movie screens may have been filled with nesting goodwives, but female viewers still gave their highest ratings to shows with strong-willed and independent heroines. Backlash dressmakers couldn't even get women to follow the most trivial of fashion prescriptions; while retailers crammed their racks with garter belts and teddies, women just kept reaching for the all-cotton Jockeys. . . .

American women have always fought the periodic efforts to force them back behind the curtain. The important question to ask about the current backlash, then, is not *whether* women are resisting, but how effectively. Millions of individual women, each in her own way, spent the last decade kicking against the backlash barricades. But much of that effort proved fruitless. While women didn't succumb to the backlash agenda, they didn't gain sufficient momentum to crash its steel-reinforced gates, either. Instead, when women tried to drive privately against the antifeminist forces of the '80s, they most often found their wheels spinning, frustration and disappointment building as they sank deeper in the same old ruts.

There are so many ways to rebel that pose no real or useful challenge to the system—like the proverbial exploited worker who screws the bolts in backward or the dutiful daughter chronically late to Sunday dinner. Some women tried to slip by the backlash checkpoint by mouthing the backlash passwords or trying to tailor the "pro-family" agenda to their own ends or by insisting that *they* were certainly not feminists. Still others resorted to the old "feminine" strategy—just be good and patient; the world will eventually take pity on women who wait.

While the '80s was an era that trumpeted the "one person can make a difference" credo, this strategy proved a blind alley on the road to equal rights. To remove the backlash wall rather than to thrash continually against it, women needed to be armed with more than their privately held grievances and goals. Indeed, to instruct each woman to struggle alone was to set each woman up, yet again, for defeat.

In the past, women have proven that they can resist in a meaningful way, when they have had a clear agenda that is unsanitized and unapologetic, a mobilized mass that is forceful and public, and a conviction that is uncompromising and relentless. On the rare occasions when these three elements have coalesced in the last two centuries, women have won their battles. The suffrage campaign faltered when its leaders resorted to accommodation and deception—daintily claiming they just viewed the vote as a form of "enlarged housekeeping." Ultimately, it was the combination of a forthright agenda, mass action, and sheer physical resistance that won the day. Suffragists organized thousands of women, filed 480 appeals to the state legislatures, launched fifty-six referendum efforts and staged forty-seven campaigns at state constitutional conventions. Even so, it wasn't until the National Woman's Party members began picketing the Capitol, chaining themselves to the White House gates and enduring imprisonment and forced feedings, that half the population finally got the vote.

Likewise, the women's liberation movement had many false starts. As political scientist Ethel Klein has observed, despite individual women's repeated efforts only 10 of the 884 women's rights bills introduced in Congress in the '60s ever passed. It took a sheer display of numbers and determination for the women's movement to force its way into public consciousness. The 1970

Women's Strike for Equality, then the largest demonstration for women's rights in history, turned the tide—inspiring a vast growth in feminist organization memberships and a flood of legal victories. Before the strike, the politicians ignored feminists. Afterward, seventy-one women's rights bills were signed into law in a matter of a few years—nearly 40 percent of all the legislation on women's rights passed in the century. . . .

Under the '80s backlash, in the very few instances where women have tried such a vocal and unapologetic strategy, they *have* managed to transform the public climate, set the agenda on their own terms, and change the minds of many individual men. The spectacular turnaround in abortion politics, pulled off by a rejuvenated pro-choice movement in 1989, is a textbook case in point. It happened when women who believed in the right to control their own bodies finally made a mighty showing of those bodies in 1989—a half billion marched on the Capitol on April 9, Washington, D.C.'s largest demonstration ever—and confronted the antiabortion protesters at the clinic doors. Among female students, too, pro-choice protests drew more undergraduates than came to the antiwar marches in the '60s. Their vast numbers steamrolled over an antiabortion crusade that seemed, only weeks earlier, on the verge of wiping out women's reproductive rights. The mass mobilization of a pro-choice coalition defused all but a few of the hundreds of antiabortion bills introduced in the state legislatures in 1989, swept pro-choice candidates into gubernatorial and congressional office and even scared Republican National Committee chairman Lee Atwater enough to relabel the GOP "an umbrella party" on the abortion question. In Idaho in 1990, one of the nation's most restrictive abortion bills was vetoed by Cecil Andrus, the state's "pro-life" governor—after pro-choice women declared a boycott of Idaho potatoes. Some feminist leaders argued against such forceful tactics. "Let the governor make his decision based on the seriousness of this issue and the Constitution, not potatoes," National Abortion Rights Action League's executive director Kate Michelman advised. But it was the boycott that clinched it. "Anytime someone threatens one of our major cash crops," Governor Andrus explained, "it becomes significant."

For most of the decade, however, the increasingly reinforced fortress of an antifeminist culture daunted women more than it galvanized them. The backlash watchtowers flashed their warning signals without cease, and like high-security floodlights, they served to blind women to their own prodigious strengths. Women of the '80s were the majority in the general population, the college campuses, the voting booths, the bookstores, at the newsstands, and before the television sets. They represented nearly half the workers in offices and spent nearly 80 percent of the consumer dollars in stores. They enjoyed an unprecedented and expanding gender advantage in both national and state elections—by the end of the '80s, a Democratic female candidate could command an instant 12- to 20-point lead from female voters simply by declaring herself pro-choice. Yet so often in this era, women seemed unaware of the weight and dynamism of their own formidable presence. . . .

That women have in their possession a vast and untapped vitality also explains one of the more baffling phenomena of the backlash—the seeming "overreaction" with which some men have greeted even the tiniest steps toward women's advancement. Maybe these men weren't overreacting after all. In the '80s, male politicians saw the widening gender gap figures. Male policymakers saw the polls indicating huge and rising majorities of women demanding economic equality, reproductive freedom, a real participation in the political process, as well as a real governmental investment in social services and a real commitment to peace. (A record gender gap of 25 percent divided the sexes on the 1991 Persian Gulf war; on the eve of battle, a majority of women opposed military intervention, while a majority of men supported it.) Male corporate heads saw the massive female consensus for child care and family leave policies and the vast female resentment over indecent pay and minimal promotions. Male evangelical leaders saw the huge numbers of "traditional" wives who were ignoring their teachings or heading for the office. All of these men understood the profound force that an American women's movement could exert if it got half a chance. It was women, tragically, who were still in the dark.

"The reason men 'overreact' is *they* get it," Eleanor Smeal, founder of the Fund for the Feminist Majority, says. "If women all got together on the same day, on the same hour, we would go over the top." That day could have been any one of the 3,650 days in the last backlash decade. But women never did capitalize on the historic advantage they enjoyed; and as the attack on equal rights gathered momentum, women's energies were diverted and ultimately exhausted in fending off antifeminism's punishing blows. What is perhaps most depressing to contemplate is what might have been. The '80s could have become American women's great leap forward.

At the start of the '90s, some forecasters—most of them advertisers and political publicists—began declaring that the next ten years was going to be "the Decade of Women." What they meant by this prognosis was not entirely clear. Were they divining a real phenomenon or just coining another "trend"? Were they suggesting that women would wield more authority in the '90s, or were they simply envisioning another nostalgia-drenched epoch in which women would adopt a softer, more "feminine" pose?

In any event, when the media set out to report this story, they had the usual trouble rounding up evidence. "I get press calls every election season," Ruth Mandel, director of the Center for the American Woman and Politics, wearily told a reporter. "But the answer is no, this isn't the year (for women)—it wasn't the year in 1986 or 1988, and it won't be in '90 or '92."

One might hope, or dream, that Mandel's gloomy prediction is proved wrong. But more productively, women can act. Because there really is no good reason why the '90s can't be their decade. Because the demographics and the opinion polls are on women's side. Because women's hour on the stage is long, long overdue. Because, whatever new obstacles are mounted against the future march toward equality, whatever new myths invented, penalties levied, opportunities rescinded, or degradations imposed, no one can ever take from the American woman the justness of her cause.

## uestions for Review and Reflection

1. How does Faludi describe the backlash?
2. Why does she feel women would turn against the women's movement?
3. Why does she feel that men "overreact" to women's advancement?
4. Why does Faludi say the 90's is the decade of the woman?

# Reading 9

Rosalind C. Barnett and Caryl Rivers, 1992

## "The Myth of the Miserable Working Woman"

In this article, Dr. Rosalind C. Barnett, senior scholar at Radcliffe College, psychologist, and researcher of women's roles in American society, reports on the working role of women, in collaboration with Caryl Rivers, professor of journalism at Boston University.

Dr. Barnett has engaged in a number of studies on women's issues, has published articles in major national news outlets, has written several books, and has received several awards for her work, including the Books for a Better Life Literary Award.

Written for *Working Woman*, this report tends to alleviate the concerns raised by Phyllis Schlafly in "The Power of the Positive Woman" (see Chapter 5, Reading 1). Men and women, these authors assert, need not have defining roles that are distinct and different; both sexes can operate on a much more coequal basis at work and at home. They conclude from their compilation of research that the workplace is harmed without women working in it, and the family unit is harmed without men playing a much more vital role. That women must be treated so differently is a myth, they contend, and is based on "disinformation that has serious consequences for the life and health of every American woman."

If you believe what you read, working women are in big trouble-stressed out, depressed, sick, risking an early death from heart attacks, and so overcome with problems at home that they make inefficient employees at work.

In fact, just the opposite is true. As a research psychologist whose career has focused on women and a journalist-critic who has studied the behavior of the media, we have extensively surveyed the latest data and research and concluded that the public is being engulfed by a tidal wave of disinformation that has serious consequences for the life and health of every American woman. Since large numbers of women began moving into the work force in the 1970s, scores of studies on their emotional and physical health have painted a very clear picture: Paid employment provides substantial health *benefits* for women. These benefits cut across income and class lines; even women who are working because they have to—not because they want to—share in them. . . .

Too often, legislation is written and policies are drafted not on the basis of the facts but on the basis of what those in power believe to be the facts. Even the much discussed *Workforce 2000* report, issued by the Department of Labor under the Reagan administration—hardly a hotbed of feminism—admitted that "most current policies were designed for a society in which men worked and women stayed home." If policies are skewed toward solutions that are aimed at reducing women's commitment to work, they will do more than harm women—they will damage companies, managers and the productivity of the American economy. . . .

But doesn't working put women at greater risk for stress-related illnesses? No. Paid work is actually associated with *reduced* anxiety and depression. In the early 1980s we reported in our book, *Lifeprints* (based on a National Science Foundation-funded study of 300 women), that working women were significantly higher in psychological well-being than those not employed. Working gave them a sense of mastery and control that homemaking didn't provide. More recent studies echo our findings. For example:

• A 1989 report by psychologist Ingrid Waldron and sociologist Jerry Jacobs of Temple University on nationwide surveys of 2,392 white and 892 black women, conducted from 1977 to 1982, found that women who held both work and family roles reported better physical and mental health than homemakers. . . .

• A University of California at Berkeley study published in 1990 followed 140 women for 22 years. At age 43, those who were homemakers had more chronic conditions than the working women and seemed more disillusioned and frustrated. The working mothers were in good health and seemed to be juggling their roles with success.

In sum, paid work offers women heightened self-esteem and enhanced mental and physical health. It's unemployment that's a major risk factor for depression in women. . . .

This isn't true only for affluent women in good jobs; working-class women share the benefits of work, according to psychologists Sandra Scarr and Deborah Phillips of the University of Virginia and Kathleen McCartney of the University of New Hampshire. In reviewing 80 studies on this subject, they reported that working-class women with children say they would not leave work even if they didn't need the money. Work offers not only income but adult companionship, social contact and a connection with the wider world that they cannot get at home. . . .

## The Advantages for Families

What about the kids? Many working parents feel they want more time with their kids, and they say so. But does maternal employment harm children? In 1989 University of Michigan psychologist Lois Hoffman reviewed 50 years of research and found that the expected negative effects never materialized. Most often, children of employed and unemployed mothers didn't differ on measures of child development. But children of both sexes with working mothers have a less sex-stereotyped view of the world because fathers in two-income families tend to do more child care.

However, when mothers work, the quality of non-parental child care is a legitimate worry. Scarr, Phillips and McCartney say there is "near consensus among developmental psychologists and early-childhood experts that child care per se does not constitute a risk factor in children's lives." What causes problems, they report, is poor-quality care and a troubled family life. The need for good child care in this country has been obvious for some time. . . .

But the real point about working women and children is that work *isn't* the point at all. There are good mothers and not-so-good mothers, and some work and some don't. When a National Academy of Sciences panel reviewed the previous 50 years of research and dozens of studies in 1982, it found no consistent effects on children from a mother's working. Work is only one of many variables, the panel concluded in *Families That Work,* and not the definitive one. . . .

## The First Shift: Women at Work

While women's own health and the well-being of their families aren't harmed by their working, what effect does this dual role have on their job performance? It's assumed that men can compartmentalize work and home lives but women will bring their home worries with them to work, making them distracted and inefficient employees.

The only spillover went in the other direction: The women brought their good feelings about their work home with them and left a bad day at home behind when they came to work; in fact, some sociological studies found that it was the *men* who brought the family stresses with them to work. "Women are able to avoid bringing the contagion of home stress into the workplace," the researchers write, "whereas the inability of men to prevent this kind of contagion is pervasive.". . .

Perhaps the most dangerous myth is that the solution to most problems women suffer is for them to drop back—or drop out. What studies actually show is a significant connection between a reduced commitment to work and increased psychological stress. . . .

As soon as a woman has any kind of difficulty—emotional, family, medical—the knee-jerk reaction is to get her off the job. No such solution is offered to men, despite the very real correlation for men between job stress and heart attacks.

What the myth of the miserable working woman obscures is the need to focus on how the *quality* of a woman's job affects her health. Media stories warn of the alleged dangers of fast-track jobs. But our *Lifeprints* study found that married women in high-prestige jobs were highest in mental well-being; another study of life stress in women reported that married career women with children suffered the least from stress. Meanwhile, few media tears are shed for the women most at risk: those in the word-processing room who have no control at work, low pay and little support at home.

Women don't need help getting out of the work force; they need help staying in it. As long as much of the media continues to capitalize on national ignorance, that help will have to come from somewhere else. (Not that an occasional letter to the editor isn't useful.) Men need to recognize that they are not just occasional helpers but vital to the success of the family unit. The corporate culture has to be reshaped so that it doesn't run totally according to patterns set by the white male workaholic. This will be good for men *and* women. The government can guarantee parental leave and affordable, available child care. (It did so in the '40s, when women were needed in the factories.) Given that Congress couldn't even get a bill guaranteeing *unpaid* family leave passed last year, this may take some doing. But hey, this is an election year.

# Q uestions for Review and Reflection

1. According to Dr. Barnett and Dr. Rivers, what is the source of the disinformation that has serious consequences for the life and health of the American woman?
2. Identify three benefits of work for women that are discussed in the article.
3. What is the role for men that is recommended in this article?
4. The authors recommend that government support a working family. Research what legislative policies have been enacted by the U.S.

Congress and your state government to support the working family since this article was written.

5. Based on your own experience, do you agree or disagree with the findings put forth in this article regarding the working woman?

## Reading 10

John Mohawk, 1992

## "Looking for Columbus: Thoughts on the Past, Present, and Future of Humanity"

John Mohawk is a member of the Seneca tribe of Native Americans, an associate professor of American studies at State University of New York, and editor of *Daybreak* newsletter, a national publication of Indian news.

Mohawk criticized the "melting pot" theory as a failed ideology for a pluralist society. He recommends an end to the "clashing" and "intermixing" and urges a respect for the "multiplicity of cultures" that make up America. His concept of pluralism embraces people from all over the world. He views America as only part of a much larger society where "difference is just a simple fact of life." The global world is made up of so many different cultures and languages; it is past time to understand and accept this reality, according to Mohawk.

Is it possible at last to look at the modern period, not as a process of crisis and decline, but as a wonderful opportunity to amalgamate and pull things together?

No area of the globe has a bloodier history than Europe. And the reason for this is the outrageous intolerance of people claiming for centuries and centuries to be the chosen ones of God, to be a special people, a "superior race of men." . . .

It is essential that we understand that the intolerance arising out of Eurocentrism is what has caused the crisis of our times. Eurocentrism not only creates anthropocentrism—which comes directly from the tradition calling upon "man" to go out and assert "dominion" over nature—but ordains that people are not open to any other thinking. I was at a discussion at the Harvard Divinity School not long ago when a speaker got up and said, "Humans are obviously superior to all other life forms on Earth." I wanted to ask him to define "superior." Without trees to create oxygen, humans can't breathe, so they are a *dead* life form. If we don't understand ourselves in relation to the very big picture of the planet, as a biological living thing, then we don't understand the world we are living in. We can make abysmally ignorant statements such as "mankind is superior to all other life forms on Earth," but, *however* you define "superior," it is immaterial to nature. Nature doesn't care what your ideologies are.

## Toward a Viable Future

For 500 years we have seen both a clashing and an intermixing of cultures. Over all but the last decade or so, America has espoused the ideology of "the melting pot," and yet that approach has failed to enrich this culture. So, we're beginning to arrive at the realization that we might have to adopt a more pluralistic approach; instead of requiring everybody to be the same, maybe we should learn to live with one another, and allow for a genuine multiplicity of cultures. We are living in a world in which difference is just a simple fact of life, but our collective thinking has yet to truly come to grips with this reality. This *has* to change.

A workable world mentality means that we are going to have to make peace with those who are different from us. We must also come together in the realization that social initiatives, social justice, and ecology have to go hand in hand. As long as people don't have enough to eat, as long as people are driven off their lands, as long as investment banks in the industrialized world finance dams that displace people in the Third and Fourth Worlds, there will be people scrambling down hillsides cutting down the forests in order to find a place to live and a way to make a living.

I offer you the suggestion that we need to reevaluate our thinking. We need to look at the old philosophies and ask ourselves whether that is where we want to put our energies. Or should we look at other peoples' ways of thinking about the world and its societies, and decide anew how human priorities and human societies ought to be constructed? We need to give ourselves permission to trust our own thinking and not allow bureaucrats and crazed guys at the pulpit to do our thinking for us. And we need to take *this* kind of ideology and make it work for us on *the land.*

We are going to have to ask ourselves what our resources are. Our first resource is human compassion, gained through the clear use of our minds, which will allow us to make the best use of the human family. And another of our best resources emerges when we think clearly about the peoples who have alternative answers to the questions that are not being answered by the society we live in. For the first time in human history it is possible to talk to the jungle-dwelling Indians of South America in a European language at a North American conference and find out what they think about the world they live in and the world we live in. It is possible for the first time to take all the knowledge of the whole family of humanity and start plotting a course toward a viable future. It is possible at last to look at the modern period, not as a process of crisis and decline, but as a wonderful opportunity to amalgamate and pull things together, and to make the world our library. It at last is possible, in other words, not only to finally find the real meaning of Columbus, but to bury it.

# [Q] uestions for Review and Reflection

1. How does Mohawk define Eurocentrism?
2. What kinds of differences does he say exist in the world that are simple facts of life?
3. What resources does Mohawk feel can be utilized to achieve a more pluralistic society?

# Reading **11**

Vine Deloria Jr., 1992

## "Afterword"

A member of the Standing Rock Sioux, Vine Deloria Jr. is a scholar of Indian affairs. He has written many books, including *Custer Died for Your Sins; An Indian Manifesto; We Talk, You Listen;* and *Behind the Trail of Broken Treaties.* He holds degrees in law and theology, and is considered a leading spokesman for American Indians.

Deloria calls for a redefinition of American democracy. This will require a revision of history that provides a true accounting of the "smallest and least significant people" in order that they be part of "the complete human heritage." Deloria maintains that we live in a global society, that "the world is now irretrievably one." A full understanding of the contributions and "virtues" represented by these previously ignored people is vital to future human development, according to Deloria, and is a step necessary for future progress.

**I**ncreasingly, American Indians are understanding the European invasion as a failure. That is to say, in spite of severe oppression, almost complete displacement, and substantial loss of religion and culture, Indians have not been completely defeated. Indeed, the hallmark of today's Indian psyche is the realization that the worst has now passed and that it is the white man with his careless attitude toward life and the environment who is actually in danger of extinction. The old Indian prophecies say that the white man's stay on these western continents will be the shortest of any who have come here. From an Indian point of view, the general theme by which to understand the history of the hemisphere would be the degree to which the whites have responded to the rhythms of the land—the degree to which they have become indigenous. From that perspective, the judgment of Europeans is severe.

American history is usually cast in the light of progress—how a wilderness was tamed and brought to production by a hardy people who created a society in which the benefits of the earth were distributed to the largest percentage of people. From a short-term perspective, there is much to be said for this interpretation. Luxuries virtually inundate the United States, and even the poorest person in this society is in a much more comfortable position than the majority of people in most other human societies. This evaluation cannot be true for all nations of the Americas, of course, but for the peoples influenced by the English tradition it is most certainly a fact. The people of the United States prefer to credit their success to an intense commitment to progress, although at odd moments the Deity does get a bit of a compliment, and progress is almost always defined as an increase in material wealth. But in recent years, as the United States has begun to resemble a Third World nation saddled with insurmountable debts, the argument about the superiority of the United States is wearing a little thin. We are now living on future wealth, not on what we are able to produce ourselves. Today we have mortgaged the future.

It is fitting that we understand the conditions which once existed in this hemisphere, because this generation is facing a particularly difficult time grasping the meaning of the American experience. History, it appears to some people, is drawing to a close—at least the view of history that has nourished, inspired, and oriented us for most of our lives. The titanic struggle known as the Cold War is over and it is no longer clear in which direction world history is moving, if indeed there is movement at all.

In a rare and almost eerie prophetic analysis of the potential contained in the world situation in 1830, Alexis de Tocqueville observed:

> The American fights against natural obstacles; the Russian is at grips with men. The former combats the wilderness and barbarism; the latter, civilization with all its arms. America's conquests are made with the plowshare, Russia's with the sword.

> To attain their aims, the former relies on personal interest and gives free scope to the unguided strength and common sense of individuals.

The latter in a sense concentrates the whole power of society in one man.

One has freedom as the principal means of action; the other has servitude.

Their point of departure is different and their paths diverse; nevertheless, each seems called by some secret design of Providence one day to hold in its hands the destinies of half the world.

To what degree has this prediction been fulfilled? Russia no longer fights men and apparently has abandoned one-man rule, but has the United States transcended its struggle with nature so that it is, in a sense, the leader of the beginning of a new global history shared by everyone?

If we have understood the rage for democracy that has recently swept the earth, toppling long-established dictatorships and gnawing at the foundations of the monolith of Chinese communism, we must come to see that even American democracy, the oldest and most prosperous on earth, faces a gigantic task of redefinition. It may well be that the United States has worn out the democratic forms which were once so comfortable and reassuring. The United States must either make a gargantuan leap forward to a new global society of peace and justice or become a relic of vested privilege that will be swept aside with the old political structures of the Old World.

Russian communism and the American experiment with democracy represented two paths which the European emergence from feudalism could have taken. That these possibilities were realized on lands away from Europe is significant because the Old World could not have survived the stresses which the escape from feudalism required. Indeed, Nazism can be regarded as the true response of Europe to its declining role in the world: the *Lebensraum* of the National Socialists was simply Russian and American imperialism written in the small space of Central Europe. If the struggle for living space has ended, and it was always a quest for a secure national identity, then our present and future task is to create, once and for all, an adequate history of the human race, a history in which even the smallest and least significant people are understood in the light of their own experiences. For Americans that means coming to grips with the real meaning of the past five centuries and understanding what actually happened between the original inhabitants of this hemisphere and those who tried to erase and replace them. . . .

We now stand at a similar threshold in human history. We do not know how the pieces will fit together yet, but we do know that the world is now irretrievably one. And the Americas stand as the crucial elements in the new order. The future writing of American history must seek to integrate the American experience into the much larger context of human strivings. It cannot be regarded as the final product of an evolutionary march toward greatness or as a unique experiment in how people should organize themselves as a society. America and Canada, Australia and New Zealand, remain the primary lands where the native and immigrant histories have not yet been reconciled. These lands yet contain mysteries about the human past which we cannot fathom. We must solve them so that they can become part of the complete human heritage.

Scott Momaday suggests at the beginning of this book that Columbus made a voyage in time as well as space, that he moved the world from the Middle Ages to the Renaissance. Since that time, we have moved beyond the Renaissance, through the Reformation and the Industrial Revolution, suffered a series of world wars, and now envision a period of relative global peace. The native peoples of the American continents suffered total inundation, lost a substantial portion of their population, and in coming into the modern world surrendered much of the natural life which had given them comfort and dignity. But they have managed to survive. Now, at a time when the virtues they represented, and continue to represent, are badly needed by the biosphere struggling to remain alive, they must be given the participatory role which they might have had in the world if the past five centuries had been different. The attitudes and beliefs that have kept the natives of the Western Hemisphere hidden and neglected must be changed so that world history becomes the story of mankind on this planet and not the selected history of a few people and their apology for what has happened to our species.

There are old Indian prophecies that forecast the coming of the white man, and some of them predict the disappearance of tribes because of the actions of these invaders. Other prophecies declare that the white man will be the shortest-lived of all those who have sought to live on these lands. We have yet to write the final chapter of the human story and we must now attempt to live out the final chapter of the American story. How closely it will resemble the contents of this book in another five centuries is for this and future generations to determine.

## Q uestions for Review and Reflection

1. What do Indian prophecies predict for the future of the white man?
2. Analyze de Tocqueville's predictions for the world and compare them to what has happened.
3. Why is it necessary to redefine democracy, according to Deloria?
4. What world view does Deloria take?

# One Nation, Many People

The United States of America is one nation made up of people from many backgrounds and origins. It began with a population of 4 million in 13 states. Today there are over 250 million people in 50 states. Combining diversity and democracy requires both tolerance for the differences that exist among people and a shared set of values that unify and create a spirit of community.

The authors of the U.S. Constitution recognized that it would have to adapt to changing circumstances. The Constitution was written in language broad enough to allow for reinterpretation and prescient enough to include an amending process.

One set of changing circumstances has led to a new relationship between the United States and Native American tribes. In 1992, Congress declared that the nation's obligations included "the protection of the sovereignty of each tribal government." To that end, Congress authorized support for an internal tribal justice system.

By the late 1980s, circumstances had changed sufficiently to permit Congress to enact more substantial reparations for Japanese Americans who had been interned during World War II. The 1988 Civil Liberties Act included an apology for excessive and precipitous actions.

Spurred by political pressures from organized groups of citizens, the United States expanded its interpretation of the Fourteenth Amendment and placed minorities and women under its equal protection umbrella. This recognition of infringement of rights has led to legislation such as the Women in Apprenticeship and Nontraditional Occupations Act, which aims to increase equal opportunities for women.

Maintaining a sense of community has always been difficult among people who do not share a common culture or history. The United States Civil Rights Commission confronted one such instance when they found newly arriving Asian Americans to be "victims of stereotype," facing "significant cultural and linguistic barriers," and an "inability to use the political process effectively," and recommended major policy initiatives to help.

Public education has been a particularly effective means of achieving commonality by contributing to a tolerance for diversity and offering an understanding and appreciation of other cultures. Recognizing that "a primary means by which a child learns is through the use of such child's native language and cultural heritage," Congress passed the Bilingual Education Act to help preserve immigrants' native cultures while they were being assimilated into American culture. Following the federal example, the state of New York incorporated a multicultural curriculum into its educational program that reflects the multiethnic, multiracial society that it serves.

Another way in which a pluralistic society manages diversity and democracy is by acknowledging the existence of distinct groups and their right to exist. When like-minded individuals form associations, they have more power to express their views. A variety of interest groups, representing minorities and women, have expressed views to Congress that they were underrepresented in management and decision-making positions in business. Such organized complaints contributed to the passage of the Civil Rights Act of 1991, which was designed to prevent employment practices with a "disparate impact" on minorities and to provide equal access to job opportunities.

The most basic form of civil rights continues to be the right to vote. To exercise that right is "the essence of a democratic society," the Supreme Court said in its 1964 *Reynolds v. Sims* case. (See Chapter 4; Reading 1.) In voting, "the individual is important, not his race, his creed or his color," wrote Justice William O. Douglas when he dissented from the majority opinion in *Wright v. Rockefeller,* a case deliberated before the *Reynolds v. Sims* case in 1964. The *Wright* plaintiffs argued that New York's reapportionment plan, which created one white and three nonwhite congressional districts, was based solely on race. Justice Hugo Black's majority decision upheld the redistricting on the grounds that its racial motivation had not been proved. In 1993, however, the Court rejected a reapportionment plan that it found was based solely on race, because it resulted in an "irrational" political district. In the *Shaw v. Reno* decision, the Court posited that such a plan "threatens to carry us further from the goal of a political system in which race no longer matters," and "reinforces the perception that members of the same racial group . . . think alike. . . . We have rejected such perceptions elsewhere as impermissible racial stereotypes."

# Reading **1**

U.S. Supreme Court, 1984

## *Roberts v. United States Jaycees,* 468 U.S. 609

The United States Jaycees, initially called the Junior Citizens, was founded in 1920 for the purpose of promoting and fostering the development of young men through civic and charitable works. The organization limited its regular, voting membership to men only, ages 18 to 35.

The Human Rights Act for Minnesota denied discrimination on the grounds of "race, color, creed, religion, disability, national origin or sex," in "public accommodations," which they defined as "a business, whose goods, services, facilities, privileges, advantages or accommodations are made available to the public." Because the Jaycees sold goods and services in exchange for membership, they fell under Minnesota's definition of a public accommodation and were ordered to accept women as full voting members. The Jaycees countered that their organization was being denied its right to free association and its right to freedom of speech, both guaranteed in the First Amendment to the Constitution.

Eventually, the case wound up in the U.S. Supreme Court. "The Jaycees has failed to demonstrate that the Act imposes any serious burdens on the male members' freedom of expressive association," and the justices stated that "we decline to indulge in the sexual stereotyping that underlies appellee's contention that, by allowing women to vote, application of the Minnesota Act will change the content or impact of the organization's speech."

In a concurring opinion, Justice Sandra Day O'Connor wrote, "The organization claims that the training it offers its members gives them an advantage in business." Such advantage was now available to women.

. . . Justice Brennan delivered the opinion of the Court.

This case requires us to address a conflict between a State's efforts to eliminate gender-based discrimination against its citizens and the constitutional freedom of association asserted by members of a private organization. In the decision under review, the Court of Appeals for the Eighth Circuit concluded that, by requiring the United States Jaycees to admit women as full voting members, the Minnesota Human Rights Act violates the First and Fourteenth Amendment rights of the organization's members. . . .

Our decisions have referred to constitutionally protected "freedom of association" in two distinct senses. In one line of decisions, the Court has concluded that choices to enter into and maintain certain intimate human relationships must . . . be secured against undue intrusion by the State because of the role of such relationships in safeguarding the individual freedom that is central to our constitutional scheme. In this respect, freedom of association receives protection as a fundamental element of personal liberty. In another set of decisions, the Court has recognized a right to associate for the purpose of engaging in those activities protected by the First Amendment—speech, assembly, petition for the redress of grievances, and the exercise of religion. The Constitution guarantees freedom of association of this kind as an indispensable means of preserving other individual liberties.

The intrinsic and instrumental features of constitutionally protected association may, of course, coincide. In particular, when the State interferes with individuals' selection of those with whom they wish to join in a common endeavor, freedom of association in both of its forms may be implicated. The Jaycees contend that this is such a case. . . .

. . . Determining the limits of state authority over an individual's freedom to enter into a particular association therefore unavoidably entails a careful assessment of where that relationship's objective characteristics locate it on a spectrum from the most intimate to the most attenuated of personal attachments. . . . We need not mark the potentially significant points on this terrain with any precision. We note only that factors that may be relevant include size, purpose, policies, selectivity, congeniality, and other characteristics that in a particular case may be pertinent. In this case, however, several features of the Jaycees clearly place the organization outside of the category of relationships worthy of this kind of constitutional protection. . . .

The undisputed facts reveal that the local chapters of the Jaycees are large and basically unselective groups. . . . Apart from age and sex, neither the national organization nor the local chapters employ any criteria for judging applicants for membership, and new members are routinely recruited and admitted with no inquiry into their backgrounds. . . .

In short, the local chapters of the Jaycees are neither small nor selective. Moreover, much of the activity central to the formation and maintenance of the association involves the participation of strangers to that relationship. Accordingly, we conclude that the Jaycees chapters lack the distinctive characteristics that might afford constitutional protection to the decision of its members to exclude women. . . .

. . . There can be no clearer example of an intrusion into the internal structure or affairs of an association than a regulation that forces the group to accept members it does not desire. Such a regulation may impair the ability of the original members to express only those views that brought them together. Freedom of association therefore plainly presupposes a freedom not to associate. . . .

The right to associate for expressive purposes is not, however, absolute. Infringements on that right may be justified by regulations adopted to serve compelling state interests, unrelated to the suppression of ideas, that cannot be achieved through means significantly less restrictive of associational freedoms. . . . We are persuaded that Minnesota's compelling interest in eradicating discrimination against its female citizens justifies the impact that application of the statute to the Jaycees may have on the male members' associational freedoms. . . .

By prohibiting gender discrimination in places of public accommodation, the Minnesota Act protects the State's citizenry from a number of serious social and personal harms. In the context of reviewing state actions under the Equal Protection Clause, this Court has frequently noted that discrimination based on archaic and overbroad assumptions about the relative needs and capacities of the sexes forces individuals to labor under stereotypical notions that often bear no relationship to their actual abilities. It thereby both deprives persons of their individual dignity and denies society the benefits of wide participation in political, economic, and cultural life. . . . Thus, in upholding Title II of the Civil Rights Act of 1964, 78 Stat. 243, 42 U.S.C. 2000a, which forbids race discrimination in public accommodations, we emphasized that its "fundamental object . . . was to vindicate 'the deprivation of personal dignity that surely accompanies denials of equal access to public establishments.' " Heart of Atlanta Motel, Inc. v. United States, *379 U.S. 241, 250* (1964). That stigmatizing injury, and the denial of equal opportunities that accompanies it, is surely felt as strongly by persons suffering discrimination on the basis of their sex as by those treated differently because of their race. . . .

In applying the Act to the Jaycees, the State has advanced those interests through the least restrictive means of achieving its ends. Indeed, the Jaycees has failed to demonstrate that the Act imposes any serious burdens on the male members' freedom of expressive association. . . .

. . . In claiming that women might have a different . . . attitude about such issues as the federal budget, school prayer, voting rights, and foreign relations, . . . or that the organization's public positions would have a different effect if the group were not "a purely young men's association," the Jaycees relies solely on unsupported generalizations about the relative interests and perspectives of men and women. . . . In the absence of a showing far more substantial than that attempted by the Jaycees, we decline to indulge in the sexual stereotyping that underlies appellee's contention that, by allowing women to vote, application of the Minnesota Act will change the content or impact of the organization's speech. . . .

# Questions for Review and Reflection

1. Who are the Jaycees?
2. Define "freedom of association."
3. What are the distinctive characteristics that afford one constitutional protection to freedom of association, as explained in this Court decision?
4. Do the Jaycees qualify for constitutional protection, according to the Supreme Court?
5. What assumptions on the part of the Jaycees did the Court reject regarding women?

# Reading 2

U.S. Congress, 1988

# The Bilingual Education Act

"Recognizing . . . that the Federal Government has a special and continuing obligation to assist in providing equal educational opportunity to limited English proficient children," the United States Congress passed the Bilingual Education Act.

Bilingual education is seen as one means of preserving immigrants' native cultures while assimilating them into their new culture. Students are permitted to learn in their own language while they are making the transition to English. This acknowledgement of the effectiveness of other languages as teaching tools is now prevalent in states with large populations of minorities. Nevertheless, the policy remains controversial. Opponents say that it slows down the learning process and hinders the mainstreaming of students. Proponents defend the program as a means of keeping students up to date in their other subjects, preserving the cultural integrity of their language, and introducing their fellow students to other languages.

## § 3282. Policy; appropriations

### (a) Policy

Recognizing—

(1) that there are large and growing numbers of children of limited English proficiency;

(2) that many of such children have a cultural heritage which differs from that of English proficient persons;

(3) that the Federal Government has a special and continuing obligation to assist in providing equal educational opportunity to limited English proficient children;

(4) that, regardless of the method of instruction, programs which serve limited English proficient students have the equally important goals of developing academic achievement and English proficiency;

(5) that the Federal Government has a special and continuing obligation to assist language minority students to acquire the English language proficiency that will enable them to become full and productive members of society;

(6) that the instructional use and development of a child's non-English native language promotes student self-esteem, subject matter achievement, and English-language acquisition;

(7) that a primary means by which a child learns is through the use of such child's native language and cultural heritage;

(8) that, therefore, large numbers of children of limited English proficiency have educational needs which can be met by the use of bilingual educational methods and techniques;

(9) that in some school districts establishment of bilingual education programs may be administratively impractical due to the presence of small numbers of students of a particular native language or because personnel who are qualified to provide bilingual instructional services are unavailable;

(10) that States and local school districts should be encouraged to determine appropriate curricula for limited English proficient students within their jurisdictions and to develop and implement appropriate instructional programs;

(11) that children of limited English proficiency have a high dropout rate and low median years of education;

(12) that the segregation of many groups of limited English proficient students remains a serious problem;

(13) that reliance on student evaluation procedures which are inappropriate for limited English proficient students have resulted in the disproportionate representation of limited English proficient students in special education, gifted and talented, and other special programs;

(14) that there is a serious shortage of teachers and educational personnel who are professionally trained and qualified to serve children of limited English proficiency;

(15) that many schools fail to meet the full instructional needs of limited English proficient students who also may be handicapped or gifted and talented;

(16) that both limited English proficient children and children whose primary language is English can benefit from bilingual education programs, and that such programs help develop our national linguistic resources and promote our international competitiveness;

(17) that research, evaluation, and data collection capabilities in the field of bilingual education need to be strengthened so as to better identify and promote those programs and instructional practices which result in effective education;

(18) that parent and community participation in bilingual education programs contributes to program effectiveness; and

(19) that because of limited English proficiency, many adults are not able to participate fully in national life, and that limited English proficient parents are often not able to participate effectively in their children's education,

the Congress declares it to be the policy of the United States, in order to establish equal educational opportunity for all children and to promote educational excellence (A) to encourage the establishment and operation, where appropriate, of educational programs using bilingual educational practices, techniques, and methods, (B) to encourage the establishment of special alternative instructional programs for students of limited English proficiency in school districts where the establishment of bilingual educational programs is not practicable or for other appropriate reasons, and (C) for those purposes, to provide financial assistance to local educational agencies, and, for certain related purposes, to State educational agencies, institutions of higher education, and community organizations. The programs assisted under this subchapter include programs in elementary and secondary schools as well as related preschool and adult programs which are designed to meet the educational needs of individuals of limited English proficiency, with particular attention to children having the greatest need for such programs. Such programs shall be designed to enable students to achieve full competence in English and to meet school grade-promotion and graduation requirements. Such programs may additionally provide for the development of student competence in a second language.

## (b) Authorization

(1) For the purpose of carrying out the provisions of this subchapter, there are authorized to be appropriated, subject to paragraph (6), $200,000,000 for the fiscal year 1989 and such sums as may be necessary for the fiscal year 1990 and for each succeeding fiscal year ending prior to October 1, 1993.

(2) There are further authorized to be appropriated to carry out the provisions of section 3302 of this title, subject to paragraph (6), such sums as may be necessary for the fiscal year 1989 and each of the 4 succeeding fiscal years.

(3) From the sums appropriated under paragraph (1) for part A of this subchapter for any fiscal year, the Secretary may reserve not to exceed 25 percent for special alternative instructional programs and related activities authorized under section 3291(a)(3) of this title and may include programs under paragraphs (2), (4), (5), and (6) of section 3291(a) of this title.

(4) From the sums appropriated under paragraph (1) for any fiscal year, the Secretary shall reserve at least 60 percent for the programs carried out under part A of this subchapter; and of this amount, at least 75 percent shall be reserved for the programs of transitional bilingual education carried out under section 3291(a)(1) of this title, and may include programs under paragraphs (2), (4), (5), and (6) of section 3291(a) of this title.

(5) From the sums appropriated under paragraph (1) for any fiscal year, the Secretary shall reserve at least 25 percent for training activities carried out under part C of this subchapter.

(6) Notwithstanding paragraphs (1) and (2), no amount in excess of $200,000,000 may be appropriated for the fiscal year 1989 to carry out the provisions of this subchapter (including section 3302 of this title).

(7) The reservation required by paragraph (3) shall not result in changing the terms, conditions, or negotiated levels of any grant awarded in fiscal year 1987 to which section 3291(d)(1)(A), 3291(d)(1)(C), or 3291(d)(2) of this title applies.

(Pub.L. 89–10, Title VII, § 7002, as added Pub.L. 100–297, Title I, § 1001, Apr. 28, 1988, 102 Stat. 274.)

# Questions for Review and Reflection

1. What are the positive aspects of the ideal of bilingual education? What are the negative aspects? Do you believe that bilingual education benefits or detracts from American society? Why?
2. The Bilingual Education Act begins with a series of statements that establish certain assumptions. Which assumptions do you agree with? Which don't you agree with?
3. In what ways does this legislation empower local school districts? In what ways does it diminish the power and autonomy of local school districts? Why?
4. Might there be any hidden agenda behind the move for bilingual education? If so, what might it be?

# Reading 3

U.S. Congress, 1988

## The Civil Liberties Act

Japanese Americans who had been forced from their homes and into internment camps following the Japanese attack on Pearl Harbor lobbied for years for an apology and financial compensation for assets lost. (See Chapter 1; Reading 4.)

President Franklin D. Roosevelt triggered the mass relocation of over 100,000 Japanese Americans with Executive Order 9066. Given little notice and enforced limits on what individuals could carry away with them, families left behind most of what they owned. Heavy losses were suffered in real and personal property. Millions of dollars were lost. The 1988 Civil Liberties Act was a remedy: $20,000 to each person who had experienced what Senator Daniel Inouye of Hawaii characterized as an event "unprecedented in the history of American civil rights deprivation."

Senator Inouye had lost his right arm in the service of the United States during World War II. His all–Japanese-American infantry unit of the 442nd Army regiment earned the distinction of being the most highly decorated in the history of the United States.

**M**r. [Daniel K.] INOUYE [D-Hawaii]. . . .

[W]hile it is true that all people of this Nation suffer during wartime, the Japanese-American internment experience is unprecedented in the history of American civil rights deprivation. I think we should recall, even if painful, that Americans of Japanese ancestry were determined by our Government to be security risks without any formal allegations or charges of disloyalty or espionage. They were arbitrarily branded disloyal solely on the grounds of racial ancestry.

No similar mass internment was deemed necessary for Americans of German or Italian ancestries, and I think we should recall and remind ourselves that in World War II, the Japanese were not our only enemies.

These Japanese-Americans who were interned could not confront their accusers or bring their case before a court. These are basic rights of all

Americans. They were incarcerated, forced to live in public communities with no privacy, and stripped of their freedom to move about as others could.

Japanese-Americans wishing to fight for this country were initially declared ineligible. However, once allowed to volunteer, they volunteered in great numbers. In fact, proportionately and percentagewise, more Japanese-Americans put on the uniform of this country during World War II, more were wounded and more were killed, even if they were restricted to serving in ethnically-restricted military units.

The individual payments acknowledge the unjust deprivation of liberty, the infliction of mental and physical suffering, and the stigma of being branded disloyal, losses not compensable under the Japanese Evacuation Claims Act of 1948. . . .

The Presidentially appointed Commission on Wartime Relocation and Internment of Civilians found no documented acts of espionage, sabotage, or fifth column activity by any, Mr. President, by any identifiable American citizen of Japanese ancestry or resident Japanese aliens on the west coast.

This was supposed to have been the rationale for this mass evacuation and mass incarceration, that these Americans were not to be trusted, that these Americans were agents of an enemy country, that these Americans would spy and carry out espionage, and this Presidentially appointed Commission, which incidentally was made up of leading citizens throughout this land—and only one member of that Commission was of Japanese ancestry—declared that there were no acts of espionage whatsoever. And sadly, the Commission in its 1983 report concluded that internment was motivated by racial prejudice, war hysteria, and a failure of political leadership. . . .

[T]he goal of S. 1009 is to benefit all citizens of our Nation by educating our citizens to preclude this event from occurring again to any other ethnic or religious group or any person suspected of being less than a loyal citizen. This bill reinforces the strength of our Constitution by reaffirming our commitment to upholding the constitutional rights of all our citizens. So, respectfully, I strongly urge its passage and in so doing once again commend and congratulate my distinguished colleague from Hawaii. . . .

Mr. MATSUNAGA. I congratulate the senior Senator from Hawaii for his excellent statement. Coming from one who served in the 442d Regimental Combat Team, the most highly decorated military unit in the entire history of the United States, and having been highly decorated with the second highest award, the Distinguished Service Cross, and having sacrificed an arm in that war, I believe what the senior Senator from Hawaii has to say should be taken most seriously. . . .

Mr. [Daniel J.] EVANS [D-Wash.]. . . . As a Senator from the State of Washington, I have a special interest in this legislation. The first group of Japanese citizens to be removed from their homes under President Roosevelt's Executive Order were from Bainbridge Island, WA. They were the first of nearly 13,000 Japanese-Americans from the State of Washington to be funneled into assembly centers and eventually into relocation facilities.

Victims of Executive Order 9066 were given very short notice that they would be sent to relocation facilities. Most were granted just a few days to abandon their homes and belongings. As a result they were forced to sell or lease their property and businesses at prices reflecting only a fraction of their worth. Substantial economic losses were incurred. Once they arrived at the relocation centers they found a quality of life which was atrocious. They were overcrowded and families suffered from an acute lack of privacy with no borders or walls to separate them from others.

Opponents of this legislation choose to ignore raw, racial prejudice woven in what was supposed to be legitimate national security justification for internment. The evacuees, however, were guilty of no crime other than the apparent crime of being of Japanese ancestry. Japanese-Americans left their homes in an atmosphere of racial prejudice and returned to the same.

What is perhaps most alarming about the Japanese internment is that it took place in the United States of America. This is the same country which has prided itself on freedom, justice, and the preservation and protection of individual rights. . . .

The $20,000 compensation that would be allotted to each victim, and the educational fund established by this legislation are a modest attempt to redress wrongs against loyal Americans. Although we cannot restore completely what already has been lost, the legislation would serve as a symbol to all that the United States can come to terms with its own tragic mistake. . . .

Mr. [Jesse A.] HELMS [R-N.C.]. . . . Nobody is, in retrospect, proud of the relocation of the Japanese-Americans during World War II, but as I said earlier, we lived in a time of terror in this country immediately after the attack on Pearl Harbor. Nobody knew what was coming next. . . . We had just been attacked by a totalitarian regime which had enjoyed a virtually unbroken string of military successes, both before and immediately after the Government of Japan attacked the United States of America. . . .

I think it is only fair to look back to that time, and recall the fact that our intelligence community told the then President of the United States, Franklin Delano Roosevelt, that there was great risk. Now we can see that it was a mistake.

I have no vision problem with respect to that. We will have 20-20 vision by hindsight, and I am perfectly willing for this Senate and this Congress to declare that this kind of thing must never happen again.

But the Senate has just voted to give the priority emphasis to money, $1.3 billion. So I think we ought to look at our priorities. . . .

For example, in 1948, Congress enacted the American Japanese Claims Act, which authorized compensation for "any claim" for damages to or loss of real or personal property "as a reasonable consequence of the evacuation or exclusion of" persons of Japanese ancestry as a result of governmental action during World War II.

I might add that this act of 1948 was subsequently amended to liberalize its compensation provisions.

Under the amended act, the Justice Department received claims seeking approximately $147 million. Ultimately, 26,568 settlements were achieved.... True enough, the American Japanese Claims Act did not include every item of damage that was or could have been suggested. It did, however, address the hardships visited upon persons of Japanese ancestry in a comprehensive, considered manner taking into account individual needs and losses, and this effort to correct injustice to individuals was in keeping with our Nation's best tradition of individual rather than collective response, and it was far more contemporaneous with the injuries to the claimants than would be any payments at this late date....

Mr. [Alan K.] SIMPSON [R-Wyo.]. . . . I was a young boy in Cody, WY, in 1941 when the war started. I was 10 then.

Two years later, at the age of 12, somewhere between the years of 12 and 13, the third largest community in Wyoming was constructed between the communities of Powell and Cody, WY, a city of 15,000 people which really literally went up overnight. And the name of it, of course, was Heart Mountain War Relocation Center, known to the people of the area simply as the "Jap Camp," a term which may be hard for us to believe now but that is what it was referred to then; swiftly built by those who had not been drafted into the war, or older men in their 40's who were not able to be taken into the war effort.

And so came into being Heart Mountain, WY, War Relocation Center. There was barbed wire around it. There were guard towers at the edges of it. It was a very imposing area. . . . I remember one night very distinctly when the scoutmaster—I was a Boy Scout, a rather nominal one, but I enjoyed the activities of the group. And he said, "We are going to go out to the War Relocation Center and have a scout meeting." I said, "Well, I mean, are there any of them out there?" . . . He said, "Yes, yes, these are American citizens, you see." And that put a new twist on it because we thought of them as something else—as aliens; we thought of them as spies; we thought of them as people who were behind wire because they were trying to do in our country.

So I shall not forget going to the Boy Scout meeting and meeting Boy Scouts from California, most of them, I recall, same merit badges, same scout sashes, same clothing.

And why not? Some of them were second- or third-generation American citizens. . . .

Then we would go downtown in Cody, WY, and there would be a sign on the restaurant that said, "No Japs allowed here." And then you would go down to another place of business, it might be a sign that said, "My son was killed at Iwo Jima. How do you think I feel?" . . .

There is no question about it being the gravest of injustices. And it may be hardly a repayable one. How do you ever really repay these people for the wages, the property, the opportunity, the education, the part of their lives lost during this period? And this taxpayer expenditure is a troubling part of the bill for me.

I have trouble with the money. An apology may be long overdue and may be so appropriate. But, coupled with money, it takes away some of the sincerity of the apology, somehow. If you did that with a friend, a lovely friend, and you said: I am sorry for what I did. I know that was very harmful to you and hurtful. But I am sorry and I apologize and I want to give you some money. . . .

Hopefully, we will conclude this debate shortly and move on to other issues of the day because this is an old and sad and very painful thing that we have reopened here in this debate. The sooner we close that wound and suture it with love and understanding and affection, we will be better off. And suturing it with money does not seem like the best way to conclude the issue.

# $\boxed{Q}$ uestions for Review and Reflection

1. Identify several reasons given for Japanese-American reparations.
2. What was the rationale during World War II for Japanese-American internment?
3. Was internment justified, in your opinion?
4. Is the compensation proposed sufficient to mend the harm done, in your opinion?

# Reading 4

U.S. Congress, 1991

# The Civil Rights Act

Traditionally, some employers have practiced discrimination in their hiring policies, claiming it is necessary to their business to do so. Others have tolerated workplace harassment of individuals based on their race, ethnicity, or gender. Under the 1991 Civil Rights Act, employers must prove a business necessity when an employment practice results in a "disparate impact" on protected groups (categories based on race, sex, religion or national origin). The employer is required to seek other means of achieving the business purpose before such an employment policy will be tolerated. The act also offers limited compensation for intentional discrimination or harassment. Punitive damages can be awarded when it is proven that the defendant acted with reckless disregard for the rights of the individual.

Congress stated that this legislation was necessary to provide additional protection against unlawful discrimination and to strengthen and improve civil rights laws.

## Civil Rights Act of 1991

*For Legislative History of Act, see Report for P.L. 102–166 in U.S.C.C. & A.N. Legislative History Section.*

**An Act to amend the Civil Rights Act of 1964 to strengthen and improve Federal civil rights laws, to provide for damages in cases of intentional employment discrimination, to clarify provisions regarding disparate impact actions, and for other purposes.**

*Be it enacted by the Senate and House of Representatives of the United States of America in Congress assembled,*

**Section 1. Short Title.**

This Act may be cited as the "Civil Rights Act of 1991".

**Sec. 2. Findings.**

The Congress finds that—

(1) additional remedies under Federal law are needed to deter unlawful harassment and intentional discrimination in the workplace;

(2) the decision of the Supreme Court in Wards Cove Packing Co. v. Atonio, 490 U.S. 642 (1989) has weakened the scope and effectiveness of Federal civil rights protections; and

(3) legislation is necessary to provide additional protections against unlawful discrimination in employment.

**Sec. 3. Purposes.**

The purposes of this Act are—

(1) to provide appropriate remedies for intentional discrimination and unlawful harassment in the workplace;

(2) to codify the concepts of "business necessity" and "job related" enunciated by the Supreme Court in Griggs v. Duke Power Co., 401 U.S. 424 (1971), and in the other Supreme Court decisions prior to Wards Cove Packing Co. v. Atonio, 490 U.S. 642 (1989);

(3) to confirm statutory authority and provide statutory guidelines for the adjudication of disparate impact suits under title VII of the Civil Rights Act of 1964 (42 U.S.C. 2000e et seq.); and

(4) to respond to recent decisions of the Supreme Court by expanding the scope of relevant civil rights statutes in order to provide adequate protection to victims of discrimination. . . .

**Sec. 105. Burden of Proof in Disparate Impact Cases.**

(a) Section 703 of the Civil Rights Act of 1964 (42 U.S.C. 2000e–2) is amended by adding at the end of the following new subsection:

"(k)(1)(A) An unlawful employment practice based on disparate impact is established under this title only if—

"(i) a complaining party demonstrates that a respondent uses a particular employment practice that causes a disparate impact on the basis of race, color, religion, sex, or national origin and the respondent fails to demonstrate that the challenged practice is job related for the position in question and consistent with business necessity; or

"(ii) the complaining party makes the demonstration described in subparagraph (C) with respect to an alternative employment practice and the respondent refuses to adopt such alternative employment practice.

"(B)(i) With respect to demonstrating that a particular employment practice causes a disparate impact as described in subparagraph (A)(i), the complaining party shall demonstrate that each particular challenged employment practice causes a disparate impact, except that if the complaining party can demonstrate to the court that the elements of a respondent's decisionmaking process are not capable of separation for analysis, the decisionmaking process may be analyzed as one employment practice.

"(ii) If the respondent demonstrates that a specific employment practice does not cause the disparate impact, the respondent shall not be required to demonstrate that such practice is required by business necessity.

"(C) The demonstration referred to by subparagraph (A)(ii) shall be in accordance with the law as it existed on June 4, 1989, with respect to the concept of 'alternative employment practice'. . . .

"(2) A demonstration that an employment practice is required by business necessity may not be used as a defense against a claim of intentional discrimination under this title.

"(3) Notwithstanding any other provision of this title, a rule barring the employment of an individual who currently and knowingly uses or possesses a controlled substance, as defined in schedules I and II of section 102(6) of the Controlled Substances Act (21 U.S.C. 802(6)), other than the use or possession of a drug taken under the supervision of a licensed health care professional, or any other use or possession authorized by the Controlled Substances Act or any other provision of Federal law, shall be considered an unlawful employment practice under this title only if such rule is adopted or applied with an intent to discriminate because of race, color, religion, sex, or national origin."

(b) No statements other than the interpretive memorandum appearing at Vol. 137 Congressional Record S 15276 (daily ed. Oct. 25, 1991) shall be considered legislative history of, or relied upon in any way as legislative history in construing or applying, any provision of this Act that relates to Wards Cove—Business necessity/cumulation/alternative business practice. . . .

## Title II—Glass Ceiling

**Sec. 201. Short Title.**
This title may be cited as the "Glass Ceiling Act of 1991".

**Sec. 202. Findings and Purpose.**
(A) Findings.—Congress finds that—

(1) despite a dramatically growing presence in the workplace, women and minorities remain underrepresented in management and decisionmaking positions in business;

(2) artificial barriers exist to the advancement of women and minorities in the workplace;

(3) United States corporations are increasingly relying on women and minorities to meet employment requirements and are increasingly aware of the advantages derived from a diverse work force;

(4) the "Glass Ceiling Initiative" undertaken by the Department of Labor, including the release of the report entitled "Report on the Glass Ceiling Initiative", has been instrumental in raising public awareness of—

(A) the underrepresentation of women and minorities at the management and decisionmaking levels in the United States work force;
(B) the underrepresentation of women and minorities in line functions in the United States work force;
(C) the lack of access for qualified women and minorities to credential-building developmental opportunities; and
(D) the desirability of eliminating artificial barriers to the advancement of women and minorities to such levels;

(5) the establishment of a commission to examine issues raised by the Glass Ceiling Initiative would help—

(A) focus greater attention on the importance of eliminating artificial barriers to the advancement of women and minorities to management and decisionmaking positions in business; and
(B) promote work force diversity.

# Questions for Review and Reflection

1. Why did Congress find additional remedies necessary to protect civil rights?
2. What are the major purposes of the 1991 act?
3. Who has the burden of proof as of 1991?
4. Define disparate impact, according to this statute and the courts.
5. Define the glass ceiling and describe who is affected by it.

# Reading 5

New York State Social Studies and Review Committee, 1991

## "One Nation, Many Peoples: A Declaration of Cultural Independence"

Education is one of the primary institutions which advances the ideals and values of a democracy. States all across the country, responding to the distinct groups of peoples with prominent cultures, have begun to advance a pluralistic approach to education. Textbooks and general curricula are infusing multicultural learning into mainstream academic disciplines. Separate ethnic- and gender-based programs and studies are being developed in high schools and colleges all over America.

A leader in this movement has been the New York State Social Studies Department, which issued a lengthy report on behalf of pluralism and inclusion, recommending a full multicultural curriculum for history and the social sciences. They wrote, "We see the social studies as the primary avenue through which the school addresses our cultural diversity and interdependence."

### Preamble

The United States is a microcosm of humanity today. No other country in the world is peopled by a greater variety of races, nationalities, and ethnic groups. But although the United States has been a great asylum for diverse peoples, it has not always been a great refuge for diverse cultures. The country has opened its doors to a multitude of nationalities, but often their cultures have not been encouraged to survive or, at best, have been kept marginal to the mainstream.

Since the 1960s, however, a profound reorientation of the self-image of Americans has been under way. Before this time the dominant model of the typical American had been conditioned primarily by the need to shape a unified nation out of a variety of contrasting and often conflicting European immigrant communities. But following the struggles for civil rights, the unprecedented increase in non-European immigration over the last two decades and the increasing recognition of our nation's indigenous heritage, there has been a fundamental change in the image of what a resident of the United States is.

With this change, which necessarily highlights the racial and ethnic pluralism of the nation, previous ideals of assimilation to an Anglo-American model have been put in question and are now slowly and sometimes painfully being set aside. Many people in the United States are no longer comfortable with the requirement, common in the past, that they shed their specific cultural differences in order to be considered American. Instead, while busily adapting to and shaping mainstream cultural ideals commonly identified as American, in recent decades many in the United States—from European and non-European backgrounds—have been encouraging a more tolerant, inclusive, and realistic vision of American identity than any that has existed in the past.

This identity, committed to the democratic principles of the nation and the nation-building in which all Americans are engaged, is progressively evolving from the past model toward a new model marked by respect for pluralism and awareness of the virtues of diversity. This situation is a current reality, and a multicultural education, anchored to the shared principles of a liberal democracy, is today less an educational innovation than a national priority.

It is fitting for New York State, host to the Statue of Liberty, to inaugurate a curriculum that reflects the rich cultural diversity of the nation. The beacon of hope welcomes not just the "wretched and poor" individuals of the world, but also the dynamic and rich cultures all people bring with them.

Two centuries after this country's founders issued a Declaration of Independence, focused on the political independence from which societies distant from the United States have continued to draw inspiration, the time has come to *recognize cultural interdependence.* We propose that the principle of respect for diverse cultures is critical to our nation, and we affirm that a right to cultural diversity exists. We believe that the schoolroom is one of the places where this cultural *interdependence* must be reflected.

It is in this spirit that we have crafted this report, "One Nation, Many Peoples." We see the social studies as the primary avenue through which the school addresses our cultural diversity and interdependence. But the study of cultural diversity and interdependence is only one goal. It is through such studies that we seek to strengthen our national commitment and world citizenship, with the development of intellectual competence in our students as the foundation. We see the social studies as directed at the development of intellectual competence in learners, with the capacity to view the world and understand it from multiple perspectives as one of the main components of such competence. Multicultural knowledge in this conception of the social studies becomes a vehicle and not a goal. Multicultural content and experience become instruments by which we enable students to develop their intelligence and to function as human and humane persons.

## I. Introduction

### Affirmation of Purpose

This Committee affirms that multicultural education should be a source of strength and pride. Multicultural education is often viewed as divisive and even as destructive of the values and beliefs which hold us together as Americans. Certainly, contemporary trends toward separation and dissolution in such disparate countries as the Soviet Union, South America, Canada, Yugoslavia, Spain, and the United Kingdom remind us that different ethnic and racial groups have often had extraordinary difficulty remaining together in nation-states. But national unity does not require that we eliminate the very diversity that is the source of our uniqueness and, indeed, of our adaptability and viability among the nations of the world. *If the United States is to continue to prosper in the 21st century, then all of its citizens, whatever their race or ethnicity, must believe that they and their ancestors have shared in the building of the country and have a stake in its success.* Thus, multicultural education, far from being a source of dissolution, is necessary for the cultural health, social stability, and economic future of New York State and the nation.

## uestions for Review and Reflection

1. In what ways is the United States a microcosm of humanity, according to the committee? Do you agree, or do you think that the American experience somehow separates us from the rest of the world?
2. How is this report a repudiation of the concept of assimilation for minority cultures? How is this an argument for a new model of multicultural pluralism? How is this a declaration of cultural interdependence?
3. How might a multicultural education policy lead to strength and pride? Which societal groups might feel threatened by this policy of multicultural education? Is there common ground?
4. Why is the social studies class important in the development of intellectual competence and learning in American society?
5. How does the committee employ recent events in the former Soviet Union, South America, Canada, Yugoslavia, Spain, and the United Kingdom to argue that separatism is destructive, while a multicultural approach benefits society more? How do events following the publication of this document further strengthen the committee's argument?

# Reading 6

U.S. Commission on Civil Rights, February 1992

## "Civil Rights Issues Facing Asian Americans in the 1990s"

The 1957 Civil Rights Act established a commission appointed by the president to investigate and make recommendations on the status of civil rights in America. Its initial focus was an investigation of the civil rights of African Americans, but its agenda expanded to include other minorities, as well as women and the disabled.

The civil rights of Asian Americans became an issue as floods of refugees came to the United States from Southeast Asia following the Vietnam War. Immigration from that part of the world surpassed Latino immigration during the 1980s.

Many Asian Americans were highly educated and professionally skilled. They often succeeded in business and other occupations, and their children became high achievers in school. At times, this caused resentment among other minority populations. Interracial animosity became very open in some neighborhoods of cities like New York and Los Angeles.

The U.S. Civil Rights Commission held a series of conferences to examine the problems facing these arriving immigrants from Vietnam, Thailand, Cambodia, Laos, and elsewhere in Asia. The report concluded that an image of the "model minority" had been cast upon the Asian American, an image that was damaging, because government agencies overlooked them when drawing up antidiscrimination policies.

The report found that, much like some of the other minority groups, Asian Americans faced language and cultural barriers as well as a lack of political representation. Recommendations were made that could provide some relief and could, in the commission's view, "be applicable to other minority groups as well."

T his report presents the results of an investigation into the civil rights issues facing Asian Americans that was undertaken as a follow-up to the commission's 1989 Asian Roundtable Conferences. Contrary to the popular perception that Asian Americans have overcome discriminatory barriers, Asian Americans still face widespread prejudice, discrimination, and denials of equal opportunity. In addition, many Asian Americans, particularly those who are immigrants, are deprived of equal access to public services, including police protection, education, health care, and the judicial system.

Several factors contribute to the civil rights problems facing today's Asian Americans. First, Asian Americans are the victims of stereotypes that are widely held among the general public. These stereotypes deprive Asian Americans of their individuality and humanity in the public's perception and often foster prejudice against Asian Americans. The "model minority" stereotype, the often-repeated contention that Asian Americans have overcome all barriers facing them and that they are a singularly successful minority group, is perhaps the most damaging of these stereotypes. This stereotype leads federal, state, and local agencies to overlook the problems facing Asian Americans, and it often causes resentment of Asian Americans within the general public.

Second, many Asian Americans, particularly immigrants, face significant cultural and linguistic barriers that prevent them from receiving equal access to public services and from participating fully in the American political process. Many Asian-American immigrants arrive in the United States with minimal facility in the English language and with little familiarity with American culture and the workings of American society. There has been a widespread failure of government at all levels and of the nation's public schools to provide for the needs of immigrant Asian Americans. Such basic needs as interpretive services to help limited-English-proficient Asian Americans in their dealings with government agencies, culturally appropriate medical care, bilingual/English as a Second Language education, and information about available public services are largely unmet.

A third, but equally important, problem confronting Asian Americans today is a lack of political representation and an inability to use the political process effectively. Asian Americans face many barriers to participation in the political process, in addition to the simple fact that many Asian Americans are not yet citizens and hence ineligible to vote. Although some Asian Americans are politically active, the large majority have very little access to political power. This lack of political empowerment leads the political leadership of the United States to overlook and sometimes ignore the needs and concerns of Asian Americans. It also leads to a failure of the political leadership to make addressing Asian-American issues a national priority.

This chapter lays out specific conclusions and recommendations. Many of the civil rights issues facing Asian Americans also confront other minority groups. For example, issues related to the rights of language minorities are equally important for other language-minority groups. Thus, many of our conclusions with respect to violations of Asian-Americans' civil rights and our recommendations for enhancing the protection of their civil rights are applicable to other minority groups as well. . . .

## Recommendation 12:

Every school system with immigrant students should have in place a comprehensive program to ease the transition of newly arrived immigrant students and their families into the American school system and into American society at large. Such a program should include intensive English as a Second Language classes offered to adults, as well as classes for children in school. . . .

## Recommendation 15:

Colleges and universities should examine thoroughly their admissions policies for adverse effects or unintentional bias against Asian Americans and put in place safeguards to prevent them. Such safeguards should include:

- providing training to admissions staff;

- routinely reviewing new policies for adverse impact;
- including Asian Americans in the admissions process; and
- making data on the racial and ethnic breakdown of applicants and admitted students available to the public when requested. . . .

## Recommendation 19:

Federal and State enforcement agencies should take aggressive steps to enforce antidiscrimination provisions with respect to the glass ceiling, including initiating compliance reviews of firms' employment practices that follow the lead of the Office of Federal Contract Compliance Programs' pilot studies of Fortune 500 companies. . . .

## Recommendation 29:

Congress should reauthorize section 203(c) of the Voting Rights Act of 1982 with the following change:

- The section should be modified to apply to language-minority groups with more than a specified minimum number rather than a percentage of citizens of voting age.

## Recommendation 30:

The Bureau of the Census should release detailed data on Asian Americans promptly, as promised.

## Recommendation 31:

The major political parties and civic organizations (e.g., the League of Women Voters) should launch a major effort to promote voter registration and political participation among Asian Americans.

# Questions for Review and Reflection

1. Identify the kinds of discrimination faced by Asian Americans, according to the commission. Are the issues any different than for other minorities, in your opinion?
2. Which government institutions does the commission feel can most effectively address the problems faced by Asian Americans?
3. Some of the commission's recommendations can apply to other minority groups. Can you identify which of those recommendations may be helpful and which may not?

# Reading 7

U.S. Congress, October 1992

## The Women in Apprenticeship and Nontraditional Occupations Act

Following the demise of the Equal Rights Amendment, the women's movement focused on economic issues. Activists lobbied for government assistance in creating more equal opportunities in employment, more child care, and more protection from fathers who fail to follow through on child-support responsibilities.

The federal government was able to assist both women and the economy by affording the means to develop much-needed skilled labor in some of the trades while at the same time creating new and nontraditional employment opportunities for women.

Congress defined nontraditional occupations as those jobs in which women made up less than 25% of the work force. They appropriated money for outreach programs and technical assistance to employers and unions "to encourage employment of women in apprenticeable . . . and nontraditional occupations."

Efforts in child care and enforcement of child-support orders continue. Congresswoman Lynn Woolsey, D-(Petaluma) CA, recently proposed legislation to the House of Representatives, under which the Internal Revenue Service would collect delinquent child-support payments and disburse the money to the child's custodial parent.

## Women in Apprenticeship and Nontraditional Occupations Act

**An Act to assist business in providing women with opportunities in apprenticeship and nontraditional occupations.**

*Be it enacted by the Senate and House of Representatives of the United States of America in Congress assembled,*

**Section 1. Short Title.**
This Act shall be cited as the "Women in apprenticeship and Nontraditional Occupations Act".

### Sec. 2. Findings; Statement of Purpose.

(a) FINDINGS.—The Congress finds that—

(1) American businesses now and for the remainder of the 20th century will face a dramatically different labor market than the one to which they have become accustomed;

(2) two in every three new entrants to the work force will be women, and to meet labor needs such women must work in all occupational areas including in apprenticeable occupations and nontraditional occupations;

(3) women face significant barriers to their full and effective participation in apprenticeable occupations and nontraditional occupations;

(4) the business community must be prepared to address the barriers that women have to such jobs in order to successfully integrate them into the work force; and

(5) few resources are available to employers and unions who need assistance in recruiting, training, and retaining women in apprenticeable occupations and other nontraditional occupations.

(b) PURPOSE.—It is the purpose of this Act to provide technical assistance to employers and labor unions to encourage employment of women in apprenticeable occupations and nontraditional occupations. Such assistance will enable business to meet the challenge of Workforce 2000 by preparing employers to successfully recruit, train, and retain women in apprenticeable occupations and non-traditional occupations and will expand the employment and self-sufficiency options of women. This purpose will be achieved by—

(1) promoting the program to employers and labor unions to inform them of the availability of technical assistance which will assist them in preparing the workplace to employ women in apprenticeable occupations and nontraditional occupations;

(2) providing grants to community-based organizations to deliver technical assistance to employers and labor unions to prepare them to recruit, train, and employ women in apprenticeable occupations and nontraditional occupations;

(3) authorizing the Department of Labor to serve as a liaison between employers, labor, and the community-based organizations providing technical assistance, through its national office and its regional administrators; and

(4) conducting a comprehensive study to examine the barriers to the participation of women in apprenticeable occupations and nontraditional occupations and to develop recommendations for the workplace to eliminate such barriers.

### Sec. 3. Outreach to Employers and Labor Unions

(a) IN GENERAL.—With funds available to the Secretary of Labor to carry out the operations of the Department of Labor in fiscal year 1994 and subsequent fiscal years, the Secretary shall carry out an outreach program to inform employers of technical assistance available under section 4(a) to assist employers to prepare the workplace to employ women in apprenticeable occupations and other nontraditional occupations.

> (1) Under such program the Secretary shall provide outreach to employers through, but not limited to, the private industry councils in each service delivery area.
>
> (2) The Secretary shall provide outreach to labor unions through, but not limited to, the building trade councils, joint apprenticeable occupations councils, and individual labor unions.

(b) PRIORITY.—The Secretary shall give priority to providing outreach to employers located in areas that have nontraditional employment and training programs specifically targeted to women.

### Sec. 4. Technical Assistance.

(a) IN GENERAL.—With funds appropriated to carry out this section, the Secretary shall make grants to community-based organizations to provide technical assistance to employers and labor unions selected under subsection (b). Such technical assistance may include—

> (1) developing outreach and orientation sessions to recruit women into the employers' apprenticeable occupations and nontraditional occupations;
>
> (2) developing preapprenticeable occupations or nontraditional skills training to prepare women for apprenticeable occupations or nontraditional occupations;
>
> (3) providing ongoing orientations for employers, unions, and workers on creating a successful environment for women in apprenticeable occupations or nontraditional occupations;
>
> (4) setting up support groups and facilitating networks for women in nontraditional occupations on or off the job site to improve their retention;
>
> (5) setting up a local computerized data base referral system to maintain a current list of tradeswomen who are available for work;
>
> (6) serving as a liaison between tradeswomen and employers and tradeswomen and labor unions to address workplace issues related to gender; and
>
> (7) conducting exit interviews with tradeswomen to evaluate their on-the-job experience and to assess the effectiveness of the program.

(b) SELECTION OF EMPLOYER AND LABOR UNIONS.—The Secretary shall select a total of 50 employers or labor unions to receive technical assistance provided with grants made under subsection (a).

## Ⓠ uestions for Review and Reflection

1. In what ways can government assist employers and unions under this law?
2. What role can the Department of Labor play?
3. Outline some programs in this law that provide technical assistance.
4. Why does the law say women should be singled out for help?

## Reading 8

U.S. Supreme Court, 1993

## *Shaw v. Reno,* 509 US—, 125 L. Ed. 2d 511, 113

Gerrymandering, a term that dates back to 1812, describes the practice of drawing voting district boundaries for political advantage. Named for Massachusetts governor Elbridge Gerry, who created a district shaped like a salamander, the skewing practice has been employed by some states to draw district boundaries that dilute minority voting power. With this racial gerrymandering, a group was fragmented into several districts so that its power was not congregated in any one.

The 1965 Voting Rights Act (see Chapter 4, Reading 3) prohibited racial gerrymandering, but the 1982 Voting Rights Amendment changed this policy, requiring states to draw lines where possible that took race into account in order to foster minority voting strength.

In 1991 North Carolina produced a redistricting plan that was challenged by voters because it appeared to have been drawn solely on the basis of race, without taking any other factors such as community or contiguousness into account.

The Supreme Court ruled 5–4 that such a plan violated the Constitution because it "reinforces the perception that members of the same racial group—regardless of their age, education, economic status, or the community in which they live—think alike." The Court feared that such a form of gerrymandering, even for remedial purposes, may "balkanize us into competing racial factions." Furthermore, they stated that it

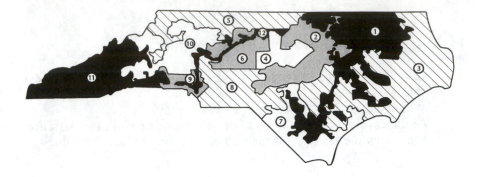

threatened to "carry us further from the goal of a political system in which race no longer matters—a goal . . . to which the Nation continues to aspire."

Justice O'Connor delivered the opinion of the Court.

**[1a]** This case involves two of the most complex and sensitive issues this Court has faced in recent years: the meaning of the constitutional "right" to vote, and the propriety of race-based state legislation designed to benefit members of historically disadvantaged racial minority groups. As a result of the 1990 census, North Carolina became entitled to a twelfth seat in the United States House of Representatives. The General Assembly enacted a reapportionment plan that included one majority-black congressional district. After the Attorney General of the United States objected to the plan pursuant to § 5 of the Voting Rights Act of 1965, 79 Stat 439, as amended, 42 USC § 1973c [42 USCS § 1973c], the General Assembly passed new legislation creating a second majority-black district. Appellants allege that the revised plan, which contains district boundary lines of dramatically irregular shape, constitutes an unconstitutional racial gerrymander. The question before us is whether appellants have stated a cognizable claim. . . .

Appellants contended that the General Assembly's revised reapportionment plan violated several provisions of the United States Constitution, including the Fourteenth Amendment. They alleged that the General Assembly deliberately "create[d] two Congressional Districts in which a majority of black voters was concentrated arbitrarily—without regard to any other considerations, such as compactness, contiguousness, geographical boundaries, or political subdivisions" with the purpose "to create Congressional Districts along racial lines" and to assure the election of two black representatives to Congress. App to Juris Statement 102a. Appellants sought declaratory and injunctive relief against the state appellees. They sought similar relief against the federal appellees, arguing, alternatively, that the federal appellees had miscontrued the Voting Rights Act or that the Act itself wasunconstitutional. . . .

[2] It is against this background that we confront the questions presented here. In our view, the District Court properly dismissed appellants' claims against the federal appellees. Our focus is on appellants' claim that the State engaged in unconstitutional racial gerrymandering. That argument strikes a powerful historical chord: It is unsettling how closely the North Carolina plan resembles the most egregious racial gerrymanders of the past. . . .

An understanding of the nature of appellants' claim is critical to our resolution of the case. In their complaint, appellants did not claim that the General Assembly's reapportionment plan unconstitutionally "diluted" white voting strength. They did not even claim to be white. Rather, appellants' complaint alleged that the deliberate segregation of voters into separate districts on the basis of race violated their constitutional right to participate in a "color-blind" electoral process. . . .

What appellants object to is redistricting legislation that is so extremely irregular on its face that it rationally can be viewed only as an effort to segregate the races for purposes of voting, without regard for traditional districting principles and without sufficiently compelling justification. . . .

A reapportionment plan that includes in one district individuals who belong to the same race, but who are otherwise widely separated by geographical and political boundaries, and who may have little in common with one another but the color of their skin, bears an uncomfortable resemblance to political apartheid. It reinforces the perception that members of the same racial group—regardless of their age, education, economic status, or the community in which they live—think alike, share the same political interests, and will prefer the same candidates at the polls. We have rejected such perceptions elsewhere as impermissible racial stereotypes. . . .

When a district obviously is created solely to effectuate the perceived common interests of one racial group, elected officials are more likely to believe that their primary obligation is to represent only the members of that group, rather than their constituency as a whole. This is altogether antithetical to our system of representative democracy. As Justice Douglas explained in his dissent in Wright v. Rockefeller nearly 30 years ago:

> "Here the individual is important, not his race, his creed, or his color. The principle of equality is at war with the notion that District A must be represented by a Negro, as it is with the notion that District B must be represented by a Caucasian, District C by a Jew, District D by a Catholic, and so on." . . .

For these reasons, we conclude that a plaintiff challenging a reapportionment statute under the Equal Protection Clause may state a claim by alleging that the legislation, though race-neutral on its face, rationally cannot be understood as anything other than an effort to separate voters into different districts on the basis of race, and that the separation lacks sufficient justification. . . .

[1e, 9c] Racial classifications of any sort pose the risk of lasting harm to our society. They reinforce the belief, held by too many for too much of our history, that individuals should be judged by the color of their skin. Racial classifications with respect to voting carry particular dangers. Racial gerrymandering, even for remedial purposes, may balkanize us into competing racial factions; it threatens to carry us further from the goal of a political system in which race no longer matters—a goal that the Fourteenth and Fifteenth Amendments embody, and to which the Nation continues to aspire. It is for these reasons that race-based districting by our state legislatures demands close judicial scrutiny.

In this case, the Attorney General suggested that North Carolina could have created a reasonably compact second majority-minority district in the south-central to southeastern part of the State. We express no view as to whether appellants successfully could have challenged such a district under the Fourteenth Amendment. We also do not decide whether appellants' complaint stated a claim under constitutional provisions other than the Fourteenth Amendment. Today we hold only that appellants have stated a claim under the Equal Protection Clause by alleging that the North Carolina General Assembly adopted a reapportionment scheme so irrational on its face that it can be understood only as an effort to segregate voters into separate voting districts because of their race, and that the separation lacks sufficient justification. If the allegation of racial gerrymandering remains uncontradicted, the District Court further must determine whether the North Carolina plan is narrowly tailored to further a compelling governmental interest. Accordingly, we reverse the judgment of the District Court and remand the case for further proceedings consistent with this opinion.

It is so ordered.

# Q uestions for Review and Reflection

1. According to this decision:

   a. What is the basis for the appellants' complaint?
   b. What constitutional rights were at issue?
   c. What constitutes political apartheid?
   d. How would the creation of these districts affect the roles of elected officials?
   e. Why are racial classifications harmful?

2. Examine the North Carolina congressional plan. Do you agree that the districts are unjustifiably irregular?

# Reading **9**

U.S. Congress, December 1993

## The Indian Tribal Justice Act

Among the many diverse peoples of the United States, Native American tribes occupy a unique position in the American democracy, constituting quasi-sovereign dependent nations within, and surrounded by, the larger country.

With the end of armed conflict between Indians and other Americans, the tribes and the federal government began their prolonged struggle to establish an appropriate relationship. The search continues for a balance that allows Native Americans to retain both their cultural identity and independence and the legal and economic protections of the United States government. Over and over again, the parties have struggled to determine where the responsibility for medical, legal, and educational services to the tribes should lie. That responsibility has shifted among Congress, state and local governments, and the tribes themselves in a changing series of federal laws—the 1924 act declaring Indians to be U.S. citizens, the Indian Reorganization Act of 1934, the Termination Acts of 1953–54, the Indian Civil Rights Act of 1968, and the Self-Determination and Assistance Act of 1975.

The Indian Tribal Justice Act of 1993 joins this list of legislative attempts to afford Native Americans such services as legal counsel for the indigent, law libraries, probation systems, and other technical assistance, without curtailing the tribes' sovereignty and self-governance.

### Indian Tribal Justice Act

**An Act to assist the development of tribal judicial systems, and for other purposes.**

*Be it enacted by the Senate and House of Representatives of the United States of America in Congress assembled,*

**Section 1. Short Title.**
This Act may be cited as the "Indian Tribal Justice Act."

**Sec. 2. Findings.**
The Congress finds and declares that—

(1) there is a government-to-government relationship between the United States and each Indian tribe;

(2) the United States has a trust responsibility to each tribal government that includes the protection of the sovereignty of each tribal government;

(3) Congress, through statutes, treaties, and the exercise of administrative authorities, has recognized the self-determination, self-reliance, and inherent sovereignty of Indian tribes;

(4) Indian tribes possess the inherent authority to establish their own form of government, including tribal justice systems;

(5) tribal justice systems are an essential part of tribal governments and serve as important forums for ensuring public health and safety and the political integrity of tribal governments;

(6) Congress and the Federal courts have repeatedly recognized tribal justice systems as the appropriate forums for the adjudication of disputes affecting personal and property rights;

(7) traditional tribal justice practices are essential to the maintenance of the culture and identity of Indian tribes and to the goals of this Act;

(8) tribal justice systems are inadequately funded, and the lack of adequate funding impairs their operation; and

(9) tribal government involvement in and commitment to improving tribal justice systems is essential to the accomplishment of the goals of this Act.

**Sec. 3. Definitions.**
For purposes of this Act:

(1) The term "Bureau" means the Bureau of Indian Affairs of the Department of the Interior.

(2) The term "Courts of Indian Offenses" means the courts established pursuant to part 11 of title 25, Code of Federal Regulations.

(3) The term "Indian tribe" means any Indian tribe, band, nation, pueblo, or other organized group or community, including any Alaska Native entity, which administers justice under its inherent authority or the authority of the United States and which is recognized as eligible for the special programs and services provided by the United States to Indian tribes because of their status as Indians.

(4) The term "judicial personnel" means any judge, magistrate, court counselor, court clerk, court administrator, bailiff, probation officer,

officer of the court, dispute resolution facilitator, or other official, employee, or volunteer within the tribal justice system.

(5) The term "Office" means the Office of Tribal Justice Support within the Bureau of Indian Affairs.

(6) The term "Secretary" means the Secretary of the Interior.

(7) The term "tribal organization" means any organization defined in section 4(1) of the Indian Self-Determination and Education Assistance Act.

(8) The term "tribal justice system" means the entire judicial branch, and employees thereof, of an Indian tribe, including (but not limited to) traditional methods and forums for dispute resolution, lower courts, appellate courts (including intertribal appellate courts), alternative dispute resolution systems, and circuit rider systems, established by inherent tribal authority whether or not they constitute a court of record.

## Title I—Tribal Justice Systems

### Sec. 101. Office of Tribal Justice Support.

(a) ESTABLISHMENT.—There is hereby established within the Bureau the Office of Tribal Justice Support. The purpose of the Office shall be to further the development, operation, and enhancement of tribal justice systems and Courts of Indian Offenses.

(b) TRANSFER OF EXISTING FUNCTIONS AND PERSONNEL.—All functions performed before the date of the enactment of this Act by the Branch of Judicial Services of the Bureau and all personnel assigned to such Branch as of the date of the enactment of this Act are hereby transferred to the Office of Tribal Justice Support. Any reference in any law, regulation, executive order, reorganization plan, or delegation of authority to the Branch of Judicial Services is deemed to be a reference to the Office of Tribal Justice Support.

(c) FUNCTIONS.—In addition to the functions transferred to the Office pursuant to subsection (b), the Office shall perform the following functions:

(1) Provide funds to Indian tribes and tribal organizations for the development, enhancement, and continuing operation of tribal justice systems.

(2) Provide technical assistance and training, including programs of continuing education and training for personnel of Courts of Indian Offenses.

(3) Study and conduct research concerning the operation of tribal justice systems.

(4) Promote cooperation and coordination among tribal justice systems and the Federal and State judiciary systems.

(5) Oversee the continuing operations of the Courts of Indian Offenses.

# Q uestions for Review and Reflection

1. According to this law:

    a. What is the importance of tribal justice systems?
    b. What is the responsibility of the United States government toward tribes and their justice systems?
    c. What steps will the United States take in order to provide for the Indian justice system?
2. Do you see any fundamental change in United States–Indian relations as a result of this act?

# 7

# The New Politics

The "New Politics" of minorities and women in the 1990s faced a much more conservative government than the 1960s. In 1994, the Republicans ran on a platform called the "Contract with America." They won both chambers of the U.S. Congress for the first time in decades and produced some major reforms.

Immigration is a public policy issue that has been debated and changed many times over the years. A recession in the early 1990s caused some Americans to resent immigrants and accuse them of taking jobs away from U.S. citizens. Aliens, both legal and illegal, were suspected of coming to America only to take advantage of the welfare benefits they could obtain. The 1996 Immigration and Reform Act requires stringent proof of legal status for purposes of employment and imposes harsh fines and penalties upon employers who hire illegal aliens. The 1996 Welfare Reform Act dramatically ends "welfare as we know it." One of its major components is termination of benefits to all aliens.

Luis Gutierrez, a Chicago congressman, champions immigrants and their contributions to the American economy, and defends, particularly, Mexican Americans, who he alleges are unfairly stereotyped as exploiting the welfare system. He urges more compassion for those struggling to make America their new home.

Asian Americans had been stereotyped as the "model minority" because of their success in education, business, and the professions. Gary Okihiro, a journalist, challenges that stamp and charges that many are victimized. A high proportion of Asian Americans live in poverty, receive a poor education, and are subject to "hate crimes."

187

Affirmative action policy has been affected by the conservatism of the 1990s and is reflected in the U.S. Supreme Court's retreat from its earlier imposition of desegregation and busing plans; it relieved school districts from rigid compliance in the face of "massive demographic changes." In *Adarand v. Pena,* the Supreme Court ruled that affirmative action would be permitted as a remedy only to redress specific discrimination.

Minorities disagreed within their own communities during the 1990s over many of the civil rights issues.

There is conflict within the Black community over affirmative action. Conservative Blacks disagree with the policy. Ward Connerly, a member of the Board of Regents for the University of California at Berkeley, chaired the California initiative to end "preferential treatment" in state hiring, contract, and admissions practices. He viewed it as fundamentally unconstitutional and successfully spearheaded the movement that ended race and gender as factors in admissions at the University of California at Berkeley. Clarence Page, Pulitzer prize-winning journalist, dispels many of the common complaints associated with affirmative action and asserts that, until there can be a level playing field and all people regardless of race or gender can start out with the same opportunities, the policy must continue.

Native Americans have internal disagreements about reservation life. Some tribes have opened casino-style gambling on their reservations, and have created hundreds of jobs and some impressive economic successes. Others object to that solution: Russell Means, an Oglala/Lakota, is a proponent of going back to long-established roots and "embracing the ideals of one's ancestors."

In the context of the "New Politics," the feminist movement has experienced division over the causes of gender inequality. Christina Hoff Sommers critiques and challenges much of the feminist research that casts women as "victims" and blames men and society. Naomi Wolf discounts the "male-bashers" and proposes that men are not "the problem." She asserts that women need to be less judgmental of men and of one another because there are no "fixed truths or tight answers about feminism."

When we consider modern education, we can observe that there is division in the academic world about multicultural education and ethnic studies. Professor Ronald Takaki commends the teaching of multiculturalism and condemns those academics who fail to tell "the whole story."

The willingness of groups to disagree within their ranks over issues integral to their pursuit of liberty and equality is a sign of health. Their strength is expressed by voting as these groups stay the course in their quest for a true reflection of "We, the People."

Jesse Jackson cautions the African-American community that they may have become complacent and need to restore the vitality of their movement by voting. Bert Corona, longtime Latino labor leader, advocates collective organization for the ballot box and also for unionization. There is strength in numbers, he urges. Eleanor Smeal, feminist leader, asserts that there is still a "gender gap" in politics that must be filled not just by women voting, but by women voting for women and getting more females into positions of power.

The 1990s reflect success in numbers of women and minorities voting and in winning elective office. Hundreds of seats in state and local offices are filled by the previously excluded groups of minorities and women. The U.S. Congress has 38 African Americans, 18 Latinos, 5 Asian Americans, 1 Native American, and 60 women. In this chapter, we witness Carl Stokes, the first Black mayor of Cleveland, Ohio, as he reviews the successes and predicts that a black man will be president in the not-too-distant future.

As the 20th century closes, minorities and women can point to impressive achievements in political and economic power. Laws have been enacted and attitudes have changed that guarantee greater "equal protection of the laws." Much remains to be done.

# Reading 1

Naomi Wolf, 1993

## "What We Can Do Now"

We have an opportunity, "an open moment," wrote Naomi Wolf, as she explained a plan to achieve real power. A Yale graduate, Rhodes scholar, public speaker, and author, Ms. Wolf introduced "power feminism" in her book, *Fire with Fire*.

During the 1980s and 1990s, as the women's movement began to realize some goals, a split occurred from within. Some of the more radical leaders blamed men for any continuing inequality and characterized women as victims of male domination. Critical of this "victim feminism," Ms. Wolf offers strategies for the 21st century to bring economic and political power to women. Hating men is not the answer; quite the contrary, women must "avoid generalizations about men that imply that their maleness is the unchangeable source of the problem."

The fight for equality can be "playful, witty, sexy, and fun," she writes and urges women to be less judgmental and more inclusive, not only of men but also of women who hold different views on feminism. "Resist the notion that there are any fixed truths or right answers about feminism, or that any one woman's way of sticking up for women is divinely better than any other woman's."

As we put power feminism into action, we must revise our day-to-day dealings with one another. Power feminism cannot work until we try to make changes in the way we treat ourselves and others. Let us:

- Avoid generalizations about men that imply that their maleness is the unchangeable source of the problem;
- Avoid generalizations about men that are totalizing: that is, that do not admit to exceptions;
- Never choose to widen the rift between the sexes when the option exists to narrow it, without censoring the truth.
- Never unreflectingly judge men in a way that we would consider sexist if men applied it to women; let us be able to explain why inequality makes the situation different, if it does;
- Distinguish between the men we love, who are on our side, and the male system of power, which we must resist. It is not "hating men" to fight sexism. But the fight against sexism must not lead to hating men;
- Resist the idea that sexual orientation is fixed and categorical, or that any one woman's sexual choices are more legitimate than any other's;
- Resist the notion that there are any fixed truths or right answers about feminism, or that any one woman's way of sticking up for women is divinely better than any other woman's;
- Practice evaluating our participation in a pro-woman effort on the basis of the goal in question rather than on the basis of whether we like the people involved and "identify" with them personally;
- Distinguish between the right to have an opinion about a woman's choices and the right to judge her;
- Challenge ourselves when we engage in "women's talk" that involves putting ourselves down or bonding over inadequacies;
- Make it socially acceptable for women to discuss their skills and achievements;
- Urge women to "come out" about the financial details of their lives and make it socially acceptable to discuss money;
- Remember and take possession of the girlhood will to power and fantasies of grandeur;
- Challenge the impulse to shy away from acknowledging the power, or admitting to the leadership skills, that we possess;
- Practice asking for more money, and urge our friends to do so;

- Examine our financial behavior, and question the sense women often have that money is polluting or masculinizing;
- Institute "Power 101" courses in high schools so girls of all backgrounds know how to debate, fund-raise, call a press conference, run a campaign, read contracts, negotiate leases and salaries, and manage a portfolio;
- If we are older, investigate our fear of younger women "taking too much" or "having it too easy"; if we are younger, pay due respect to the women who paved our way;
- Challenge our reflexive unease at the sight of another woman with "too much"; question the ritual in which we bond with other women by putting down achievers or leaders;
- Claim our dark side and take responsibility for it. Acknowledge that impulses toward aggression, retaliation, dominance, and cruelty are as innate to women as they are to men;
- Abandon the double standard that women as well as men impose on female political leaders;
- Give our daughters room for the "bad girl" to survive;
- Welcome dissent and differences of opinion among women; foster debate; create rituals—the equivalent of men's handshakes—in which women in conflict with one another express not conciliation but mutual respect;
- Visualize having the power we seek; then imagine the very worst thing that will happen if we attain it. Does it destroy us? Or do we survive, and even have a good time?
- Distinguish personal emotional connections that must be preserved from situations in which business, politics, or simple justice means that a connection may be disrupted or renegotiated;
- Create private pantheons—in our minds or even in a scrapbook, in a shrine, or on a bulletin board—of women, real or mythical, who braved dissent, created controversy, showed leadership, and wielded power. History texts and biographies are helpful because they show that our demands for power are not so unheard-of, or even so pioneering;
- Abandon the notion that the fight for equality has to be gloomy; take every opportunity to make it playful, witty, sexy, and fun. . . .

Historians agree that just after the Revolutionary War, the Civil War, and World War I, women failed to take advantage of what they called "the open moment." This is another open moment.

Whatever feminism is to you, to me it is at heart the logical extension of democracy. Power feminism's use of realpolitik and capitalism for the next stage of women's empowerment is not selfish, not "selling out," not imitating men, not accommodating to a less radical position. "Radical" comes from the Latin word for "root." Nothing is more radical than going to the roots of power.

If we continue to distrust the power of our imaginations, our money, and our words, we hand over victory to those who want the majority to remain silent. By dint of sheer numbers and a handful of change, women have already begun to win. Are we psychologically prepared to see this potential for victory in our lifetime? Will we take up the responsibility to contribute the hidden perspectives of women to the policies of the twenty-first century, which will sorely need them in order to ensure the well-being of everyone, male as well as female?

We have reached a moment at which sexual inequality, which we think of as being the texture and taste of femininity itself, can begin to become a quaint memory of the old country—if we are not too attached to it to let it go.

# Questions for Review and Reflection

1. Analyze the psychological strategies recommended by Wolf in terms of old feminism versus new feminism.
2. What do you think Wolf means by "power feminism"?
3. Wolf states that women have another "open moment." What do you think she means by that?

# Reading 2

Carl Stokes, 1993

## "Racial Equality and Appreciation of Diversity in our Urban Communities: How Far Have We Come?"

Carl Stokes represents the progress that has been made in race relations in the 20th century. He was Cleveland's first Black mayor, elected by an overwhelmingly white constituency. This is only a "microcosm" of what has happened across the United States, according to Stokes.

He itemizes a list of success stories: African Americans as state legislators, federal officers, judges, mayors; in the 1990s America celebrated its first Black governor, Doug Wilder, and its first Black chairman of the Joint Chiefs of Staff, General Colin Powell. Stokes anticipates that within 20 years, the United States will have its first African-American president. He credits "a fundamental decency" in a nation that is "still molding the kind of democracy it wants to be."

Twenty-five years ago, people told me that a black man could not be elected mayor of a major American city—particularly if the population of that city was majority white. I asked them "why not." They told me "because its never been done." I did it.

Today, the question tantalizing our nation, is when, if ever, the United States will elect an African American as its President. It seems to me that the discussion of the election of a black president is not "if" or "when," but "who." "When" is necessarily subordinate to and conditioned upon the unique persona of "who" will be that maker of history.

But there is no question in my mind that there will be an African American elected President of the United States. And it could easily occur within the next twenty years. . . .

In 1661, while still a colony, Virginia was the first to pass statutory recognition of slavery. And its unremitting struggle against the Union as the oldest of the Confederate states is a matter of history. Yet, in 1986, Doug Wilder was elected its Lieutenant Governor, and in 1990, the over 85 percent white population of Virginia elected Wilder their Governor over his white opponent, the elected Attorney General.

What a feat. This country had quietly gone from slavery in 1865, to the election of a black man in 1990 to the chief executive officer of one of its fifty states.

In the interim, over 300 black men and women have been elected mayor of their cities—indeed, the six largest cities in our nation have been led by African American mayors; the number of black congresspersons has ballooned from none in 1900, to 40 today, many of them chairs of major committees; most state legislatures have black members occupying varying degrees of power; the school boards and city councils in every large city are led or dominated by their black elected members; several states have black officials elected state-wide; the police chiefs of most of the largest industrial cities are black; black judges, elected and appointed, are serving from the municipal level to the highest state courts, and in the Federal district and appellate courts, and the U.S. Supreme Court; and the current Chairman of the Joint Chiefs of Staff of the U.S. military forces is a black man, General Colin Powell.

General Powell's current position as head of the military is of great significance to one of my generation. When I was in the U.S. Army from 1945 to 1947, there were only a few black lieutenants, almost no captains, black majors or colonels, and with the exception of Benjamin O. Davis, Sr., generals were not to be thought of. We were totally segregated in our living quarters and training facilities. We were generally denied the opportunity to serve in combat, and relegated to driving trucks. Today, 45 years later, the boss of all the armed services, an African American, General Colin Powell. . . .

This does not mean that racial bias and prejudice is not existent in the political market place. It means that racial animosities are not uniform and not universally employed. It means that more often than noticed, American's acknowledged racism, is well off-set by a fundamental decency in a nation still molding the kind of democracy it wants to be. It means that there is a framework in this country within which the individual can cause the system to respond to his or her appeal to the best that is in us. It means that the opportunity to rise to one's level is a fact; that the precept that "all men are created equal" has credence when viewed from the realities of those who have succeeded; and that the democratic principles on which this nation was formed, continue to evolve and expand and to fulfill the promise of a Democracy that has yet to reach full bloom.

##  uestions for Review and Reflection

1. According to Carl Stokes:

   a. What legislative acts have advanced Black political participation?
   b. What are some of the most significant political achievements for Blacks?
   c. Is there reason to be optimistic regarding the future for Blacks in politics?
   d. An African American can become president of the United States in the near future, according to Mr. Stokes. Why does he believe this?

# Reading 3

Gary Okihiro, 1993

## "The Victimization of Asians in America"

Director of Asian American Studies at Cornell University, Dr. Gary Okihiro delivered this lecture while a visiting professor at Amherst College. His presentation challenges the myth of the "model minority," a term used to describe Asian Americans.

Many of the immigrants who came from Asia were educated; many had solid job skills and a flair for entrepreneurship.

As a result, they flourished in business and their children excelled in school. Young Asian Americans had high graduation rates from both high school and college. Their parents entered the professions and commerce. But, Professor Okihiro cautioned, occurring at the same time is a very different experience for so many other Asian Americans: poverty, discrimination, low wages, and disparate educational opportunities. The stereotype of a "model minority" actually works against the Asian American, he submits, and causes a backlash of resentment and prejudice.

He details "the victimization of Asians" much like all of the other minorities and cites antimiscegenation laws, segregated schools, Japanese-American internment, and pervasive discrimination as examples of the United States' failure to enforce the equal protection of laws. Asian Americans fought back, he says, and through their contributions to the civil rights movement, brought about a broader definition of equality.

Asked which of the country's ethnic minorities has been subjected to the most discrimination and the worst injustices," observed sociologist William Petersen in 1966, "very few persons would even think of answering: 'The Japanese Americans.' Yet, if the question refers to persons alive today, that may well be the correct reply. Like the Negroes, the Japanese have been the object of color prejudice." . . .

Writing in the aftermath of the 1965 Watts riot in Los Angeles, Petersen noted that normally the treatment accorded to America's Japanese would have created a "problem minority," like blacks, characterized by low incomes, poor health and education, high crime rates, and unstable families. Race prejudice, inferior schools, and social ostracism, common wisdom argued, tended to produce a "cumulative degradation" such that even after a formal end to segregation and discrimination, "the minority's reaction to them is likely to be negative—either self-defeating apathy or a hatred so all-consuming as to be self-destructive." . . .

But the history of Japanese Americans, countered Petersen, challenges that generalization about America's minorities. "Every attempt to hamper their progress resulted only in enhancing their determination to succeed." . . .

Indeed, Asian Americans as a whole—not just Japanese Americans—have been held up as America's "model minority." . . .

All those reports are built upon the basic argument that although Asian Americans were victims of war and inhumanity, race prejudice and hatred, poverty and injustice, they overcame those obstacles through their culture—their family and ethnic solidarity, religion and work ethic, morals and values. . . .

The Asian American struggle for inclusion within the American community, as migrants and citizens, was principally based upon the constitutional guarantee of equal protection. As neither white nor black, Asians were deemed "aliens ineligible to citizenship" and were denied the privileges of life, liberty, and property, exemplified by their exclusion from the white courtroom, restrictions placed upon their language and their choice of spouses and livelihoods, and land laws that limited their access to real property. . . .

## The Contemporary Struggle Against Anti-Asian Prejudice

If Asian Americans are no longer victimized in quite the same way as in the past, it is in large measure because they protested against injustice and inequality in countless fields and factories, courts and legislatures, schools and street corners. And that contest over their civil liberties continues to this day, despite the popular and widespread notion of the "model minority." . . .

A *Wall Street Journal* and NBC News poll conducted in the spring of 1991 showed that a majority of Americans believed that there was no discrimination against Asian Americans. In fact, some held that Asian Americans received "too many special advantages." Among those "special advantages," no doubt, is the racial privilege of culture whereby Asians are programmed to succeed, especially in economic affairs, as purported by a number of current popular books. But a 1992 report of the U.S. Commission on Civil Rights concluded that "bigotry and violence against Asian Americans remains a serious national problem today," and contrary to popular opinion, "Asian Americans still face widespread prejudice, discrimination, and denials of equal opportunity." Contributory to that anti-Asianism, explained the report, were race prejudice, economic competition, misunderstanding, and resentment over the real or imagined success of Asian Americans. The idea that Asian Americans posed an exemplar to other minorities, the idea that Asians had overcome all barriers to succeed in America, the idea that Asian Americans had even "outwhited the whites," was the very idea that fueled hatred of and denied equal opportunity to that vaunted group.

A prominent aspect of the notion of contemporary success is that despite past victimization, Asian Americans have, through quiet fortitude, patience, and hard work, attained their heralded status. They did not become a "problem minority," nor did they manipulate their victimization for economic or political advantage, or so the argument goes. But the historical record shows that Asians, like African Americans and Latinos, worked the edges, insofar as they were permitted, and struggled mightily to make inroads toward the center and the full promise of American democracy. Asian Americans enjoined the civil rights movement, broadly construed, for legal, economic, and social equality—for inclusion within the definition of America. That effort for inclusion was not a self-serving drive for gain at the expense of others, but expanded the meaning and application of the American creed, and helped to protect and guarantee the civil liberties of all Americans. This we must remember. The victimization of any group reduces the humanity and hence freedoms of both victims and victimizers; equally, the struggle against victimization secures the humanity and freedoms of both victims and victimizers. And therein rests the true significance of minorities, of Asians in America.

## Questions for Review and Reflection

1. Compare the discrimination that Asian Americans confront with that of other minority groups.
2. Do you see differences in the way that Asian Americans deal with discrimination, compared to other minority groups?
3. Why are Asian Americans viewed as a "model minority"?

# Reading 4

Christina Hoff Sommers, 1994

## *Who Stole Feminism?*

Professor of Philosophy at Clark University, Christina Hoff Sommers has written articles for many publications including the *Wall Street Journal, The New Republic,* and the *Chicago Tribune.* She indicts the feminist movement for being full of "female chauvinists" who have betrayed women. Her book criticizes those she labels "gender feminists," who claim that women are still controlled by and submissive to male dominance. She challenges the results of many of their published studies that support the victimization charge, and accuses them of having faulty and even false data and research.

"I am a feminist who does not like what feminism has become," Professor Sommers declares. She advocates a need to educate and alert young women to this "dangerous new agenda that threatens our most cherished ideals and sets women against men in all spheres of life."

## Preface

American feminism is currently dominated by a group of women who seek to persuade the public that American women are not the free creatures we think we are. The leaders and theorists of the women's movement believe that our society is best described as a patriarchy, a "male hegemony," a "sex/gender system" in which the dominant gender works to keep women cowering and submissive. The feminists who hold this divisive view of our social and political reality believe we are in a gender war, and they are eager to disseminate stories of atrocity that are designed to alert women to their plight. The "gender feminists" (as I shall call them) believe that all our institutions, from the state to the family to the grade schools, perpetuate male dominance. Believing that women are virtually under siege, gender feminists naturally seek recruits to their side of the gender war. They seek support. They seek vindication. They seek ammunition.

Not everyone, including many women who consider themselves feminists, is convinced that contemporary American women live in an oppressive "male hegemony." To confound the skeptics and persuade the undecided, the gender feminists are constantly on the lookout for proof, for the smoking gun, the telling fact that will drive home to the public how profoundly the system is rigged against women. To rally women to their cause, it is not enough to remind us that many brutal and selfish men harm women. They must persuade us that the system itself sanctions male brutality. They must convince us that the oppression of women, sustained from generation to generation, is a structural feature of our society. . . .

I recently told a friend that I was coming across a lot of mistakes and misleading data in feminist studies. "It's a mess," I said. "Are you sure you want to write about it?" she asked. "The far right will use what you find to attack all women. It will harm the women who are working in such problem areas as battery and wage discrimination. Why do anything to endanger our fragile gains?" My friend's questions were sobering, and I want to underscore at the outset that I do not mean to confuse the women who work in the trenches to help the victims of true abuse and discrimination with the gender feminists whose falsehoods and exaggerations are muddying the waters of American feminism. These feminist ideologues are helping no one; on the contrary, their divisive and resentful philosophy adds to the woes of our society and hurts legitimate feminism. Not only are women who suffer real abuse not helped by untruths, they are in fact harmed by inaccuracies and exaggerations. . . .

American women owe an incalculable debt to the classically liberal feminists who came before us and fought long and hard, and ultimately with spectacular success, to gain for women the rights that the men of this country had taken for granted for over two hundred years. Exposing the hypocrisy of the gender feminists will not jeopardize those achievements. . . .

The women currently manning—womanning—the feminist ramparts do not take well to criticism. How could they? As they see it, they are dealing with a massive epidemic of male atrocity and a constituency of benighted women who have yet to comprehend the seriousness of their predicament. Hence, male critics must be "sexist" and "reactionary," and female critics "traitors," "collaborators," or "backlashers." This kind of reaction has had a powerful inhibiting effect. It has alienated and silenced women and men alike.

I have been moved to write this book because I am a feminist who does not like what feminism has become. The new gender feminism is badly in need of scrutiny. Only forthright appraisals can diminish its inordinate and divisive influence. If others join in a frank and honest critique, before long a more representative and less doctrinaire feminism will again pick up the reins. But that is not likely to happen without a fight. . . .

But who will challenge them? The answer to that question transcends the politics of liberalism and conservatism. Too often, those who find fault with the intolerance of the feminist ideologues are tarred as right-wing reactionaries. It is true that "the right" has tended to be more alarmed about the censoriousness of the "liberal" left. But there are relatively few conservatives in our educational institutions and cultural temples, and it would be most unrealistic to count on them to be very effective in combatting gender feminism. Nor, if we judge by the sorry record of their faintheartedness in the academic world, should we count on intellectual men to engage the gender feminists in open battle. So the unpleasant but necessary task of confrontation falls to women who believe in free expression and who scorn those who would stifle it. Such women waged and won the battle for the suffrage and for all the basic rights American women now enjoy. Such women are still in the majority, but out of a lack of awareness of the extent of the problem or a reluctance to criticize their zealous sisters, they have remained silent. The price has been great—the ideologues have made off with the women's movement. . . .

Classical equity feminism is very much alive in the hearts of American women. It is unfortunate that part of its energies must now be diverted to defend the women's movement from the grave threat posed to it by the gender feminist ideologues. Ironically a concerted effort to deal with the threat may well prove revitalizing to the languishing mainstream. Getting out from under the stifling, condescending ministrations of the ideologues is a bracing cause and an exhilarating necessary step for the truly liberated women to take. When enough women take it, the gender feminists' lack of a constituency among American women will be exposed, and their power structure will not survive.

# **Q** uestions for Review and Reflection

1. According to Christina Hoff Sommers:

   a. American feminism is dominated by "gender feminists." Define what she means by that term.

b. Why do American women owe a debt to the "classically liberal feminists"?

c. There is a problem with the many studies produced by "gender feminists." What is wrong with some of these studies?

d. Define "classical equity feminism."

# Reading 5

Mario T. Garcia, 1994

## Memories of Chicano History: The Life and Narrative of Bert Corona

"Pensamientos" means memories in Spanish. These memories are Bert Corona's and are shared with Mario T. Garcia in a book about Corona's life as a community organizer and labor activist.

Corona has worked as a labor leader throughout his life and with some of the great leaders of the Hispanic civil rights and labor movements—people such as Cesar Chavez, Luisa Moreno, and Frank Lopez. Corona helped to found the Mexican American Political Association (MAPA), a distinguished Latino advocacy group. He also served on the U.S. Civil Rights Commission in the 1960s.

In these reflections on his life, Corona comments on the future for Latinos in the United States, is "optimistic" about a coming together of the different Latino groups, and calls upon young Latinos to create that collective strength. ". . . [y]ou have to develop a philosophy or an ideology that inspires you to accept the need for social change," he says, one that will provide the vision, commitment, and tenacity necessary for progressive leadership.

### "Pensamientos"

Some proclaimed the 1980s as the "Decade of the Hispanic." I'm afraid that I was never quite sure what that meant or in whose interest this proclamation was being made. I can't accept the idea that a particular decade belongs to a particular group. I have no problem with the idea that Hispanics or Latinos are going to accelerate their struggle for social change. But it can't and shouldn't be done in isolation from other forces that are also struggling for social justice.

. . . Latinos are going to be presented with some major opportunities in the 1990s. One of these will be increased political representation. At the federal level, we'll elect additional people to the House of Representatives and perhaps elect a senator or two. At the state and local levels, we may win some governorships, and we'll definitely see more Latinos in the statehouses and on city councils, county boards, and school boards. . . .

The opportunities, issues, and challenges that the Chicano/Latino communities will face in the 1990s and beyond have a lot to do with the quality of leadership. I frankly think that we've never before had as many prominent and competent leaders as we have today. This is true not only politically but also in academia, the arts, the media, and business. These men and women can stand on their own achievements, and they are more and more becoming interested in correcting many of the social ills they see around them. We have more lawyers, doctors, and educators than we have ever had in our history.

A distinguishing characteristic of this leadership is that, regardless of political ideology, the people who are part of it are extremely knowledgeable. You can't be a leader—certainly not a national Latino leader—and be unaware of the issues affecting the Latino communities. You've got to have at your fingertips the data about education, poverty, immigration, and so on. You must have this knowledge in order to qualify as a national leader. . . .

Although I'm optimistic about the future of our leadership, at the same time I think we should be as critical of our leaders as we feel the need to be. This is especially true for our elected leadership. We have to expect and demand that our leaders who are elected or appointed to office reflect the needs and aspirations of our people and that they work to better our communities. We've got to be very hard on them on this issue of accountability. On the other hand, I don't think we should make the mistake of demanding from them a level of activity and participation that only saints can bear. We have to keep in mind that they're human beings.

And we should never assume that they know all about our problems just because they're Latino. I remember that when we went to lobby in Congress on the immigration issue, someone said, "There's no need to go and talk to the Hispanic Congressional Caucus, because they know all about this issue." Well, as it turned out, they didn't know all about this issue; they had to be informed just like anybody else. I think that we should deal with our Latino elected officials just as we would with any other elected officials. We should expect the same of Latino leaders as we would of anyone else. . . .

I believe in the American dream—or at least in my version of it. I interpret it as a hope and a wish, which has not been completely fulfilled for all Americans such as Latinos and other racial minorities. It's similar to the dream of the Mexican Revolution, which also promised freedom, equality, and democracy. Clearly, that hasn't been fully achieved. In both cases, they're unfulfilled dreams. . . .

If I can pass anything on to younger people, it would be that, based on my experiences, successful community organization depends on establishing as broad a coalition as possible, regardless of personality differences, organizational differences, or political differences. I would also insist that the essentials of strong, effective leadership are consistency and stubbornness in pursuit of one's goals. But to have a goal, you have to develop a philosophy or an ideology that inspires you to accept the need for social change. With that vision, commitment, and tenacity, strong progressive leadership is possible.

I've known too many young people who will tell me, "Mister Corona, I really want to work for my *gente,* my people. I don't want to make a lot of money; I just want to be with my *gente.*" That's a very noble expression, but you still need to know *why* you want to be with your *gente.* To do what? You can't just do something because you think it's cool or glamorous, because pretty soon this will wear off unless you have a broader and deeper understanding of your commitment.

My advice to young people who want to work in the community is that if they can develop those qualities or characteristics I've mentioned, they'll be able to find their niche, where they can get people together to build collective strength. This is how they'll become leaders. It can be done.

# Questions for Review and Reflection

1. According to Bert Corona:
   a. What is bringing the Latino community together under the common term "Hispanic"?
   b. What is meant by the "Decade of the Hispanic"?
   c. Identify some of the opportunities presented to Latinos in the 1990s.

# Reading 6

Russell Means, 1995

## *Where White Men Fear to Tread*

Russell Means is an Oglala/Lakota Native American. In the 1960s he was the leader of the American Indian Movement (AIM). Today he is a producer, singer, activist, and author, and continues his efforts on behalf of what he calls the Native American way of life.

Mr. Means describes white Americans as wasteful, alienated, and materialistic, "none of which produces satisfaction." Native Americans, too, have lost their way, he alleges, and recommends as a solution for both peoples—the Indian way of life. "Indians must rejoin the family circle," he urges, by returning to their roots and serving as a model to non-Native Americans. "Let us embrace the ideals of our ancestors and show the white man how to find peace."


In the last century, Eurocentric male-oriented nations, the United States foremost among them, have tried to force the rest of the world to become just like them—the most wasteful people on earth. America wastes its energy, its water, its land, its food, its forests, and its people. . . .

Sadly, the white man equates happiness with the pleasing of his senses. My Uncle Matthew King used to shake his head and say, "The white man is like a little child; you have to be patient with him." But Grandmother Earth is running out of patience. What Eurocentric societies have done to indigenous peoples all over the world they are now doing to themselves—poisoning the land and air and water, abusing one another as they abuse our sacred Grandmother. We are approaching the abyss of species suicide.

In their arrogance, science addicts who call themselves environmentalists blather about those who are destroying the earth. They miss the point. They are destroying *themselves,* not the earth. No matter what industrialized societies do to themselves and to the human race, the earth has eons to heal itself. . . .

Industrial society creates alienation. More and more people of every color can no longer bear the strain of living in artificial surroundings. They have worked and fought their way up through the ranks of automatons, they have accumulated wealth and position, they have sacrificed their souls to their corporate masters' bottom lines—but materialism did not bring inner satisfaction. They have a few ties to the land. Their families are scattered across the country—grandparents in Sun Belt retirement towns, parents in Chicago or New York or Denver, children in Seattle or Cincinnati or Philadelphia. They don't know where they came from or where they are going. They are driftwood.

. . . [m]y people became like those rootless ones. In some urban areas, a third generation of Indian people has reached maturity without ever feeling a connection to the land their forebears revered. . . . Urban assimilation over the last three decades threatens to accomplish the destruction of Indian culture as efficiently as cavalry raids and massacres.

It is not too late to restore Indian values to the generations growing up far from their land. Unfortunately, the more "educated" we Indians get, the more embarrassed we are about our origins. We lose confidence in our heritage and its institutions. Instead of respecting our elders, who were raised in wisdom and whose traditional role was to teach succeeding generations, we pay them only lip service. If they can't speak English, we rarely ask their advice on decisions of any importance. Even when we do, it is because something has gone wrong in our lives and we want the old guys to give us an immediate fix. We want redemption—just like Christians who pray to Jesus. When our elders offer insight and thoughtful questions instead of absolution or cookbook-style instructions, people go away disappointed and disillusioned. . . .

If we are to survive as a people our future must be our past—rejoining the family circle. Return to our traditional clan system. Because it resolves conflict peacefully, the clan system also ensures individual liberty. The extended family and the core-family unit—my term for what whites call the "nuclear" family—are essential in building community self-determination, and it is the community that provides the only means for us to preserve the institutions that traditionally guided every aspect of our lives as human beings. The white man could learn this from us.

We must become independent nations to show non-Indians how to perceive us as men and women and children with our own view of the world, people with good reasons for being who we are. When we become as real to other races as they are to themselves, when they get to know us as human beings instead of two-dimensional symbols, they will no longer be able to demonize and dehumanize us. . . .

How does one attain freedom? How can we fight city hall? The BIA? The federal government? How can we succeed in reestablishing our individual rights as guaranteed by the Constitution? It's as simple as this—people of every color must stand up on their hind feet and begin to act like human beings. Start with yourself! Understand that freedom is responsibility. Before you can champion individual rights, you must recognize that you cannot be free and accept government handouts, whether they are federal farm subsidies, corporate subsidization, aid for dependent children, or state-paid medical care. The next step, in the words of Kwame Touré (formerly Stokely Carmichael), is to organize, organize, organize. Take your message to the streets—but even though government is not going to give away anything, force begets only brutality and injustice. I have swallowed my share of official violence, and I now feel that real change cannot come except through non-violence.

My goal is to return to Pine Ridge and rebuild my own extended family on land that once belonged to my father. I will build a treatment center with therapy based on traditional values, where Indian people will learn to improve their relationships without confrontation. I will establish a total-immersion school to teach Lakota children the beauty and superiority of their people's sciences, knowledge, and wisdom. In that way, I will begin to rebuild the Independent Oglala Nation. I have sworn on the sacred pipe that in my lifetime, I will see a free and independent Indian nation, responsible for its own economic destiny, beholden to no government, and recognized by the world community. I hope it will be the Lakota, but if not, then the Dene or Miskito or Cree or Hawaiian or Inuit. . . .

I want Indian youths to take heart, to have faith. I want them to know that although the white man insists that they are wasting their miserable lives by living with few material goods on reservations or in ghettos, their lives can be good if they live as true Indians, faithful to the principles of their ancestors. I want them to know that the Great Mystery is there for everyone and has a path for them. It is not strict and narrow. It winds and twists and branches off in every direction, but as long as they follow it freely and respectfully, it will take them where they are meant to go.

One of the white man's enduring myths is about a great leader called Moses, who lived long ago when my ancestors were still a free people and his tribes were captives in Egypt. Moses went to the pharaoh and begged, "Let my people go." Greedy and stubborn, the pharaoh did not listen, so the god of Israel sent plagues to punish and frighten the Egyptians. Today, my people's tribes are captives of the white man's greed and stubbornness. His plagues punish us all—with choking clouds of unbreathable air, poisoned water, soil desecrated with chemicals and radioactivity, violence stalking every community, homeless people crowding streets and parks, parents abusing children, legions of addicts sniffing or eating or smoking or injecting drugs, hospitals filled with people dying of cancer or heart disease or AIDS. And even worse may be yet to come, for the white man shows no sign of changing his ways. Just as the pharaoh ignored Moses, the U.S. government did not hear my forebears. I say to my nation and to all indigenous peoples: To hell with the pharaoh! Let us embrace the ideals of our ancestors. Let us show the white man how to find peace of mind by living in harmony with the universe. Let us show him how to honor and protect our Grandmother. Let *us* go.

## $\boxed{Q}$ uestions for Review and Reflection

1. According to Russell Means:

   a. What is a "Eurocentric society"?
   b. How do Native Americans define "immortality"?
   c. How does industrialization contribute to alienation?
   d. What are the benefits of "rejoining the family circle"?
   e. How does the story of Moses apply to today's issues?

# Reading 7

Luis Gutierrez, 1995

## "The New Assault on Immigrants"

Congressman Luis Gutierrez is the first Hispanic to be elected to the U.S. House of Representatives. A graduate of Northeastern

Illinois University, Representative Gutierrez has been a school teacher, a social worker, and a member of Chicago's city council.

Although his article focuses on Chicago's immigration issues, his remarks apply to the problems that immigrant populations face across the country. For example, the Immigration Reform and Control Act of 1987 requires employers to provide proof of the legal status of their employees. The act stemmed from charges that "illegals" entered the country to qualify for welfare and medical benefits or to get free education for their children. He claims in this article that immigrants are blamed unfairly for all of the nation's economic and social problems, and, in particular, Latinos are singled out as "uneducated, unwilling to work and unable to contribute. . . ."

As a leader himself, he asks all leaders to "remember our history, learn our facts and find our voices to speak out for fairness and tolerance. . . ."

Anti-immigrant backlash, too, seems to flow in waves, and in recent years, we've seen public discussion about immigration grow increasingly ugly and more divisive. Listen closely to the rhetoric coming out of state capitals from Sacramento to Tallahassee. Note the tone of radio talk shows. Study the legislation being proposed in Washington and across the country. From welfare reform to health care, immigrants—these new immigrants—are the target of the legislative and rhetorical equivalent of rocks aimed at their heads. . . .

The cumulative effect of this assault has been to make blaming immigrants for our nation's economic and social woes an accepted part of our political and cultural debate. . . .

We've heard the charges for years: immigrants are draining our resources. They force Americans into unemployment. They are tearing the fabric of our society apart by demanding to speak their own language and have their own culture. . . .

The economic blame, the unemployment worries, the corrupting of culture and language—this fingerpointing is as old as the Mayflower. The intensity of the debate regarding the perceived problems of immigration blinds far too many of us to learning from history. Keeping in mind a historical perspective would serve well to remind us of the foolishness of targeting a single group of immigrants or a particular wave of immigration as "different." How seriously can we take the opponents of immigration today when we realize that the same urgent crisis they believe Mexicans are bringing across our border today their forbears vehemently argued were brought by Poles and Italians many decades ago. . . .

Unfortunately, today many of the voices of intolerance have a pronounced racial edge less evident in the battles between the Germans and English in

Pennsylvania, or the Poles, Lithuanians and Bohemians of Chicago's past. That immigrant-bashing has become meaner and more personal seems to me clearly related to the fact that so many of our new immigrants are traveling here not from Europe but from Asia and Latin America.

The stakes have been raised, and that is why any of us who cares about the future of immigration—and particularly Latino leaders—must meet the challenge that the voices of intolerance and division are raising. . . .

Immigrants to this country are not fighting for a handout; they are not here merely for a student loan or food stamps or access to a free clinic. What they are interested in is something much simpler, much more basic. They are fighting to have all of the opportunities that they are denied in their native countries: a chance to work at a decent job and make a decent living, the opportunity to educate their children, the opportunity to have decent shelter and clothing. They want to contribute to a better America.

The facts speak clearly. The stereotype of immigrants, particularly Latino immigrants, as uneducated, unwilling to work and unable to contribute to our economy and our society simply does not hold true. By any objective standard, the immigrant population in the US today is as productive and beneficial to the national economy and culture as it has ever been in our nation's history. . . .

In the past, America has struggled and fought and eventually overcome the voices of intolerance to implement immigration policies that do not break our budget and allow immigrants to grow and thrive in our country.

Today's immigrant groups need the same leadership. And not just quiet leadership. They need outspoken public figures and grassroots activism that spread the message of immigrant rights and contributions. Challenging anti-immigrant rhetoric is not very popular these days, but it has never been more important, and more people need to be willing to carry on this struggle.

## The Pleasures of Diversity

The congressional district I represent is a community filled with people who celebrate America while honoring and remembering the nations they have left behind. People express genuine ethnic pride on St. Patrick's Day and Columbus Day, and they receive a day off of work to honor Casimer Pulaski, a Polish immigrant who fought heroically during the Revolutionary War.

There are ethnic restaurants, kitchens and grocery stores; you hear Polish and Italian and Korean and of course Spanish being spoken on the streets. And, while the district is full of ethnic diversity and pride, it has its share of ethnic strife, too.

Immigrants made my district, made my city, and their leaders fought for their rights. The Slavs worked to elect Anton Cermak mayor. When an assassin ended his term, their domination gave way to the Irish, who elected decades of mayors from Edmond Kelley to Martin Kennelly to Richard M. Daley—all of whom were careful to slate ethnically backed tickets. Immigrant groups have not always gotten along, but they never lacked leaders who fought for them.

Now is the time for the leaders of the new immigrants to stand up against division and intolerance, and to explain in clear terms that the new wave of immigrants—from Mexico and Guatemala, from Honduras and Cuba, from El Salvador and Nicaragua—is contributing just as immigrants before them did.

No less a figure than Benjamin Franklin was so frightened of German immigration that he wrote, "all the advantages we have will, in my opinion, be not able to preserve our language, and even our government will become precarious." Franklin was wrong about Germans in 1753. The politicians, talk-radio hosts and editorial writers who fear the new immigrants are just as wrong today.

Leaders must remember our history, learn our facts and find our voices to speak out for fairness and tolerance, and to remind ourselves that new immigrants, like the old ones, are ready to give back as much as and more than they take—economically, culturally, and socially.

# Questions for Review and Reflection

1. According to Luis Gutierrez:

   a. Immigrants are coming to America for what reason?
   b. What contributions do immigrants make to the country?
   c. What are the charges that are historically made against immigrants?
   d. Compare the charges against immigrants that were made early in the century with those being made against immigrants today. Are they the same or different?
   e. Why are Latino immigrants singled out?
   f. What were Benjamin Franklin's concerns about immigrants? Are they different from today's concerns?

# Reading 8

Barbara Koeppel, 1995

## "The Progressive Interview: Eleanor Smeal"

Eleanor Smeal is a political activist, a major figure in the women's movement, and a leader in the National Organization for Women (NOW) and the fund for the Feminist Majority. She has called for a separate feminist political party because the

Republican and Democratic parties are not progressive enough on women's issues.

In this interview by writer Barbara Koeppel, Ms. Smeal itemizes the number of gains women have made in recent years—from education to jobs to more equal pay. Despite these and other achievements, a 1990 government report describes a "glass ceiling" that still exists, a point on the success ladder beyond which women cannot climb.

Ms. Smeal believes that this "gender gap" can be repaired only through political power. One strategy is voter registration, getting women to vote is the key to power, and "where possible, to vote for women."

**Q:** Let's talk about the women's movement. What do you think are its most important gains?

**Smeal:** First, there's the obvious—education. Before the late 1960s, women were just 3 percent of law students and 8 percent of medical students. Now, we're 40 percent of both. More girls are going to college. Before, there were quotas. For example, when I went to Duke, the university wouldn't accept more than 25 percent female students. Now, women are 52 percent of all undergrads.

Second, we have more choices about the occupations we enter. In the 1960s, women were in only 20 percent of all job categories, mostly in those predominantly filled by women, such as secretaries, teachers, and nurses. At the same time, we accounted for less than 1 percent of dentists, veterinarians, and engineers. Now, we account for 25 to 30 percent of *all* professions. On the surface, this may seem a minor improvement. But given where we were just three decades ago, it's more like an explosion.

What is most important is the change in consciousness, both for women and men—but mostly for women. In the 1960s, people didn't even think discrimination existed. So we had to first prove it did—for example, documenting that women were paid less for doing the same work. But even that wasn't enough, because we then had to show it was *wrong*—since the thinking in those days was that it was OK for men to earn more at the same job, because they had to support families. Now, 80 percent of the public think women should have comparable pay.

Another gain is that we now have sex-discrimination laws, and society recognizes that everyone has the right to work without being harassed.

Also, the public finally recognized that violence against women is widespread—and that it cuts across class lines. Before, there were only a few battered-women's shelters. Now there are hundreds. And consciousness-raising was crucial in all these areas.

Of course, another obvious change is that abortions were legalized and clinics now exist where women can obtain them. These changes are particularly important for low-income women, who use the clinics most, because rich women could always get abortions if they needed to. Also, there's more funding for women's diseases, like breast cancer.

**Q:**  A lot of advances in education and job opportunities have benefited mostly upper-income women. What about the others?

**Smeal:**  Because of affirmative-action laws, a lot more job categories opened up to working-class women—say, as police and firefighters, or in construction. Though the numbers are still small nationwide—for example, women are just 8 percent of all police—they account for as much as 40 percent in a big city like Pittsburgh.

Also, because of a 1978 law, women can't lose jobs when they become pregnant. And this affects lower-income women even more than upper-income ones.

The Feminist Majority organizes around the affirmative-action message—making the point that it keeps the doors open for them, that it *has* made a difference to their paychecks and kinds of jobs they can now work in. Where affirmative action has worked, as in education, it has equaled things out.

**Q:**  But women still don't account for a large proportion in the occupations you mentioned.

**Smeal:**  Yes, it's true the numbers are small in each. But if you add them all together, they're substantial. Also, pay scales have been narrowed. When we started the crusade in the early 1970s, women earned fifty-nine cents to the males' dollar. Now, women get a bit over 70 percent of what men earn overall. That's not good enough, but it's clearly an improvement. Even then, we have to be honest and qualify this. You see, part of the reason the gap has closed is that men's wages have dropped—because the higher-paid, union, manufacturing jobs have been lost and men are earning far less at service-sector jobs. That said, we still calculate about half the gain in women's pay has been due to our wages having risen. And it's important for men to understand that women getting paid less is a threat to their *own* wages, particularly now that they're in the service sector.

**Q:**  Now for the down-side. What hasn't changed?

**Smeal:**  The worst thing is that there's still horrific violence against women—in all economic groups. Before, it was behind closed doors. We exposed the problem and now it's well known—four million women a year are badly beaten, and violence is the leading cause of women from fifteen to forty-four entering emergency rooms.

Second, women are very underpaid and are not economically independent. Their average income is still very low—less than $14,000 a year. Generally, they, along with kids and the elderly, are the ones earning the minimum wage.

**Q:** How does this square with your statement that women are in many more occupations and the pay gap has narrowed?

**Smeal:** If you look at predominantly women's jobs, like secretaries, they are still the lower end and terribly underpaid. And they are trapped in these jobs. Also, many are in the underground economy, like domestics, who earn near the minimum wage and can't report their income—because they can't afford to pay taxes. So if you add them into the calculations, plus all the part-time workers who can't get more work and don't get benefits, you get a fuller picture.

**Q:** You have worked for many years with NOW and the Feminist Majority. How do they differ?

**Smeal:** We start from a different premise, and emphasize different strategies, although we complement each other in many ways. NOW, which is a chapter-based grassroots movement, believes we have to raise consciousness and educate the public. But the Feminist Majority feels consciousness has already been raised, that we already have majority support. So we feel we need a strategy to empower that majority to find a way to enable feminists to govern. To do this, we concentrate on initiatives and state referendums, like the one on affirmative action in California, on abortion in Oregon, and equal rights in Iowa, in 1992. And when women take an active role in these struggles, they also learn how to empower themselves.

**Q:** How did you fare with the referendums?

**Smeal:** We won in Oregon and lost, by only four percentage points, in Iowa. Some people feel these fights are too costly for us to get involved in, that we should use our resources, which are small, in other ways. But we feel strongly that we need to enter these battles. We took on the opposition and are winning. We won the bulk of the abortion referendums—to the point that you don't see these so much any more. We even passed a pro-choice referendum in Nevada in 1992. In Oregon, where the referendum was on requiring teenage girls to get parental consent for an abortion, only 20 percent opposed it when we began.

We feel we have to activate the political gender gap, since studies on this clearly show that women are more concerned about social issues. We need to mobilize more women to vote. And, where possible, to vote for women. The more women in power, the more change there will be. . . .

**Q:** What can we expect of the women's movement now? Where's it headed?

**Smeal:** The women's movement is growing, despite what is said. From our polls, women want different things, and empowering them will lead to change. Feminist ideas *have* permeated, especially among women, who do vote differently. And having power would help create a society that is more interested in human concerns.

# Questions for Review and Reflection

1. According to Eleanor Smeal:

   a. How does the Feminist Majority differ from NOW?
   b. Which issues are women most concerned with?

# Reading 9

Ward Connerly, 1996

## "With Liberty And Justice For All"

The solution to equal opportunity in Ward Connerly's view is an end to Affirmative Action. (See Chapter 5; Readings 5 and 7.) As a member of the Board of Regents for the University of California at Berkeley, Mr. Connerly led a controversial assault on Affirmative Action policies that brought about an end to race-based preferences in the university's admissions program.

He later chaired the California Civil Rights Initiative that passed and ended any preference given to women and minorities in California's hiring and contract policies. Mr. Connerly states a belief in the democratic values of "the supremacy of the individual, equal opportunity for the individual, and zero tolerance for discrimination."

In his view, affirmative action militates against those values; instead, he relies on "America's passion for fairness."

When we become citizens of this nation, at birth or otherwise, we get a warranty. That warranty is supposed to be honored by every government franchise in every village and hamlet of this nation. It is not transferable, and it is good for the life of the vehicle.

We are guaranteed the right to vote, the right to due process, the right to be free, not to be enslaved, as long as we conduct ourselves in accordance with the laws of our nation, and the right to equal treatment under the law, regardless of our race, color, sex, religion, or national origin. These are rights which attach to us as individuals, not as members of a group.

This warranty has not always been honored for some of us. Because of the color of our skin or the place from whence we came, some of us were denied the right to vote, we were enslaved, we were denied due process, and the equal treatment granted to others was not ours to enjoy. . . .

But, the past is a ghost that can destroy our future. It is dangerous to dwell upon it. To focus on America's mistakes is to disregard its virtues.

This nation has a passion for fairness. That passion is evidence in our constitution, in the bill of rights, in executive orders, in court decisions but, most of all, it courses through the arteries of our culture. . . .

Affirmative Action has its roots in that passion for fairness. When President Lyndon Johnson explained Affirmative Action to the nation, it is significant that he said, you can't bring a man to the starting line who has been hobbled by chains and expect him to run the race competitively.

Fairness suggested that the nation pursue Affirmative Action to compensate black Americans for the wrong that had been done. Affirmative Action was a technique for jump starting the process of integrating black Americans into the fabric of American society, for changing the culture of America from an exclusive society into an inclusive one.

I believe Affirmative Action was meant to be temporary. It was meant to be a stronger dose of equal opportunity for individuals, and the prescription was intended to expire when the body politic had developed sufficient immunity to the virus of prejudice and discrimination. It was not meant to be a system of preferences that would harm innocent people. The rationale for Affirmative Action thirty years ago was a moral one.

Three decades later, Affirmative Action is permanent and firmly entrenched as a matter of public policy. It has its own constituency that is prepared to defend its continuation at any cost, not because of any moral imperative, but because it has become the battleground for a political and economic war that has racial self-interest as its centerpiece.

Affirmative Action, as most of us originally understood the term, enjoyed the support of a majority of Americans. Many Americans still support this concept as long as it does not involve preferences. Preferences, on the other hand, were wrong at the outset and are wrong today. . . .

When this nation began its use of Affirmative Action decades ago, America's racial landscape was rather clear. There was the dominant white majority and the oppressed black minority. Today, we have several dozen racial and ethnic categories in California.

There is no dominant majority and there is no oppressed minority. Within a few years, the group which will numerically be the largest is Hispanic. Our racial tensions are no longer just black and white. They are black and Korean. Black and Hispanic. White and Hispanic. Russian and Hispanic. Every conceivable racial conflict is present and lurking somewhere beneath the surface, in California. How, then, do we decide who among us should receive a preference?

A direct product of our diversity is the emergence of a whole new set of racial configurations and problems which defy the old racial order. Yet, Affirmative Action operates as if the old order was still in place, as if our racial dilemma was still black against white.

The end of Affirmative Action will be difficult for black Americans. It is our nature not to be trusting of the good will of whites. It is instinctive for us to harbor the belief that our rights will only be as secure as the amount of ammunition issued to the federal troops to protect us. Well, it is time to let the troops go home and to place our faith in the American system of democracy, in America's passion for fairness.

It is time for black Americans to enter the arena of democracy instead of seeing ourselves as spectators. This is our land, not Africa. The blood and sweat of black Americans can be found in the pot of democracy in just as great a quantity as that of others. It is time for black Americans to proudly accept America as their land, the land of opportunity. . . .

I am terrified at the prospect of what can become of us if we maintain our existing preferences policies. In police departments, in fire departments, in middle class homes throughout California, there is a growing perception that if I am white, I and my kids will not have an equal opportunity to succeed. No matter where it comes from, if anyone among us believes the warranty is not being honored, we have a duty to investigate the legitimacy of their complaint and to make it right if their complaint is proven to be valid. . . .

There are those who say that racism and sexism are not dead in America, and they are correct. But, racism and sexism in our society do not justify our government giving a preference to Jose over Chang because Susan's father discriminated against Willie's father fifty years ago. Not in America.

If you are a student of history, you know that every now and then, the opportunity to alter the course of human events presents itself. Such is now the occasion for the people of this nation. . . .

The opportunity is to resume that noble journey of building an inclusive family of Americans in which men and women of all races and colors can work and play in harmony, with mutual respect, and expecting nothing more than an equal opportunity to compete and from that competition we can build that more perfect union of which our forefathers dreamed. . . .

If there is any lesson that we can learn from the rest of the world, it is the fact that America's experiment with democracy will fail if we divide our people into racial enclaves and allocate jobs, contracts and college educations on the basis of group identity. . . .

We can continue down the path of numerical parity, racial preferences, and a continuing preoccupation with the concept of race. We can continue perpetuating the outdated premise on which racial preferences are based: that blacks, women and other minorities are incapable of competing without a handicap.

Or, we can return to the fundamentals of our democracy: the supremacy of the individual, equal opportunity for the individual, and zero tolerance for discrimination. . . .

Let us not mourn the death of Affirmative Action. Instead, let us proclaim our belief that the spirit of equal opportunity, which Affirmative Action engendered, has become a permanent feature of America's social, economic and political landscape. Let us have faith in our own sense of fair play.

# [Q] uestions for Review and Reflection

1. According to Ward Connerly:

   a. What could cause America's experiment with democracy to fail?
   b. What is the "outdated premise" upon which Affirmative Action is based?
   c. What are the fundamentals of American democracy?
   d. Has Affirmative Action accomplished anything?

# Reading **10**

Ronald Takaki, 1996

## "At the End of the Century: The 'Culture Wars' in the U.S."

Professor Ronald Takaki is the director of Asian American and Ethnic Studies at the University of California, Berkeley, and an author of many books on the subject of "multiculturalism," a term used to characterize the multiplicity of cultures that exist within heterogeneous North America. In this collection of perspectives on race and ethnicity, he and some of his contributors critique some of the views of other scholars.

Professor Takaki objects to those who make up a "conservative backlash against multiculturalism" (see Chapter 6; Reading 5) and praises institutions that "promote cultural diversity." He insists that it is important for Americans to understand that "the American ideal of human rights and dignity still remains a dream deferred" for people of color. "Cultural diversity" refers to the many cultures that exist within the United States, not limited to race and ethnicity but inclusive of gender, sexual preference, religion, and other "cultures" found in the United States.

His collection explores the two major cultural pluralist theories: "the assimilationist theory seeking to explain race relations in terms of the incorporation of minorities into the white mainstream versus the internal colonialist theory contending that peoples of color in the U.S. represent colonized groups."

The full story needs to be told, writes Takaki, because understanding "the making and meaning of a multicultural United States is especially crucial at this moment."

As we approach the twenty-first century, we are offered two meditations on the meaning of this transition to what might be either a new order or new chaos in the world. What we are witnessing, claims Francis Fukuyama, is the "end of history." Liberal democracy, he trumpets, remains "the only coherent" political ideology. Capitalism with its "free market" has succeeded in producing new levels of material prosperity in the industrially developed countries and also many Third World countries. Traditional identities of tribe and ethnicity are being replaced by rational forms of social organization based on efficiency and natural rights. John Lukacs is not so sanguine, however. "The twentieth century is now over," he observes. "It was a short century. It lasted seventy-five years—from 1914 to 1989." Its end is being accompanied by explosions of "tribalisms" throughout the world. Both Fukuyama and Lukacs compel us to examine the United States at the conclusion of the century.

As Americans experience the end of the twentieth century, many of them have been anxiously wondering about the future. The sound and fury of the 1992 Los Angeles conflagration over the Rodney King issue highlighted the reality of race and its multiracial dimensions—the presence not only of African Americans but also Hispanics and Asian Americans. . . .

Ironically, this crisis is occurring at the very moment of what Fukuyama celebrates as the triumph of liberal democracy and capitalism led by the United States. As the Cold War concluded, Americans found the age of their nation's global economic ascendancy coming to an end. . . . Complex and multidimensional, the current crisis represents what Lukacs terms the end of the "American Century."

Within the context of these racial tensions and economic problems have emerged the "culture wars." More than ever before, as whites approach the time when they will become a minority, many of them are perplexed about America's national identity and future as one people. . . .

Cultural pluralist scholars continue to operate largely within the river banks of two major theories—the assimilationist theory seeking to explain race relations in terms of the incorporation of minorities into the white mainstream versus the internal colonialist theory contending that peoples of color in the U.S. represent colonized groups. Both paradigms assume the existence of a racial hierarchy in terms of white and black, or white and people of color. But they become woefully inadequate to explain tensions between different groups of color such as the antagonism between African Americans and Korean Americans. Crucial to any effort to address this need for new theory and new multicultural analysis is the re-visioning of history. Scholars need to approach the past from a broad and comparative perspective in order to comprehend the dynamic, dialectical process in which different groups came together from different shores to create a new society in North America.

This need for an understanding of the making and meaning of a multicultural United States is especially crucial at this moment. Contrary to Fukuyama, we have not reached the end of history. In order for democracy to emerge in a country, Fukuyama notes, its citizens must share a strong sense of national unity and accept one another's rights. This made democracy possible in Britain, France, and the United States. Thus democracy is linked to national identity. Actually, in the United States, rights and nationality have not been extended to all groups. Liberal democracy and capitalism must still address the continuing economic and racial inequality in America itself. The American ideal of human rights and dignity still remains for many citizens of color a dream deferred; the material abundance of the "free market" continues to be enjoyed by a privileged group. Fukuyama argues that the problem of racial inequality is not "insoluble on the basis of liberal principles." But his optimism does not resonate reassurance to a society witnessing escalating racial tensions and conflicts. Indeed, Fukuyama's very celebratory insistence that history has ended only shrouds the explosive reality Lukacs describes as tribalism—identities and interests based on ethnicity.

# Questions for Review and Reflection

1. According to Professor Takaki:

   a. What are the fallacies in Francis Fukuyama's thesis?
   b. Explain the racial hierarchy paradigm that he lays out.
   c. Can liberal democracy solve the racial tensions that exist in American society?

# Reading 11

Jesse Jackson, 1996

## "It's Up to Us"

The Reverend Jesse Jackson has been a major participant in the Civil Rights movement. He is an acknowledged spokesperson for the disadvantaged in the United States and around the world as he works for human rights and social justice.

Jesse Jackson served closely with Reverend Martin Luther King Jr. and was by his side at the time of King's assassination. He has earned over 40 honorary degrees for his work, has run for the office of president of the United States twice, and serves as president of the National Rainbow Coalition.

In these remarks, made shortly before the 1996 election, Reverend Jackson emphasizes the importance of the vote to achieve power for African Americans. He describes a "right-wing offensive" that must be challenged and cautions that "[T]oo many people think of the Civil Rights Movement as something in the past tense." He fears that African Americans have become complacent and are not working to maintain all of the achievements struggled for in the past. "We must once again become drum majors for justice."

We need a new freedom movement. A new freedom movement in our cities: Most major cities have a new jail and a new stadium. They stand as two mountains with dark urban canyons in between.

A freedom movement for our youths, especially young Black men now being jailed in numbers that exceed those of Black men jailed in South Africa under apartheid.

A movement for families now working harder for less, at the mercy of merging, purging corporations seeking overseas profits.

And for our children: Nearly one out of two Black children is in poverty. Our children deserve better.

This is the time to fight back with disciplined, direct action—and with our votes. We must not forget that a vote is a valuable weapon. If someone gives you a weapon to protect yourself, your family and your community, then you must use it.

Those who vote have more influence than those who don't. A vote does not translate automatically into granted wishes, but it does increase your chances of having your needs addressed. Every vote counts.

Those who came before us paid a heavy price in sweat and blood to win the right to vote. Now our people will pay a heavy price in sweat and tears if we don't use that right well. Too many people think of the Civil Rights Movement as something in the past tense. But the cry for freedom must continue to go out because so much of what we have gained is now under assault.

Republican extremists are trying to cut back on our legislative seats and our judicial appointments, our ability to sue for economic discrimination and the amount we can sue for. Medicaid and Medicare are under attack. . . .

We hold the margin of victory in our hands.

Yet no small movement for change can lead us to the promised land. Our civil-rights organizations, the Women's Movement, our labor unions, our church networks—all of us must work together to reverse the right-wing offensive. We will return to our roots; walk the picket lines, impose our own economic sanctions and take the initiative and responsibility to reclaim our youths. . . .

Just as personal responsibility deals with ethical behavior, it must also address public policy. The threats to Black America today are not all spiritual; many are political or legislative or corporate.

So we cannot ignore the political process. The political system will put our freedom movement's agenda into law. Our freedom movement will maintain the moral clarity *and* keep pressure on the political system to acknowledge our needs. . . .

Still, many of us are giants with grasshopper complexes. In 1994, 9 million Blacks were unregistered. Too many of us were rocks just lying around. This year we must all become cornerstones for a new freedom movement.

Dr. King's dream of jobs, peace and justice is a solution to the social, economic and political ills that confront us, as well as the moral and spiritual crisis we find ourselves in.

We must remind the country of that dream; we must once again become drum majors for justice. We, the people, have the power. Keep hope alive!

# Q uestions for Review and Reflection

1. According to Reverend Jackson:

   a. What would be the purpose of a new freedom movement?
   b. Why is the political process the means to achieve the purposes of a new freedom movement?
   c. Is the new freedom movement an extension of Dr. King's movement?

# Reading 12

Clarence Page, 1996

## "Supply-Side Affirmative Action"

Pulitzer prize–winning columnist for the *Chicago Tribune*, Clarence Page has earned a seat in Chicago's Journalism Hall of Fame. His syndicated column appears regularly as does he on a variety of television talk shows.

*Showing My Color* is a series of Page's essays on race in the United States. He believes in the American ideal of equal opportunity and argues that affirmative action does what it was intended to do, enhance equal opportunity. He takes each commonly held view against the policy, challenges its "myths," and acknowledges its "merits."

"Supply-side affirmative action" which translated means education, job training, and apprenticeship programs, is his solution. Keep the policy going until the United States has built up "the supply of qualified applicants for the new jobs."

Arguments against affirmative action fall under the following general categories:

*"We don't need it anymore."* The work of early feminists and the civil rights movement did their job, but now it is time to move on. The nation has outgrown employment and educational discrimination. Nonwhite skin may actually be an advantage in many businesses and schools. The market is ultimately color-blind and would be fair, if only those infernal lawyers and government regulators would get out of the way.

*Comment:* Americans hate intrusions into their marketplace, unless the intrusions benefit them. I would argue that bias is as natural as xenophobia and as common as apple pie. Until opportunities are equalized enough to encourage women and minorities to have more trust in the free marketplace, there will be a glaring demand for extraordinary measures to target what is actually only a quite modest amount of jobs, scholarships, and contracts to minorities.

*"Racism has reversed."* This is David Duke's claim. Whites, particularly white males, now suffer a distinct disadvantage in the workplace and in college applications. Affirmative action sets racial "quotas" that only reinforce prejudices. Besides, two wrongs do not make a right.

*Comment:* Not anymore. Conservative court decisions in the 1990s actually have shifted the burden of proof in hiring, promotions, publicly funded scholarships, and contract set-aside cases from whites and males to minorities and women. If women and minorities ever had a time of supremacy under the law, it is gone. Conservative court opinions have worked hastily to restore white male primacy. . . .

*"Give meritocracy a chance."* Free market zealots like University of Chicago law professor Richard Epstein, who believes all "irrational discrimination" would disappear in an unfettered marketplace, have called for the elimination of anti-discrimination laws, saying the market will punish those who turn aside talented workers or customers with money in their pockets just because of race or ethnicity. D'Souza agrees with Epstein's bold assertion that anti-discrimination laws actually get in the way of women and minorities who would prefer to hire family members. He calls for an end to all anti-discrimination laws except those that apply solely to government.

*Comment:* "Merit" by whose standard? Market forces do count, but so do culture and personal prejudices. Segregation cost white businesses valuable consumer business, yet, even in the North, where it was required only by local custom, not by government, many refused to serve blacks anyway. . . .

*"It encourages balkanization."* Affirmative action opens social wedges that threatens to replace the basic American melting pot creed with a new "balkanization."

*Comment:* Anyone who thinks American society was *less* balkanized in the 1950s and 1960s was not only color-blind but also quite deaf to the complaints of people of color. If there was less racial or gender friction in major newsrooms, campuses, and other workplaces, it is only because there was no race or gender in them except white men.

Racism and sexism have not disappeared, it is widely agreed, they have only become more subtle—"gone underground"—making them less easy to detect, harder to root out. . . .

Each of these arguments has some merit and much myth. Left to our own devices, most of us unfortunately will discriminate, often in ways too subtle for us to notice even when we do it. Either way, such irrational discrimination occurs and is not healthy for a diverse society. . . .

The wrongs committed by affirmative action are constantly overblown. At the newspaper where I work, I have received mail from people who allege episodes of reverse discrimination. Since I have experienced the sting of racial discrimination in jobs, housing, and public access, I sympathize with them, but not by much. After all, if they have a legitimate complaint, they can do the same thing I would do. They can file a complaint with the proper federal, state, or local authorities. Many white males do, and many win. Many receive sizable judgments. Some even have famous Supreme Court cases like "Bakke," "Weber," and "Crosson" named after them. . . .

Nor does it settle the argument to say affirmative action is unfair to "meritocracy," America's cherished traditions of rewarding effort by "deserving" individuals. Americans have always had a wide array of exotic standards for determining "merit." For example, I have a blond-haired, blue-eyed friend of

Scandinavian descent who is a Washington lawyer; he told me, jokingly, that he "got into Harvard thanks to affirmative action for Nebraskans."

Another, who happens to be a Greek-American college professor, tells me he is "convinced I got into Dartmouth because I was the only application they got from Albuquerque that year. I'm sure some talented Jewish kid from New York was kept out so I could get in."

Indeed, geographic diversity was practiced by college and university admissions officers long before affirmative action came along. Few people would deny Harvard the right to choose from a broader pool of qualified applicants than just Philips Exeter graduates from New England. Nor have I seen valiant efforts put forth to dismantle preferences for promising athletes or the children of alumni or major contributors. But let a university's admissions criteria take race or ethnicity into account, and suddenly the alarms are sounded. . . .

Most affirmative action attempts to push change from the demand side, forcing private companies, agencies, and institutions to seek out women and minorities and lure them in. Some do a better job than others. Supply-side affirmative action works from the side of increasing educational and training opportunities and, as a result, the talent pool.

It does not set quotas. It does not hold white males back at the door while ushering women and minorities inside. Instead, it works to improve the supply of qualified talent from which to choose. It opens its doors to everyone, but makes a special outreach effort to women and minorities who may not have felt welcome in the past. Instead of sitting back and waiting for women or minorities to appear at the door, practitioners of supply-side affirmative action take a hard look at their own companies or agencies. Assisted by diversity consultants or simply by employees, they look for signs of racism and sexism that might not have been immediately apparent to the white males who traditionally dominated the workplace. . . .

America will not have racial equality until opportunities are equalized, beginning at the preschool level, to build up the supply of qualified applicants for the new jobs emerging in information-age America. The American ideal of equal opportunity still produces rewards, when it is given a real try. It needs to be tried more often. Affirmative action is not a perfect remedy, but it beats the alternative, if the only alternative is to do nothing.

# Questions for Review and Reflection

1. According to Clarence Page:

    a. How have conservative courts restored white primacy?
    b. What is balkanization and does affirmative action contribute to it?
    c. Does affirmative action policy set quotas?
    d. Why is the policy of affirmative action still necessary?

# Democracy in the Twenty-First Century

**L**iberty is an unfinished business," wrote the American Civil Liberties Union some years ago. Similarly unfinished is the full expression of equality that results in a truly democratic form of government. As this century ends, the United States continues to struggle with its diversity and democracy. How much of a role should government play in guaranteeing equal opportunities? Can affirmative action bring about equality of results? Can diverse groups agree on core values, or do cultural differences make that impossible? Liberty and equality have advanced dramatically from where they began in principle in the Declaration of Independence.

There is a question whether Jefferson meant only men when he said that all men are created equal; in fact, women, then, were excluded from full political participation. Today, women not only enjoy full participation but they exceed men in total percentage of voter turnout. Women are winning higher and higher elective offices; there is speculation that both the Republicans and Democrats will select a woman to be a vice-presidential candidate in the next presidential election year. Women can enter the trades and professions, own and operate companies, purchase property, become managers and CEOs. In the workplace, women and men no longer have to tolerate sexual harassment. The Supreme Court has taken language from the 1964 Civil Rights Act and interpreted it to mean that sexual conduct that a "reasonable person" would find offensive or that creates a "hostile work environment" is a violation of federal law. In *Harris v. Forklift Systems,* they extended the concept even further to include verbal abuse of a sexual nature. Education became more inclusive when the Supreme

Court ruled in *United States v. Virginia et al.* that previously all-male, state supported military academies must admit women.

Despite these and other successes, there remain many unresolved issues in the women's movement. Abortion is in controversy as support of civil rights for the unborn grows. Equal pay for women has not been achieved. More federally and state-funded day-care facilities, more resources allocated to women's sports, more equal opportunities in the military—these are some of the issues that will carry over into the 21st century.

The 1990 census reflects some of the issues facing Asian Americans in the 21st century. That census report indicates a growing median family income for Asian Americans, slightly ahead of whites. However, much of their community continues to hold low-wage jobs; they face discrimination, despite the stereotype of "model minority" they carry. According to the 1990 census, Asian Americans make up approximately 3 percent of the total population; one-half million have arrived from Vietnam since 1973. President Clinton's remarks to the Asian-Pacific American Caucus reflect their significance, as he comments on their contributions to American life.

Native Americans have won some significant victories in recent history in terms of remedies for past government violations of treaty obligations. They enjoy greater and greater religious freedom, most recently because Congress enacted the American Indian Religious Freedom Act. Economic development on many Indian reservations is growing, and gambling casinos are making some tribes wealthy. At the same time, the U.S. government has withdrawn or curtailed many of the earlier welfare programs for reservations. The Native American Housing Assistance and Self-Determination Act is one step toward restoring some help to the poverty that plagues most reservation families. President Clinton's historic meeting with all tribal leaders is a signal that government is renewing its commitment to tribal sovereignty and economic independence. Such a partnership will be the goal in the 21st century.

Twenty-three million Hispanics live in the United States. As their numbers grow, they have been organizing and are becoming a strong presence in the economics and politics of the United States. Having the U.S. government recognize Hispanic Heritage Month reflects the new rank of the Hispanic community. However, there has been a backlash toward Hispanics and other immigrants in the 1990s. Efforts to reduce or eliminate assistance to aliens, whether legal or not, have had strong support across the country. Bilingual education is in jeopardy in many states as people demand English-only classrooms. Hispanics are themselves divided on this and other issues that will carry over into the 21st century.

As the ethnic and cultural groups become veterans in the civil rights movement, new groups are born. The disabled, the elderly, and gay and lesbian rights will express their views and ask that their voices be heard.

# Reading **1**

## *Harris v. Forklift Systems, Inc.,*
## No. 92-1168

Sexual harassment is a form of gender discrimination banned in Title VII of the 1964 Civil Rights Act. (See Chapter 4; Reading 2.) What it entails is still being determined by the courts. The Supreme Court has stated that it is sexual conduct that a "reasonable person" would find offensive and that creates a "hostile working environment." It could include an expectation of some sort of sexual favor in exchange for a raise in pay or job advancement.

*Harris v. Forklift Systems* expanded the definition to include verbal abuse of a sexual nature. "When the workplace is permeated with 'discriminatory intimidation, ridicule, and insult' . . . Title VII is violated."

Much controversy continues about what constitutes sexual harassment but all agree that it is conduct that women or men no longer should have to tolerate.

Justice O'Connor delivered the opinion of the Court.

In this case we consider the definition of a discriminatory "abusive work environment" (also known as a "hostile work environment") under Title VII of the Civil Rights Act of 1964.

Teresa Harris worked as a manager at Forklift Systems, Inc., an equipment rental company, from April 1985 until October 1987. Charles Hardy was Forklift's president.

The Magistrate found that, throughout Harris's time at Forklift, Hardy often insulted her because of her gender and often made her the target of unwanted sexual innuendos. . . .

Harris then sued Forklift, claiming that Hardy's conduct had created an abusive work environment for her because of her gender. . . .

Title VII of the Civil Rights Act of 1964 makes it "an unlawful employment practice for an employer . . . to discriminate against any individual with respect to his compensation, terms, conditions, or privileges of employment, because of such individual's race, color, religion, sex, or national origin." . . . When the workplace is permeated with "discriminatory intimidation, ridicule, and insult" that is "sufficiently severe or pervasive to alter the conditions of the victim's employment and create an abusive working environment," Title VII is violated.

This standard, which we reaffirm today, takes a middle path between making actionable any conduct that is merely offensive and requiring the conduct to cause a tangible psychological injury. . . . Conduct that is not severe or pervasive enough to create an objectively hostile or abusive work environment—an environment that a reasonable person would find hostile or abusive—is beyond Title VII's purview. . . .

This is not, and by its nature cannot be, a mathematically precise test. . . . But we can say that whether an environment is "hostile" or "abusive" can be determined only by looking at all the circumstances. These may include the frequency of the discriminatory conduct; its severity; whether it is physically threatening or humiliating, or a mere offensive utterance; and whether it unreasonably interferes with an employee's work performance. The effect on the employee's psychological well-being is, of course, relevant to determining whether the plaintiff actually found the environment abusive. But while psychological harm, like any other relevant factor, may be taken into account, no single factor is required. . . .

Though the District Court did conclude that the work environment was not "intimidating or abusive to [Harris]," it did so only after finding that the conduct was not "so severe as to be expected to seriously affect plaintiff's psychological well-being" and that Harris was not "subjectively so offended that she suffered injury." The District Court's application of these incorrect standards may well have influenced its ultimate conclusion, especially given that the court found this to be a "close case."

We therefore reverse the judgment of the Court of Appeals, and remand the case for further proceedings consistent with this opinion.

*So ordered.*

# Questions for Review and Reflection

1. On what legislative act does the Court rely for its definition of a discriminatory "abusive work environment"?
2. Which individuals are protected against such discrimination?
3. On what constitutional amendment does the Court's decision rely?
4. What circumstances might create a "hostile" or "abusive" work environment?
5. Did the conditions in the Harris case rise to a "hostile" or "abusive" work environment, in your opinion?

# Reading 2

U.S. Congress, 1994

## The American Indian Religious Freedom Act Amendments of 1994

The protection and preservation of Native American culture has increasingly become the responsibility and desire of the United States government. One centuries-old practice is to use peyote in religious rites. Such ceremonial use was exempt from drug laws in over half the states until the Supreme Court ruled against it in the early 1990s. The Court reasoned that the First Amendment did not protect such use and that only the legislative branch had the power to authorize the custom.

Congress responded by amending the original American Indian Religious Freedom Act of 1978 to include "the traditional ceremonial use of the peyote cactus as a religious sacrament."

The Act of August 11, 1978 (42 U.S.C. 1996), commonly referred to as the "American Indian Religious Freedom Act", is amended by adding at the end thereof the following new section:

Sec. 3. (a) The Congress finds and declares that—

(1) for many Indian people, the traditional ceremonial use of the peyote cactus as a religious sacrament has for centuries been integral to a way of life, and significant in perpetuating Indian tribes and cultures;

(2) since 1965, this ceremonial use of peyote by Indians has been protected by Federal regulation;

(3) while at least 28 States have enacted laws which are similar to, or are in conformance with, the Federal regulation which protects the ceremonial use of peyote by Indian religious practitioners, 22 States have not done so, and this lack of uniformity has created hardship for Indian people who participate in such religious ceremonies;

(4) the Supreme Court of the United States, in the case of Employment Division v. Smith, 494 U.S. 872 (1990), held that the First Amendment does not protect Indian practitioners who use peyote in Indian religious ceremonies, and also raised uncertainty whether this religious practice would be protected under the compelling State interest standard; and

(5) the lack of adequate and clear legal protection for the religious use of peyote by Indians may serve to stigmatize and marginalize Indian tribes and cultures, and increase the risk that they will be exposed to discriminatory treatment. . . .

# Q uestions for Review and Reflection

1. On what grounds does the law justify the use of peyote?
2. In general, how has state law handled the use of peyote by Native Americans?
3. What was the Supreme Court's ruling on the use of peyote?
4. Does the legislative act override the Supreme Court's decision?

# Reading 3

President William J. Clinton, 1994

## Remarks to Native American and Native Alaskan Tribal Leaders

The U.S. population contains over 1 million Native Americans; about half of them live on reservations. They have their own tribal governments and are gaining greater economic independence through loans and federal partnership programs. Although not completely sovereign, U.S. Indian tribes have been incrementally granted more and more self-determination by Congress, from the time they achieved full citizenship status in 1924 and obtained the right to vote to the present.

The Indian Gaming Regulatory Act of 1988 opened up new economic opportunities for Native Americans. The law permits Indian tribes to offer casino-style gambling not subject to state taxation on their reservations. Recently, some states have begun to challenge the law, alleging lost revenues and unfair competition.

President Clinton is the first U.S. president to have met with all of the tribal leaders in the country. In his remarks in this reading, he reaffirms a government pledge that includes gaming, as Native Americans move toward more self-determination.

I believe in your rich heritage and in our common heritage. What you have done to retain your identity, your dignity, and your faith in the face of often immeasurable obstacles is profoundly moving, an example of the enduring strength of the human spirit. . . .

In every relationship between our people, our first principle must be to respect your right to remain who you are and to live the way you wish to live. And I believe the best way to do that is to acknowledge the unique government-to-government relationship we have enjoyed over time. Today I reaffirm our commitment to self-determination for tribal governments. I pledge to fulfill the trust obligations of the Federal Government. I vow to honor and respect tribal sovereignty based upon our unique historic relationship. And I pledge to continue my efforts to protect your right to fully exercise your faith as you wish.

Let me speak for a moment about religious freedom, something precious to you, something deeply enshrined in our Constitution. For many of you, traditional religions and ceremonies are the essence of your culture and your very existence. Last year, I was pleased to sign a law that restored certain constitutional protections for those who want to express their faith in this country. . . .

This then is our first principle: respecting your values, your religions, your identity, and your sovereignty. This brings us to the second principle that should guide our relationship: We must dramatically improve the Federal Government's relationships with the tribes and become full partners with the tribal nations. . . .

All governments must work better. We must simply be more responsive to the people we serve and to each other. It's the only way we'll be able to do good things with the resources we have. I know that you agree with that. More and more of you are moving to assume fuller control of your governments. Many are moving aggressively to take responsibility for operating your own programs. Each year the Bureau of Indian Affairs is providing more technical services and fewer direct services.

One avenue for greater tribal control is through self-governance contracts. There are about 30 self-compacting tribes today. We're working with Congress to raise that number by 20 tribes every year. We'd like self-governance to become a permanent program. But we must ensure services will still be provided to the smaller tribes that do not choose to participate. . . .

We must do more to create jobs, raise incomes, and develop capital for new businesses. . . .

At my direction, the Vice President has established a working group on Indian economic development as part of our Community Enterprise Board. I've asked them to study the recommendations from last year's National Indian Economic Summit and to consult fully with you every step of the way. Our goal is clear: to work with you to enhance economic development in every tribe. I'd like to emphasize that what I have asked them to do in this issue, I asked them to do on all issues. This great, historic meeting today must be the beginning of our new partnership, not the end of it.

I'd like to make a point about economic development that has to do with gaming. As a former Governor, I understand some of the concerns that the Governors have raised. But as President, I know that gaming gives you a competitive edge when you've had precious few. And the benefits often extend to surrounding communities in full measure. Some of you are now able to invest more in housing and health care and child care and infrastructure and taking care of your elders. I know that gaming is controversial, even among tribes. As many of you have acknowledged, it's also important that tribal governments continue to diversify their economies. Many of you are working with congressional leaders, Governors, and Secretary Babbitt to resolve tough issues. . . .

The Great Law of the Six Nations Iroquois Confederacy contained this advice: "In our every deliberation, we must consider the impact of our decision on the next seven generations." We are stewards; we are caretakers. That standard will keep us great if we have the vision of your forefathers.

As we look back on the American journey, the test ahead is always whether we are moving in the right direction of more tolerance, wider justice, and greater opportunity for all. It is the direction that counts, always the direction. And our choices will set that direction.

Of course, as you well know, our history has not always been a proud one. But our future can be, and that is up to us. Together we can open the greatest era of cooperation, understanding, and respect among our people ever. I know that we will. And when we do, the judgment of history will be that the President of the United States and the leaders of the sovereign Indian nations met and kept faith with each other and our common heritage and together lifted our great nations to a new and better place.

Thank you all.

## $\boxed{\text{Q}}$ uestions for Review and Reflection

1. According to President Clinton:

   a. What lessons can Native Americans teach?
   b. Should Native American religious practices have constitutional protection?
   c. How can a stronger partnership be built with Native Americans?

# Reading 4

President William J. Clinton, 1996

## Proclamation 6919—National Hispanic Heritage Month, 1996

The U.S. has always attracted people from Mexico, Cuba, and other Latin American countries, despite the discrimination they faced when they arrived.

Hispanics are the second largest ethnic group in the United States today and are predicted to be California's largest racial group in the 21st century. They are becoming politically organized and are winning political office.

Hispanic Heritage Month is to honor their contributions and advancement.

### A Proclamation

America draws strength from the extraordinary diversity of its people. Our national character is enhanced by citizens who maintain and honor cultural customs brought from other lands. Hispanics, who have long been part of this tradition, were the earliest European settlers of this great Nation, with the Spanish founding cities in Florida in the 1500's, and Mexicans establishing homesteads in the Southwest in the 1600's. Puerto Ricans became U.S. citizens in 1917, and other Latinos over the years, including Cubans and Central Americans, came to the United States in search of democracy, freedom, and a better way of life.

Hispanics, who are of all races, distinguish themselves as a community by fostering connections rooted in the Spanish language. Their diverse and vibrant culture includes elements originating in Spain, North America, Central America, South America, and the Caribbean. Hispanics share deep family values, recognize their obligations to the less fortunate of our society, protect their children, cherish freedom, and fulfill their patriotic duty to defend their country. . . .

Sadly, we recently lost one of our great countrymen, Dr. Hector P. Garcia of Corpus Christi, Texas. A member of the U.S. Commission on Civil Rights and a recipient of the Presidential Medal of Freedom, he is best remembered for his service to the Latino community, founding the American GI Forum to defend the civil rights of Hispanic veterans and organizing one of the first civil rights marches in the 1940's.

Many other Hispanic sons and daughters have served our country with distinction, making important contributions in the arts and sciences, the business world, academia, government, agriculture, and the Armed Forces. Helping to preserve the democracy and freedom all Americans enjoy, Hispanics have served in the United States Armed Forces in proportions much larger than their percentage of the population. Since World War I, our Nation has awarded the Medal of Honor, our highest military honor, to more Latinos than any other ethnic group.

Today, let us honor Hispanics for their example of community and patriotism, and for the richness of their contribution to this great land.

Now, Therefore, I, William J. Clinton, President of the United States of America, do hereby proclaim September 15 through October 15, 1996, as National Hispanic Heritage Month. I call upon all government officials, educators, and people of the United States to honor this observance with appropriate programs, ceremonies, and activities, and encourage all Americans to rededicate themselves to the pursuit of equality.

# $\boxed{Q}$ uestions for Review and Reflection

1. According to President Clinton:

   a. Who is included under the term "Hispanic"?
   b. What contributions have Hispanics made to this country?
   c. Why is Hector Garcia singled out?

# Reading 5

President William J. Clinton, 1996

## Remarks at the Congressional Asian-Pacific American Caucus Institute Dinner

Asian immigration increased rapidly following the 1965 Immigration Act. (See Chapter 4; Reading 5.) By 1990, there were 7 million people from Asian countries; by the year 2000, it is predicted there will be approximately 12 million, or 5 percent of the population. People from China, Japan, Korea, Vietnam, and other Asian-Pacific countries are advancing in both economics and politics.

The public image of Asian Americans is one of success; yet, there continues to be exclusion and discrimination with "hate crimes" on the rise. (See Chapter 6; Reading 6.)

President Clinton's remarks affirm the accomplishments and contributions of so many "who trace their roots to Asia and the islands of the Pacific," and call for a "full partnership" with all who come to seek a better life.

"If we unite and make a virtue out of our diversity, there is no country as well-positioned for the 21st century as the United States."

As we debate the issue of immigration again this year, we should never forget that America is a great country because we have welcomed successive generations of immigrants to our shores. Because we are a nation of laws we should do everything we can and we should do more than we have to, to stop illegal immigration. I have done more than has previously been done. But we should avoid bashing immigrants. We are nearly, all of us, immigrants or the children or grandchildren or great-grandchildren of immigrants. The Native Americans were here first, and I think they crossed an ice cap to get here.

This is a country founded on a certain set of ideas, a certain set of values, a certain set of principles. And anybody willing to embrace them, to work hard to make the most of their own lives, to be responsible, can be an American citizen. That is the special thing about the United States, and we should never forget it. . . .

Three and a half years ago when I took the Oath of Office, I did so with a clear vision of what I hoped our country could be like as we move into the 21st century. I wanted this to be a country where every person, without regard to race or gender or income, would have a chance to live out his or her dreams. I wanted this to be a country where we were coming together around our basic values, not being driven apart for cheap, short-term political reasons. . . .

If you think about so much of the political rhetoric we have heard in America for, well, a long time now, it seems to be designed to divide people, to make neighbors look upon their neighbors as if they're almost alien, to make people believe that public servants that are otherwise perfectly normal people are somehow capable of the utmost depravity.

The truth is, this is a pretty great country, or we wouldn't be here after over 200 years. And we should have our debates and our differences and our heated debates on public policy. But we ought to do it in a way that says that we realize that we all love our country, we all love our Constitution, and we know we're going up or down together. And if we persist in dividing ourselves against one another, we will weaken America. If we unite and make a virtue out of our diversity, there is no country as well-positioned for the 21st century as the United States. . . .

The main thing I want to say to all of you tonight is that, again, I thank you for your contributions to America. And I thank you for the people you have supplied, both within and without the administration, who have advanced our cause. I think that your devotion to learning, to hard work, to family, to the ideas of entrepreneurialism and the idea of engagement with the rest of the world, these are the kinds of things that will keep America great in the 21st century.

We can go into the next century with a country where everybody who is willing to work for it can live out their dreams. We can maintain this country as the world's strongest force for peace and freedom and prosperity. But if we are going to do it, we must be committed to that third element of our vision: We have to be committed to bringing this country together around a mutual ethic of responsibility instead of letting ourselves be divided by differences that ultimately don't matter nearly as much as our devotion to our shared ideals.

You can help bring this country together as well as move it forward, and I'm convinced we can't do one without the other. Asian-Pacific Americans have done both and done them brilliantly. I ask for your continued support as we try to make sure that our entire country does the same.

Thank you, and God bless you all.

## Questions for Review and Reflection

1. What special attributes of Asian Americans does President Clinton highlight in his remarks?
2. What are the ideals that the country should attempt to achieve as it enters the 21st century?

## Reading 6

U.S. Supreme Court, 1996

## *United States v. Virginia et al.,* Nos. 94-1941 and 94-2107

"Equal protection of the laws" has been an elusive right for women. Protection has been slow to come and not complete. Laws are subject to some scrutiny when they treat women differently but not to the same "strict scrutiny" test applied to laws that treat racial groups differently.

Violation of the "equal protection clause" of the Fourteenth Amendment is at issue when the state of Virginia is challenged for financing the Virginia Military Institute (VMI) as a single-sex school, excluding women from admission.

The state of Virginia argued that exclusiveness was necessary because of the unique regimen that was demanded of cadets at VMI. The Federal Appeals Court permitted VMI to experiment with a parallel course for women which became a four-year state-sponsored undergraduate program (called the Virginia Women's Institute for Leadership) at Mary Baldwin College. However, women found this an unacceptable alternative. They sued, claiming the program did not provide equal opportunity and was of inferior quality compared to VMI's respected program and reputation.

The case went to the U.S. Supreme Court which ruled that "women seeking and fit for a VMI quality education cannot be offered anything less, under the State's obligation to afford them genuinely equal protection."

Although this case did not rule out all single-sex education, it did bring an end to the male-only admissions policy at another prestigious military academy, The Citadel, in South Carolina.

J ustice Ginsburg delivered the opinion of the Court.

Founded in 1839, VMI is today the sole single sex school among Virginia's 15 public institutions of higher learning. VMI's distinctive mission is to produce "citizen soldiers," men prepared for leadership in civilian life and in military service. VMI pursues this mission through pervasive training of a kind not available anywhere else in Virginia. Assigning prime place to character development, VMI uses an "adversative method" modeled on English public schools and once characteristic of military instruction. VMI constantly endeavors to instill physical and mental discipline in its cadets and impart to them a strong moral code. The school's graduates leave VMI with heightened comprehension of their capacity to deal with duress and stress, and a large sense of accomplishment for completing the hazardous course.

VMI has notably succeeded in its mission to produce leaders; among its alumni are military generals, Members of Congress, and business executives. The school's alumni overwhelmingly perceive that their VMI training helped them to realize their personal goals. VMI's endowment reflects the loyalty of its graduates; VMI has the largest per student endowment of all undergraduate institutions in the Nation.

Neither the goal of producing citizen soldiers nor VMI's implementing methodology is inherently unsuitable to women. And the school's impressive record in producing leaders has made admission desirable to some women. Nevertheless, Virginia has elected to preserve exclusively for men the advantages and opportunities a VMI education affords. . . .

VMI, too, offers an educational opportunity no other Virginia institution provides, and the school's "prestige"—associated with its success in developing "citizen soldiers"—is unequaled. Virginia has closed this facility to its daughters and, instead, has devised for them a "parallel program," with a faculty less impressively credentialed and less well paid, more limited course offerings, fewer opportunities for military training and for scientific specialization. . . . VMI, beyond question, "possesses to a far greater degree" than the VWIL program "those qualities which are incapable of objective measurement but which make for greatness in a . . . school," including "position and influence of the alumni, standing in the community, traditions, and prestige.". . . Women seeking and fit for a VMI quality education cannot be offered anything less, under the State's obligation to afford them genuinely equal protection. . . .

There is no reason to believe that the admission of women capable of all the activities required of VMI cadets would destroy the Institute rather than enhance its capacity to serve the "more perfect Union."

For the reasons stated, the initial judgment of the Court of Appeals, 976 F. 2d 890 (CA4 1992), is affirmed, the final judgment of the Court of Appeals, 44 F. 3d 1229 (CA4 1995), is reversed, and the case is remanded for further proceedings consistent with this opinion.

*It is so ordered.*

# Questions for Review and Reflection

1. What is an "adversative method" of instruction?
2. What unique quality of education is offered by VMI that cannot be reproduced in a "parallel program"?
3. What is the state's obligation to women seeking a VMI education?

# Reading 7

U.S. Congress, 1996

# The Native American Housing Assistance and Self-Determination Act

The Native American Housing Assistance and Self-Determination Act establishes a continuation of Indian self-government along with federal assistance "to aid families and individuals seeking affordable homes in safe and healthy environments" and to "allow families to prosper without government involvement in their day-to-day activities."

Although still subject to congressional authority, Native American reservations have achieved a semi-autonomous status that recognizes "a unique relationship between the Government of the United States and the governments of Indian tribes and a unique Federal responsibility to Indian people . . . so that they are able to take greater responsibility for their own economic condition. . . ."

T he Congress finds that—

(1) the Federal Government has a responsibility to promote the general welfare of the Nation—

(A) by using Federal resources to aid families and individuals seeking affordable homes in safe and healthy environments and, in particular, assisting responsible, deserving citizens who cannot provide fully for themselves because of temporary circumstances or factors beyond their control;

(B) by working to ensure a thriving national economy and a strong private housing market; and

(C) by developing effective partnerships among the Federal Government, State, tribal, and local governments, and private entities that allow government to accept responsibility for fostering the development of a healthy marketplace and allow families to prosper without government involvement in their day-to-day activities;

(2) there exists a unique relationship between the Government of the United States and the governments of Indian tribes and a unique Federal responsibility to Indian people;

(3) the Constitution of the United States invests the Congress with plenary power over the field of Indian affairs, and through treaties, statutes, and historical relations with Indian tribes, the United States has undertaken a unique trust responsibility to protect and support Indian tribes and Indian people;

(4) the Congress, through treaties, statutes, and the general course of dealing with Indian tribes, has assumed a trust responsibility for the protection and preservation of Indian tribes and for working with tribes and their members to improve their housing conditions and socioeconomic status so that they are able to take greater responsibility for their own economic condition; . . .

(7) Federal assistance to meet these responsibilities should be provided in a manner that recognizes the right of Indian self-determination and tribal self-governance by making such assistance available directly to the Indian tribes or tribally designated entities under authorities similar to those accorded Indian tribes in Public Law 93-638 (25 U.S.C. 450 et seq.).

# Questions for Review and Reflection

1. Congress recognizes a unique responsibility toward Native Americans. What is it?
2. What are some of the specific resources being made available to Native Americans as a result of this act?
3. Define the relationship between the U.S. government and Native Americans, according to this document.

# Sources

## Chapter 1

Reading 1: Alice Stone Blackwell, "Why Should Women Vote?" In *Pamphlets in American History,* 1917. (National American Woman Suffrage Association, Headquarters, Warren, Ohio).

Reading 2: The League of United Latin-American Citizens, Aims and Objectives of the League of United Latin-American Citizens, 1929. O. Douglas Weeks, "The League of United Latin-American Citizens: A Texas-Mexican Civic Organization," *Southwestern Political and Social Science Quarterly,* December 1929.

Reading 3: Luther Standing Bear, Reprinted from *Land of the Spotted Eagle* by Luther Standing Bear, by permission of the University of Nebraska Press. Copyright © 1960 by May Jones.

Reading 4: Mike Masaoka, Testimony before Congress. Statement during hearings before the House Select Committee Investigating Defense Migration, 77th Cong., 2nd sess. (1942), p. 11137.

Reading 5: Ralph Bunche, *The Political Status of the Negro after FDR,* Dewey Grantham, ed. (Chicago: University of Chicago Press, 1973), pp. 102–18.

## Chapter 2

Reading 1: United States Congress, The Indian Reorganization Act of 1934. 73rd Cong., 2nd sess., ch. 576.

Reading 2: Harry Truman, Executive Order 9981. *Federal Register* (Washington, DC: U.S. Government Printing Office), p. 4313.

Reading 3: United States Congress, The Evacuation Claims Act of 1948. 80th Cong., 2nd sess. 62 stat., ch. 814.

Reading 4: United States Supreme Court, *Brown v. Board of Education,* 347 U.S. 483 (1954).

Reading 5: United States Supreme Court, *Hernandez v. Texas,* 347 U.S. 475 (1954).

## Chapter 3

Reading 1: Martin Luther King Jr., Letter from a Birmingham Jail. In Martin Luther King Jr., *Why We Can't Wait* (New York: Harper & Row, 1964), pp. 77–100. Reprinted by arrangement with The Heirs to the Estate of Martin Luther King Jr., c/o Writers House, Inc., as agent for the proprietor. Copyright © 1963 by Martin Luther King Jr.; copyright © renewed 1991 by Coretta Scott King.

Reading 2: Betty Friedan, *The Feminine Mystique* (New York: Dell Books, 1963), pp. 362–64. Copyright © 1983, 1974, 1973, 1963 by Betty Friedan. Reprinted by permission of W. W. Norton & Company, Inc.

Reading 3: Martin Luther King Jr., "I Have a Dream" Speech. In James M. Washington, ed., *A Testament of Hope: The Essential Writings of Martin L. King* (New York: HarperCollins, 1986, pp. 217–20. Reprinted by arrangement with The Heirs to the Estate of Martin Luther King Jr., c/o Writers House, Inc., as agent for the proprietor. Copyright © 1963 by Martin Luther King Jr.; copyright © renewed 1991 by Coretta Scott King.

Reading 4: Malcolm X, Speech to New York Meeting. In George Breitman and Betty Shabazz, eds., *Malcolm X Speaks* (New York: Pathfinder Press, 1989), pp. 45–59. Copyright © 1965, 1989 by Betty Shabazz and Pathfinder Press. Reprinted by permission.

Reading 5: The National Organization for Women, Organizing Statement. In Betty Friedan, *It Changed My Life* (New York: Random House, 1976), pp. 87–92. Copyright © 1963, 1964, 1966, 1970, 1971, 1972, 1973, 1974, 1975, 1976, 1985, 1991, 1998 by Betty Friedan. Reprinted by permission of Curtis Brown, Ltd.

Reading 6: Reies Tijerina, Letter from a Santa Fe Jail. In Wayne Moquin and Charles van Doren, *A Documentary History of the Mexican-Americans* (New York: Praeger, 1971), pp. 374–77. Reproduced by permission of Greenwood Publishing Group, Inc., Westport, CT.

Reading 7: Delano Grape Workers, Proclamation. In Wayne Moquin and Charles van Doren, *A Documentary History of the Mexican-Americans* (New York: Praeger, 1971), pp. 363–65. Reproduced by permission of Greenwood Publishing Group, Inc., Westport, CT.

Reading 8: Theodore H. E. Chen, "Silent Minority: The Oriental-American's Plight," *Los Angeles Times,* June 8, 1969, p. F7.

Reading 9: Citizens' Council on the Status of Women, "The Proposed Equal Rights Amendment to the U.S. Constitution—A Memorandum," *Congressional Record,* 92nd Cong., 2nd sess., vol. 118, part 8, pp. 9684–9686.

Reading 10: National Council on Indian Opportunity, Statement of Indian Members. In Alvin Josephy, ed., *Red Power* (American Heritage Press, 1971), p. 192–208. Copyright © 1971 by Alvin Josephy. Reprinted by permission of the author.

Reading 11: Armando Rodriguez, Testimony to Congress. *Congressional Record,* 91st Cong., 2nd sess., pp. 5154–56.

Reading 12: Mary Frances Berry, *Black Resistance/White Law.* From *Black Resistance/White Law* by Mary Frances Berry. Copyright © 1971, 1994 by Mary Frances Berry. Used by permission of Viking Penguin, a division of Penguin Putnam, Inc.

Reading 13: James W. Chin, "The Subtlety of Prejudice." In William Dudley and John C. Chalberg, eds., *Asian Americans: Opposing Viewpoints* (Greenhaven Press, 1997), pp. 180–83.

Reading 14: Cesar Chavez, An Interview. In *Cesar Chavez: Autobiography of La Causa* (New York: W. W. Norton, 1975), pp. 536–39.

## Chapter 4

Reading 1: United States Supreme Court, *Reynolds v. Sims* 377 U.S. 533 (1964).

Reading 2: United States Congress, The Civil Rights Act of 1964. *U.S. Code Annotated,* P.L. 88-352, 78 Stat. 241, Title 42.

Reading 3: United States Congress, The Voting Rights Act of 1964. *U.S. Code Annotated,* P.L. 89-110, 79 Stat. 437, Title 42.

Reading 4: Hubert Humphrey, Civil Rights Commission Report. *In Congress and the Nation* (Washington, DC: Congressional Quarterly Press, 1965), p. 1642.

Reading 5: United States Congress, The Immigration and Naturalization Act of 1965, P.L. 89-236, Stat. 1965, vol. 79, part 1.

Reading 6: Lyndon B. Johnson, Howard University Speech. In *Public Papers of Lyndon B. Johnson,* vol. 2 (Washington, DC: U.S. Government Printing Office, 1966).

Reading 7: Lyndon B. Johnson, Executive Order 11246. *Federal Register,* no. 12319 (Washington, DC: U.S. Government Printing Office, 1971).

Reading 8: Richard M. Nixon, Message to Congress. In *Public Papers of the Presidents of the United States, January 1–December 31, 1970* (Washington, DC: U.S. Government Printing Office, 1971).

Reading 9: United States Supreme Court, *Reed v. Reed,* 404 U.S. 71 (1971).

Reading 10: United States Supreme Court, *Roe v. Wade,* 410 U.S. 113 (1973).

Reading 11: United States Congress, The Indian Self-Determination and Assistance Act of 1975. In *U.S. Statutes at Large,* vol. 88, part 2 (Washington, DC: U.S. Government Printing Office, 1976), pp. 2203–17.

Reading 12: State of California, The California Agricultural Labor Relations Act of 1975. In *West Annotated Code,* Labor Sections (St. Paul: West Publishing, 1989), pp. 298–305.

## Chapter 5

Reading 1: Phyllis Schlafly, *The Power of the Positive Woman* (New York: Arlington House, 1977). From *The Power of the Positive Woman* by Phyllis Schlafly. Copyright © 1977 by Phyllis Schlafly. Reprinted by permission of Arlington House, Inc., a division of Crown Publishers, Inc.

Reading 2: Clarence Thomas, "No Room at the Inn: The Loneliness of the Black Conservative" (Heritage Foundation, 1987). Reprinted in *Policy Review,* Fall 1991, pp. 72–78.

Reading 3: Thurgood Marshall, Speech on the Bicentennial of the Constitution. In Bruce Stinebrickner, ed., *Annual Editions: American Government, 1994/95* (Guilford, CT: The Dushkin Publishing Group), pp. 53–54.

Reading 4: Herbert Hill, "Race, Affirmative Action, and the Constitution." In George McKenna and Stanley Feingold, eds., *Taking Sides: Clashing Views on Controversial Political Issues* (Guilford, CT: The Dushkin Publishing Group, 1993), pp. 194–99.

Reading 5: Joaquin Avila, *Latino Political Empowerment.* Pamphlet published privately by Joaquin Avila, 1988, Linda Stone, ed., pp. 20–25.

Reading 6: Shelby Steele, *The Content of Our Character: A New Vision of Race in America* (New York: St. Martin's Press, 1990). From *The Content of Our Character: A New Vision of Race in America* by Shelby Steele. Copyright © 1990 by Shelby Steele. Reprinted by permission of St. Martin's Press, Inc.

Reading 7: Linda Chavez, *Out of the Barrio: Toward a New Politics of*

*Hispanic Assimilation* (New York: Basic Books, 1991). From *Out of the Barrio* by Linda Chavez. Copyright © 1991 by BasicBooks, a division of HarperCollins Publishers.

Reading 8: Susan Faludi, *Backlash: The Undeclared War against American Women* From *Backlash: The Undeclared War against American Women* by Susan Faludi. Copyright © 1991 by Susan Faludi. Reprinted by permission of Crown Publishers, Inc.

Reading 9: Rosalind C. Barnett and Caryl Rivers. "The Myth of the Miserable Working Woman." First appeared in *Working Woman,* February 1992. Written by R. Barnett and C. Rivers. Reprinted by permission of MacDonald Communications Corporation. Copyright © 1998 by MacDonald Communications Corporation, www.workingwomanmag.com.

Reading 10: John Mohawk, "Looking for Columbus: Thoughts on the Past, Present, and Future of Humanity." In M. Annette Jaimes, ed., *The State of Native-Americans, Genocide, Colonization and Resistance* (Boston: South End Press, 1992), pp. 439–44.

Reading 11: Vine Deloria Jr., "Afterword." In Alvin Josephy, ed., *America in 1492* (New York: Alfred A. Knopf, 1992), pp. 429–43. Copyright © 1992 by Alfred A. Knopf, a division of Random House, Inc. Reprinted by permission of the publisher.

## Chapter 6

Reading 1: United States Supreme Court, *Roberts v. United States Jaycees,* 468 U.S. 609 (1984).

Reading 2: United States Congress, The Bilingual Education Act of 1988. P.L. 88-10, 102 Stat. 274, Title 20.

Reading 3: United States Congress, The Civil Liberties Act of 1988. In *Historic Documents of 1988* (Washington, DC: Congressional Quarterly Press, April 1988), pp. 290–295.

Reading 4: United States Congress, The Civil Rights Act of 1991. *U.S. Congressional and Administrative Codes,* P.L. 102-166 (St. Paul: West Publishing, 1991).

Reading 5: New York State Social Studies and Review Committee, "One Nation, Many Peoples: A Declaration of Cultural Independence." In *Historic Documents* (Washington, DC: Congressional Quarterly Press, 1992), pp. 333–48.

Reading 6: United States Commission on Civil Rights, "Civil Rights Issues Facing Asian Americans in the 1990s." Pursuant to P.L. 98-183 (Washington, DC: U.S. Government Printing Office, 1992).

Reading 7: United States Congress, The Women in Apprenticeship and Nontraditional Occupations Act of 1992. *U.S. Code Annotated,* P.L. 102–530, October 27, 1992.

Reading 8: United States Supreme Court, *Shaw v. Reno,* 509 US—, 125 L. Ed. 2d 511, 113 (1993).

Reading 9: United States Congress, The Indian Tribal Justice Act of 1993. U.S. Code Annotated, P.L. 103-176, December 3, 1993.

## Chapter 7

Reading 1: Naomi Wolf, "What We Can Do Now." From *Fire with Fire* by Naomi Wolf (New York: Random House, 1993). Copyright © 1993 by Naomi Wolf. Reprinted by permission of Random House, Inc.

Reading 2: Carl Stokes, Excerpts from "Racial Equality and Appreciation of Diversity in our Urban Communities: How Far Have We Come?" From *Vital Speeches of the Day,* February 19, 1993.

Reading 3: Gary Okihiro, "The Victimization of Asians in America," *The World & I,* April 1993. This article appeared in the April 1993 issue and is reprinted with permission from *The World & I,* a publication of The Washington Times Corporation. Copyright © 1993.

Reading 4: Christina Hoff Sommers, *Who Stole Feminism?* (New York: Simon & Schuster, 1994). From *Who Stole Feminism?* by Christina Hoff Sommers. Copyright © 1994 by Christina Sommers. Reprinted by permission of Simon & Schuster.

Reading 5: Mario T. Garcia, *Memories of Chicano History: The Life and Narrative of Bert Corona* (Berkeley: University of California Press, 1994). Copyright © 1994 by the Regents of the University of California.

Reading 6: Russell Means with Marvin J. Wolf, *Where White Men Fear to Tread.* From *Where White Men Fear to Tread* by Russell Means and Marvin J. Wolf. Copyright © by Russell Means and Marvin J. Wolf. Reprinted by permission of St. Martin's Press.

Reading 7: Luis Gutierrez, "The New Assault on Immigrants," *Social Policy,* Summer 1995, pp. 56–63.

Reading 8: Barbara Koeppel, "The Progressive Interview: Eleanor Smeal," *The Progressive,* November 1995. Reprinted by permission of *The Progressive,* 409 East Main Street, Madison, WI 53703.

Reading 9: Ward Connerly, 1996. "With Liberty and Justice for All," In *Vital Speeches of the Day,* May 1, 1996, pp. 434–37.

Reading 10: Ronald Takaki, "At the End of the Century: The 'Culture Wars' in the U.S." From Ronald Takaki, ed., *From Different Shores: Perspectives on Race and Ethnicity in America,* First Edition. Copyright © 1987, 1994 by Ronald Takaki.

Used by permission of the Oxford University Press, Inc.

Reading 11: Jesse Jackson, "It's Up to Us," *Essence,* Volume 27, Issue 7 (November 1996).

Reading 12: Clarence Page, "Supply-side Affirmative Action." From *Showing My Color* by Clarence Page. Copyright © 1996 by Clarence Page. Reprinted by permission of HarperCollins Publishers, Inc.

## Chapter 8

Reading 1: United States Supreme Court, *Harris v. Forklift Systems, Inc.,* No. 92-1168 (1993).

Reading 2: United States Congress, The American Indian Religious Freedom Act Amendments of 1994. P.L. 103-344, 108 Stat. 3125.

Reading 3: William J. Clinton, Remarks to Native American and Native Alaskan Tribal Leaders, *Public Papers of the President,* Book 1 (Washington, DC: U.S. Government Printing Office, 1994).

Reading 4: William J. Clinton, Proclamation 6919—National Hispanic Heritage Month, *Weekly Compilation of Presidential Documents* (Washington, DC: Office of the Federal Register, 1996), vol. 32, no. 38, pp. 1749–1826.

Reading 5: William J. Clinton, Remarks at the Congressional Asian-Pacific American Caucus Institute Dinner, 1996, *Weekly Compilation of Presidential Documents* (Washington, DC: Office of the Federal Register, 1996), vol. 32, no. 20, pp. 835–82.

Reading 6: United States Supreme Court, *United States v. Virginia et al.,* Nos. 94-1941 and 94-2107 (1996).

Reading 7: United States Congress, The Native American Housing Assistance and Self-Determination Act of 1996. P.L. 104-330, 104th Cong.